Accelerators

Accelerators

Successful Venture Creation and Growth

Edited by

Mike Wright

Professor of Entrepreneurship and Director of the Centre for Management Buyout Research, Imperial College Business School, London, UK, and Visiting Professor, University of Ghent, Belgium and ETH Zurich, Switzerland

Israel Drori

Head of the Department of Organization Sciences and Chaired Professor of Organization and Globalization, Faculty of Social Science, VU, Amsterdam, the Netherlands

Edward Elgar
PUBLISHING

Cheltenham, UK • Northampton, MA, USA

Published by
Edward Elgar Publishing Limited
The Lypiatts
15 Lansdown Road
Cheltenham
Glos GL50 2JA
UK

Edward Elgar Publishing, Inc.
William Pratt House
9 Dewey Court
Northampton
Massachusetts 01060
USA

A catalogue record for this book
is available from the British Library

Library of Congress Control Number: 2018931725

This book is available electronically in the **Elgar**online
Business subject collection
DOI 10.4337/9781786434098

ISBN 978 1 78643 408 1 (cased)
ISBN 978 1 78643 409 8 (eBook)

Typeset by Servis Filmsetting Ltd, Stockport, Cheshire
Printed and bound in Great Britain by TJ International Ltd, Padstow

Contents

Contributors

Martin Bliemel is a Senior Lecturer and Director of the Diploma in Innovation at the new Faculty of Transdisciplinary Innovation at the University of Technology Sydney (UTS). He is a member of the advisory committee for the Australian Centre for Entrepreneurship Research Exchange (ACERE) and for the Amway Global Entrepreneurship Report. Martin's research interests include entrepreneurial networks, acceleration, education, and research commercialization. His research has been published in several prestigious journals including *Nature Nanotechnology*, *Entrepreneurship Theory and Practice* and the *Entrepreneurship Research Journal*.

Massimo G. Colombo is Full Professor of Economics of Technical Change at Politecnico di Milano, where he serves as the Deputy Dean for Research at Politecnico di Milano School of Management. His research interests include entrepreneurship and entrepreneurial finance, economics of innovation, economics of organizational design and industrial economics.

Israel (Issy) Drori (PhD, UCLA) is Head of the Department of Organization Sciences and a Chaired Professor of Organization and Globalization at the Faculty of Social Science, VU, Amsterdam. He has held visiting professorships at the Faculty of Management, Tel Aviv University; Ross School of Business, University of Michigan; Simon Fraser University; Oxford University; Tisnghua University, Beijing; and Hitotsubashi University, Tokyo. He has published ten books and numerous articles in journals such as *Academy of Management Journal, American Sociological Review, Organization Science, Public Administration Review* and *Organization Studies*.

Ricardo Flores is an Assistant Professor at the Peter B. Gustavson School of Business, University of Victoria. He received his PhD in Organizational Theory and International Business from the University of Illinois at Urbana-Champaign. His work has appeared in internationally recognized journals such as the *Journal of International Business Studies, Multinational Business Review* and *Research in the Sociology of Organizations*. Ricardo's research interests are multiple but broadly associated with cross-national and transformational organizational-centered processes.

Jyun-Ying (Trent) Fu is an Assistant Professor at National Chengchi University, Taiwan. His research interests cover corporate governance, entrepreneurial finance and business accelerators.

Juanita Gonzalez-Uribe is an Assistant Professor at the London School of Economics (LSE). Her research focuses on entrepreneurship, private equity and innovation. Her work on the interaction between venture capital and innovation has won several prizes including the Kauffman Dissertation Award (2012) and the Coller Prize Award London (2013).

Saskia de Klerk is Senior Lecturer and Higher Degree Coordinator at the School of Business, UNSW Canberra. She teaches foundations of management, international business and business planning. Her research interests are broad, but include career development, networking, innovation and entrepreneurship.

Jochen Koch is Professor of Management and Organization and Director of the Centre for Entrepreneurship Research (CfER) at the European University Viadrina in Frankfurt (Oder), Germany. His research interests include organizational creativity, organizational routines and practices, and the theory of strategic and organizational path dependence.

Michael Leatherbee is an Assistant Professor at the Industrial and Systems Engineering Department at Pontificia Universidad Católica de Chile. He is the Academic Director of the Evidence-based Policy and Innovation Research Lab, board member of Start-Up Chile and IncubaUC business accelerators, and member of the Chile-California Council. His research focuses on strategy, entrepreneurship and policies.

Morgan P. Miles recently became Professor of Entrepreneurship at Charles Stuart University. Prior to that, he was Professor of Entrepreneurship and Innovation at the University of Canterbury. He holds a DBA in Marketing from Mississippi State University. Currently, he is working with the Department of Industry on entrepreneurial support program policies dealing specifically with accelerators and incubators.

Cristina Rossi-Lamastra holds a PhD in Economics of Innovation from Sant'Anna School of Advanced Studies in Pisa. She is currently Associate Professor at the Politecnico di Milano School of Management. Her research interests are in the area of entrepreneurship, organizational economics and open innovation.

Jonas Van Hove is a researcher at ETH Zurich. His main research areas are related to the dynamics of entrepreneurial ecosystems, incubation models, and academic entrepreneurship with a specific focus on acceleration of deep tech ventures.

Iris Vanaelst is a Senior Researcher at the Department of Innovation, Entrepreneurship and Service Management at Ghent University. Her research interests include entrepreneurial teams in innovative high-tech startups, the entrepreneurial university and student entrepreneurship.

Laurens Vandeweghe is a PhD applicant at Imperial College Business School, London. His research interests revolve around business accelerators and organizational legitimation.

Matthias Wenzel is a post-doctoral researcher at the Chair of Management and Organization at the European University Viadrina in Frankfurt (Oder), Germany. He conducts research on strategy as practice, disruptive innovation and path dependence.

Mike Wright is Professor of Entrepreneurship and Director of the Centre for Management Buy-out Research, Imperial College Business School, and Visiting Professor at the University of Ghent and ETH Zurich. He is an editor of the *Academy of Management Perspectives*, Chair of the Society for the Advancement of Management Studies and a Fellow of the British Academy. He has published over 50 books and 450 academic articles on entrepreneurial finance, academic entrepreneurship, management buyouts, returnee entrepreneurs and habitual entrepreneurs.

Ronit Yitshaki is an Assistant Professor at the Department of Economics and Business Administration at Ariel University. Her research interests include startups' acceleration processes, social entrepreneurship, entrepreneurial motivations and opportunity recognition, entrepreneurial identities and psychology of entrepreneurship.

1. Accelerators: characteristics, trends and the new entrepreneurial ecosystem

Israel Drori and Mike Wright

INTRODUCTION

The emergence of accelerators is a notable development in the landscape of new entrepreneurial ecosystems, which include social media, data analytics and internet-based business applications. Recently, accelerators have drawn the attention of entrepreneurship scholars who, examining accelerators' characteristics (Adkins, 2011; Fishback et al., 2007), distinguish them from incubators (Barbero et al., 2014; Hausberg and Korreck, 2017; Hoffman and Radojecich-Kelly, 2012; Isabelle, 2013; Mian et al., 2016). There is also a growing body of scholarship that has sought to develop a taxonomy (Dempwolf et al., 2014) and examine accelerators as a part of emerging ecosystems (Sparks, 2013).

Accelerators in their current forms are part of a relatively recent but rapidly growing phenomenon. They encompass a wide range of organizational types, private and public, aimed at enhancing the capabilities of start-ups through educational programming and processes (Clarysse et al., 2015; Pauwels et al., 2016). While engaging in growing individual start-ups, accelerators are developing new ecosystems and fostering communities of innovation. Thus, accelerators can affect the economy and society in multiple ways, far beyond the direct effects they may have on start-up performance, including influencing the rate and distribution of innovations and the flow of entrepreneurial knowledge and new ideas within and across industrial sectors and countries. Furthermore, various types of accelerators are the source of a wide range of innovations in different fields, such as high-tech, green technology, urban development, transportation, e-commerce, social media and energy.

In this sense, Cohen and Hochberg (2014) provide a "narrow" definition by conceiving accelerators as an organizational form that creates a process for training and exposing start-ups to their ecosystem, in other words, "a fixed-term, cohort-based program, including mentorship and educational components, that culminates in a public pitch event or demo day" (p. 4). However, such a narrow definition ignores the essential functions of accelerators related to their modus operandi, objectives, participants and ecosystem. Accordingly, we offer the following definition:

> An accelerator is a generic organizational form that aims to stimulate entrepreneurship. It is structured to provide an intensive, limited-period educational program, including mentoring and networking for the cohort of start-up participants selected for each program, to improve their ability to attract investment following the demo day at the end of the program. Accelerators are organizations that serve as gatekeepers and validators of promising business innovations through their embeddedness in their respective ecosystems and, thus, take an active and salient role in socio-economic and technological advancement.

In this chapter, we first describe the variety of structures, processes and outcomes characterizing accelerators, based on our field research in accelerators across Europe, Israel and the US, and follow with an overview of the book, concluding with a summary of how accelerators are the building blocks of the new economy's innovative ecosystems.

TRENDS IN ACCELERATORS

Internationally, there has been a rapid growth in the number of accelerators in recent years. In the US, the increasing trend identified by Hochberg (2016) up to 2013 has continued through 2015 (Hathaway, 2016) (Figure 1.1). Bone et al. (2017) found that at the end of 2016 there were 205 incubators, 163 accelerators, 11 pre-accelerators, 7 virtual accelerators and 4 virtual incubators active in the UK.

The growth of accelerators has been especially marked in certain cities. Particularly notable is the continued increase in the annual number of accelerators founded in London and hence in the cumulative number of accelerators (Figure 1.2a). In contrast, there has been a decline in the annual number of accelerators created in Paris, although the total cumulative number of accelerators present is still increasing. This number surged in 2017 triggered by the opening of Station F, noted as the world's largest startup facility (Figure 1.2b). In Berlin, after a rapid rise in 2015, there appears to have been a sharp drop in the number of accelerators created in 2016 (Figure 1.2c). The environment for the development of accelerators in these cities is discussed in more detail in Chapter 8. A rapid increase in other cities is also evident, including in emerging economies. For example, Goswami et al. (2018) note that while the first accelerator in Bangalore,

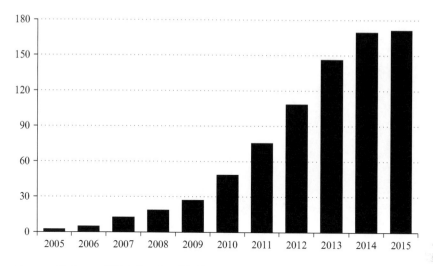

Source: Hathaway (2016). Based on Pitchbook data.

Figure 1.1   US accelerator pool by year

India was launched in 2008, there were 14 accelerators by the end of 2016, four of which were created from April through August 2016.

Because of the fluidity in defining accelerators and their different characteristics as outlined below, estimating their numbers can be challenging. For example, estimates of the number of active accelerators in Israel for 2015 vary from more than 260 (http://www.ivc-online.com) to a more conservative estimate of 90 (for detailed information about accelerators in Israel see: http://www.geektime.com/2016/05/25/do-israeli-accelerators-and-incuba tors-produce-successful-startups-heres-our-full-report/). Accelerators in Israel are of different types: corporate (such as IBM, Coca-Cola, Tyco, AOL, Orange Deutsche Telekom, Intel, Samsung, Yahoo), social, public (government, municipality, academic or kibbutzim affiliation), non-governmental and venture capital (VC) affiliated (such as JVP or Vertex). Some accelerators are joint ventures with other countries (e.g. TechCode, China).

CHARACTERISTICS OF ACCELERATORS

Accelerators are a unique organizational form; their structure and operational process is relatively basic and requires "lean" managerial personnel and resources. The essence of the accelerating program is extensive

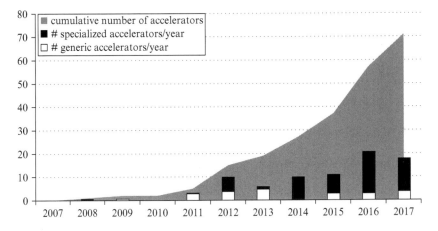

Source: Authors' calculations.

Figure 1.2a   Accelerators in London

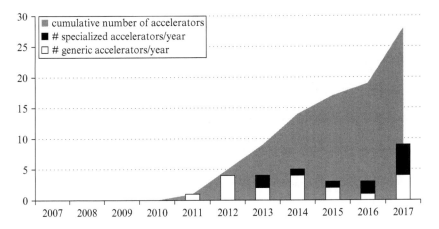

Source: Authors' calculations.

Figure 1.2b   Accelerators in Paris

training on entrepreneurship-related issues, along with preparation for a
demo day, although as we shall see not all accelerators have a formal demo
day. It is "a crash course on entrepreneurship, 300 intensive hours, and it
reminds me of an exclusive MBA" claims one of the participants we interviewed (in March 2016). However, accelerators play an important role not

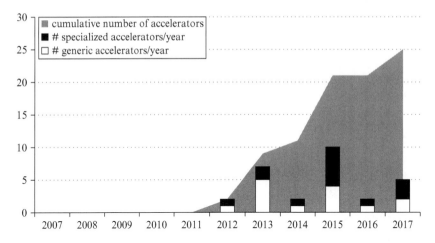

Source: Authors' calculations.

Figure 1.2c   Accelerators in Berlin

only in developing the start-ups participating in their respective programs but also in influencing the entrepreneurial ecosystem. In this sense, accelerators serve as brokers, linking start-ups with the environment. There are two features of brokerage. The first, internal, feature is associated with the accelerator's program, mainly outsourcing of expertise and mentoring. The second, which is external, is related to the networking function and the accelerator's role in shaping the innovation and the entrepreneurship landscape of its sector.

The following sections are devoted to the analysis of the dominant characteristics of accelerators. First we analyze accelerators, using the lens of a temporary organization within a permanent organization. This is followed by reviewing accelerators' internal characteristics, mainly structure, ownership and process, and then outlining external characteristics, including accessibility, validity and legitimacy.

ACCELERATORS AND TEMPORARY ORGANIZATION

Whereas accelerators are usually owned or affiliated with different types of organizations, public or private, their "*modus operandi*" is highly influenced by the temporal nature of the process associated with their offering to start-ups. When considering the traditional understanding of the temporal aspect of organization, indeed, accelerators are organizing temporary activity as part of a permanent organization. However, in understanding the ideational, strategic and operational nature of accelerators, it is useful to view accelerators using a temporal organization lens (Bakker et al., 2016). Recently, Burke and Morley (2016) defined temporary organizations as "a temporary bounded group of interdependent organization actors, formed to complete a complex task" (p. 1237). Using this definition, we present two main features that are the core of the accelerator form of organizing, and their characteristics can best be understood by the temporary dimension of accelerators. These features are (1) participants and (2) organization. Both could be beneficial for further research on accelerators using a temporary organization perspective.

1. *Participants*   Understanding the core meaning of participation in an accelerator program entails a recognition by the start-ups that they are participating in an educational-skill-oriented program which is limited in time. It is a curricula-based program designed to provide specific knowledge pertaining to managing and operating a newly founded firm, including issues beyond technology or product, such as accounting, recruiting, legal aspects of intellectual property, teamwork or consumer behavior. The other distinct offerings of the accelerator, which are also temporary in nature, are mentoring and exposure to varied communities of investors and other stakeholders that have the capacity to facilitate growth of new firms (e.g. accounting firms, established companies). The main thrust of participating in an accelerator program is the idea that effective learning and knowledge is linked to entrepreneurship and technology and is limited in time. Furthermore, selected start-ups accept the leadership and the requirements of the accelerator's management. The nature of participation raises many empirical and theoretical issues, including what is the lasting contribution of the start-ups to the accelerator's educational program? What is the relevance of the program to individual start-ups, particularly in cases of diverse selection in terms of field or technology? What is the effect of the limited time spent in the program and the opportunity cost for the individual start-up? Another aspect of temporality related to the participants is the nature of inter-team relations. Much work on teams in start-ups has drawn on the idea of changing team composition, division of tasks and expertise in accordance with the start-up's progression in its business development (e.g. Drori et al., 2009; Vanaelst et al., 2006). Studying accelerators may provide opportunities to explore neglected aspects of temporary organization, such

as questions related not only to internal start-ups' team dynamics but also inter-team relations with other firms in the cohort, collaboration or competition, and the development and change of these relations over the entire duration of the program.

2. *Organizations*   The fact that most accelerators are affiliated with a permanent organization raises a series of issues stemming from the potential conflict and tension between the accelerator and its "owner" organization. A key issue is associated with the degree and the scope of autonomy versus embeddedness (Burke and Morley, 2016). Our ongoing research on the different types of accelerators reveals a variety of strategies pertaining to the degree of ownership and the objectives of the owner organization. For example, we found that accelerators that are part of non-governmental organizations (NGOs) whose objectives are related to general societal issues, such as fostering innovation or economic development, enjoy a wide degree of autonomy in terms of criteria of selection, content development, structure and operation of the program. In contrast, accelerators that are part of a distinct public sector organization, such as a municipality, or are financed by corporations or VC, are limited in their autonomy. To a certain degree, they are embedded within their parent organization. This is despite the fact that the accelerator is an independent unit in terms of management, value proposition or service, and is not an integral part of the core activities of the parent organization. However, the accelerator could serve as a hotbed for innovation related to the parent organization's services and technology. Embeddedness also implies that the accelerator is fully financed by the firm that appointed its management and usually allocates space within the firm boundaries (e.g. accelerators affiliated with IBM, Microsoft or Coca-Cola). Thus, accelerators as organizational settings present a promising opportunity to research the fundamental issues of autonomy and embeddedness that mark the relationship between permanent and temporary organizations.

Accelerators' Internal Characteristics

Structure

Asked to describe the essence of accelerators as organizational structures designed to host and grow start-ups, an experienced accelerator manager replied:

> An accelerator is first and foremost a kind of school for entrepreneurs. An accelerator is organized in such a way that it provides the pragmatic knowledge and the tools, including learning from one another and linkage to the ecosystem, high-tech and investment experts, lawyers, accountants and program alumni. (Guy, interview with the authors, February 2016)

By and large, the program follows a workshop model. Each meeting is devoted to a different subject, usually elaborated by an expert in the field. One of the accelerator's managers described the educational program as "buffet style": it is up to the participants to pick and choose from predesigned offerings the workshops or activities they consider suitable and helpful.

The topics offered are relatively wide-ranging, especially in accelerators with a diverse cohort in terms of business models and industries. For example, in one of the accelerators we studied, the educational program is essentially divided into two components. The first includes professionally oriented workshops on subjects such as marketing, client relations, branding, business and product cycles, finance and investment, legal issues, the hiring of new employees and technology. These workshops are generic in nature and provide expert knowledge considered relevant for beginner entrepreneurs. The second part of the program involves activities that provide expert skills in the "soft" but crucial areas for start-ups, such as how to build a team, networking, pitching, leadership or dealing with growth of the venture. The latter activities are mainly based on testimonies and lessons-learned narratives of experienced entrepreneurs, combining both failure and success stories. A key component of the entire educational program is an intensive question-and-answer session following each activity, and discussion on the relevance for start-up survival and growth of the subjects covered by the accelerator's educational program.

An important aspect of the program is its fit with the stages and the nature of the start-up. The fit between the program and the start-up depends on the start-up's stage in terms of development of the idea, the technology, the product and the team, in addition to a necessary fit with market and customers. Early-stage start-ups have different requirements, needs and concerns than more mature ventures. In our discussions, founders that consider their companies more mature tend to view a large part of the educational program as redundant and a waste of time. As Yaakov, founder of a start-up in the field of agriculture, claims:

> We already have customers and proven technology. We decided to participate in the program because we thought that the benefits would exceed the cost of spending time in class and not with our customers or writing program lines. Even if we learn things, and second-guess, we are not going to change

our business model. The challenge for the accelerator is to tailor the program to diverse participants, once it decides to adopt a diverse selection policy. (Interview with the authors, May 2016)

Furthermore, the structure of the program dictates an orderly and structured work regimen, which allows the start-ups to focus on problems such as solving technology-related issues or gaining a deeper understanding of their product or market. Participation in the program forces start-up founders to tackle many of their basic assumptions regarding the viability of their business models and to adopt and internalize working and thinking habits and practices that are more conducive to an orderly regime than the chaotic and informal structure characterizing start-ups in their nascent period (Drori et al., 2009).

Ownership and participation
Accelerators are varied in terms of their owners and affiliations. Generally, they are created and sponsored by either public or private sectors. Moreover, public accelerators (e.g. those operated by municipalities, NGOs, academic institutions) as well as corporate or privately owned accelerators can have heterogeneous participants in terms of life-cycle, content (start-ups with only an idea and a basic team versus those already with customers), technology (concept, demo, beta site), geographical location (city, region, national, international) or investment status (pre-seed, seed, round A). The selected start-ups may be similar, being part of the same industry, mainly horizontally or vertically, but diverse with regard to role and specialization. Yet other accelerators may recruit a cohort of heterogeneous start-ups, with no common ground. These choices depend on the ownership and goals of the accelerator. There are differences between London, Paris and Berlin in terms of the relative importance of generic versus specialized accelerators, but in general a trend over time has been towards more specialized accelerators (Figures 1.2a, 1.2b, 1.2c).

Although designing a program that fits the needs of a diverse cohort may appear difficult, some programs are generic in terms of the topics they cover, regardless of technology, stage, size or industry of the respective participants. As Uri, the founder of a cybersecurity company participating in Microsoft's accelerator program, explains:

In our batch, we were from different sectors, technology areas and even maturity. This variety makes it difficult to benefit from the concrete insights and help from our peers, but sometimes we got a brilliant idea from someone who is in the tourism business. The program was not tailor made, and we spent precious time on redundant subjects, which are nice to have but not relevant to our field of cybersecurity. (Interview with the authors, January 2016)

Thus, specialized accelerators, both publicly and privately owned, may select for a certain cohort only those start-ups sharing similar interests (e.g. in the fields of energy, transportation or clean tech). Other accelerators may be more generalized, selecting diverse start-ups for a certain cohort (e.g. fin-tech, e-commerce, clean tech). The type and stage of start-up in terms of idea, technology, team, market and finance selected to their program are major considerations for accelerator owners. The accelerator's selection of start-ups, structure, program and key performance indicators (KPIs) is contingent on the type of ownership and its respective objective. Indeed, a VC-affiliated accelerator is interested mainly in deal flow and eventually financing the most promising participants. Academically affiliated accelerators, on the other hand, are interested in providing relevant entrepreneurial training to students, while NGO-affiliated accelerators may frame a mission that relates to the societal objective of enhancing quality of life.

Process

Accelerators follow a linear process, starting with the selection of start-ups, offering educational programming and mentoring, and culminating with a demo day, an event that celebrates the start-up's graduation by pitching to investors and other industry actors. The demo day is also an event that provides an opportunity for the accelerator to reassert its position and legitimacy as an important actor in shaping the new economy's ecosystem through identifying and growing start-ups. As one of the accelerator's managers contends:

> The demo day is an opportunity for the start-ups to show what they have, but it is also an opportunity for us to strengthen our relations with our current networks and expand them by inviting new players. It is an opportunity to show the quality of our program and our commitment to build and maintain the Israeli entrepreneurial ecosystem. (Interview with the authors, July 2016)

For commercially oriented accelerators, the process of acceleration serves as a selection tool for the close monitoring of the progress of the start-up and an assessment of its value and potential. In this sense, VC-sponsored accelerators, for example, utilize the program for their investment decision making. The manager of a VC accelerator explains:

> We are selecting the best start-up so we first enhance our deal flow. We are providing them with space and "pizza money" and charge eight percent equity. We have an excellent network, but no less important, we are promising the start-ups that we will invest, ourselves, in the best. I know, this creates pressure and tension, but also healthy competition. Sometimes, the selected start-ups decline to participate because of the consequences of not being selected for investment

by us, which they think will tarnish their chances to raise money. (Interview with the authors, February 2016)

Cooperation among start-ups is usually considered an asset. In the bylaws of the program of a notable accelerator based in Tel Aviv, Israel, two out of the five items refer to collaboration, including a mandate to "respect one another and be curious and aware of the other's dilemmas and problems, and be a friend to one another." (The first item refers to mandatory attendance and a commitment to "be present, physically and mentally.") Accelerators engage in both explicit and implicit activities to encourage collaboration. Starting with the physical layout, start-ups usually work in a common open space and engage in specialized sessions devoted to providing comments and advising one another on various issues, from technology to marketing. By interacting closely with others, comparing and sharing problems, dilemmas and frustrations, the accelerator provides a supportive environment based not only on the program but also on the peer support of those who have undergone a similar process. One of the accelerator's managers asserts:

Cooperation among the participants is crucial. We start with the selection process. One important criterion is choosing the start-ups. Then, in many of our activities, we work with mixed groups, so each person can bring in his or her insight and knowledge. We encourage the start-ups to help each other in solving practical issues concerning technology, marketing, recruitment or even business strategy. So we can even identify mentors among the start-ups. By encouraging cooperation, we complement the program by sharing the knowledge and experience of the participants. (Interview with the authors, April 2016)

The benefit of cooperation is reiterated by one of the accelerator's participants: "I got more from the other participants than from the mentors and the program. Once you open up and are willing to share your dilemmas with others, you get creative advice" (Eran, interview with the authors, February 2016).

Accelerators' External Characteristics

Accessibility
Accelerators evaluate themselves on various KPIs, including their internal objectives and the outcomes of the accelerating program in terms of the sum of its participants' KPIs. Accordingly, the effectiveness of providing access to resources, networking or mentors is contingent upon the start-ups' willingness and ability to use the accelerator's varied offerings. The assumption is that the accelerator provides "optimum accessibility

to the inputs needed for the successful raising of investment" (accelerator manager, interview with the authors, February 2016), but the benefits are dependent on the start-ups themselves.

A distinct aspect of accessibility is related to the accelerator's objective of encouraging innovative start-ups, disruptive technologies and creative services. In this sense, accelerators perceive themselves as agents of change that feed into the ecosystem stream of innovations and the respective enterprises that attempt to disseminate these innovative products or services, for either profit or non-profit purposes. In particular, corporate accelerators such as those operated by Microsoft or IBM justify the rationale for having an in-house accelerator, in spite of the cost and the status as a non-profit activity, as a link to the dynamic innovative sector of start-ups. The general managers of the Microsoft accelerator claim:

> Start-ups are a hotbed for innovations. Through the accelerator's participants, we are able to develop new ideas and technological solutions. We are tapping on potential sources of new innovation and new technology. We are a behemoth, and we sometimes are not linked to the new cool things individual entrepreneurs are doing. Through the accelerator, we have access to innovation and at the same time, we disseminate our cloud technology, the Azure. (Interview with the authors, August 2016)

Furthermore, the technological solutions and other lessons learned regarding growing start-ups accumulated by the accelerators are usually disseminated from cohort to cohort. Such accessibility of knowledge makes the accelerator an effective organizational form for growing new firms. As the accelerator accumulates experience and knowledge, it operates more effectively. Dani, an accelerator manager, stated:

> We learn from every cohort, always new things in technology, products, marketing or business. This is our asset. Sometimes, it is an automatic understanding of what to do and not to do, or intuition regarding how to develop a promising business plan, and what investor or team member is needed. (Interview with the authors, March 2016)

In sum, accelerators play an important social and economic role as an organizational form that not only identifies opportunities for innovation, but also facilitates their distribution in the environment.

Validity and legitimacy

Accelerators are well-linked organizations within their respective ecosystems. In many cases, accelerators see themselves as the creators of the ecosystem. One of the notable Israeli accelerators in the field of transportation developed a network of all the organizational players that deal with transportation and related issues, including the private and public sectors, academia and start-ups. Being in the bridging position enables the accelerator to be one of the key actors that shape the agenda of the sector, to generate important information that helps in designing its activity and to provide effective validation for the start-ups that graduate from its program.

An important aspect of legitimacy is the standing and reputation of the accelerators. In numerous discussions with start-ups' founders, we have found that the issue of the selection of accelerators strongly influences their decision to apply and participate in a given accelerator's program. For example, being selected by the Microsoft accelerator implies high prospects for exposure to the best investors; it is a door opener. As one of the founders explains:

> Microsoft provides you not only material resources, their Azure, but also bestows on us their reputation, the possibility to be acquired by them and to be respected as an important player in the industry.
> Participation in the program is like a "Kosher" stamp. It signals to everyone that you are an innovative and worthy start up. (Rami, interview with the authors, May 2016)

Thus, a connection to Microsoft's reputation, standing and network is seen as an asset that the start-up acquires, in addition to its business idea, product, technology or service; an asset that bestows validity and legitimacy.

Another important factor with regard to legitimacy is the use of the accelerator's close network. Inbal, the founder of a renowned accelerator in Tel Aviv, explains: "We are not a local accelerator. We are offering to the start-up a global network, by using our alumni [of the specific technological army unit that founded the accelerator], which are operating in places such as Silicon Valley or Berlin" (Interview with the authors, January 2016). Indeed, a distinct class of accelerators could be termed "network accelerators," whose main objective is to serve as brokers of a kind, a link between the start-up and the investors. Their legitimacy resides in their ability to match appropriate investors to the start-ups and, at the same time, to benefit from "finders' fees."

An accelerator's internal design may also be used as a tool in its legitimation strategies. Specifically, incorporating distinguished partners in an industry as sponsors of a designated cohort enhances both internal and external legitimacy, among start-ups and external organizations, respectively.

Validation is considered a by-product of the acceleration process. It embodies various aspects. The first is validation of the start-up's product, market or technology. Some accelerators search for ideas and teams, and provide the platform—work space and some resources. The accelerator may be very active in assisting the start-up in developing the business model and/or the company itself. In this sense, accelerators serve as coaches, steering the start-up towards obtaining investment. Another form of validity concerns the reputation of the accelerator as a hub for promising start-ups. Successful accelerators, claims one of our interviewees, a journalist who covers the Israeli high-tech industry, "develop a reputation for selecting the best start-up in terms of ideas and teams and upgrading their abilities considerably. In this way, they signal to investors that their start-ups are dependable and promising. In this way, accelerators provide a quality assurance stamp" (Interview with the authors, May 2016). Thus, accelerators signal to the ecosystem that the start-up has undergone an adequate selection process, in addition to an educational program that improves its capabilities.

The role of validator puts pressure on accelerators to focus their program on those aspects important to investors, sometimes at the expense of their other mission. For example, an accelerator's manager testifies:

> I have to compete with other accelerators for my position as a leading validator, so I align my KPI to fit the market need, devoting, for example, too many sessions to branding and less to other social activities. Eventually, I decided to limit my role as validator only for early stage start-ups. (Interview with the authors, February 2016)

Accelerators are organizations that influence their ecosystem through the implementation of programs aimed at preparing and providing start-ups with business and investment opportunities. Lean organizations in terms of structure and management, accelerators focus on the strategic idea that their programs do not stand alone; their quality and impact are dependent upon the accelerator's standing and embeddedness in its ecosystem. A thick network of mentors, sponsors, alumni and other key players, such as investors or specialized consultants, enables accelerators not only to attract promising start-ups, but also to maintain a reputation as validators. Thus, an effective accelerator is considered a bridge between those who initiate an enterprise (founders of start-ups) and those who can help an enterprise take off (investors, adopters of technology or product). Accelerators usually execute a linear program, starting with the selection of start-ups and continuing with intensive learning curricula that are highly diverse in terms of content and format. An integral part of the program is mentoring on the one hand and peer cooperation on the other. The official acceleration program ends with a demo day, a pitch, an event that exposes both the start-ups and the accelerator to potential investors and other gatekeepers of emerging ecosystems. Although small in size and limited in its objectives, the accelerator is an enterprise in its own right, an organization that specializes in learning and connecting through both its

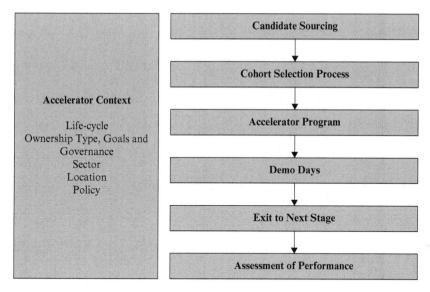

Figure 1.3   Accelerator process life-cycle

own knowledge and output and its ability to harness actors and forces in the environment for the purpose of facilitating and simplifying the work of entrepreneurs.

STRUCTURE OF THE BOOK

This book is structured on the basis of the life-cycle of accelerator programs for new ventures (Figure 1.3). This life-cycle starts with the means by which potential candidate ventures are sourced; the selection process for each cohort, the nature of the accelerator program, the nature and role of demo days; issues relating to the exit from the program and the next stage in the venture's life-cycle, including seeking investors; and the assessment of the performance of the ventures in each cohort and of the accelerator itself. These elements in the life-cycle process are analyzed in the context of how they are impacted by different dimensions of context.

Acceleration Themes

The chapters comprising the principal content of this book draw on evidence worldwide from developed and developing economies, including the

US, UK, France, Germany, the EU, Australia and Chile. They cover the following themes.

In Chapter 2, Matthias Wenzel and Jochen Koch develop conceptual arguments on *what* and *how* accelerators accelerate. Based on the literature on strategy process, they draw two conceptual distinctions that relate to the object of acceleration (strategic core versus strategic periphery) and the processual patterns of acceleration (forwarding versus leaping). They then use these distinctions to conceptualize and discuss four ways in which accelerators can accelerate the business development of new ventures. They argue that start-up acceleration seems to be largely aimed at forwarding and leaping the strategic periphery instead of the strategic core. This chapter extends the emerging literature on accelerators by making the case for considering and examining start-up acceleration as a process and offering a more specific and nuanced understanding of how it occurs.

In Chapter 3, Laurens Vandeweghe and Trent Fu provide a micro-lens on business accelerators' governance practices by examining how accelerators manage their external networks and internal organizations to achieve their organizational goals. As such, they look both at how accelerators coordinate autonomous stakeholders such as partners, investors and portfolio companies within a network form of governance and at how accelerators are monitored and controlled internally to preside over the day-to-day activities by organizational governance mechanisms. They classify accelerators based on their sponsorship (i.e. corporate, private, public), indicating that such sponsorship differences influence the ways in which accelerators are governed both from an external-network perspective and from an internal organizational perspective, and illustrate this by applying this dual perspective to the cases of AppCampus, Techstars and Start-Up Chile.

Ronit Yitshaki and Israel Drori focus in Chapter 4 on the important aspect of the accelerators' design structure and operation that concerns mentoring. By mentoring they refer to the process of learning and coaching provided by the accelerators to their participating start-ups by groups of experts with relevant knowledge and experience in founding and managing new ventures. Using detailed interview and observational data from Israel, they show that the mentoring process provides a bridge between the accelerator, the start-up and the ecosystem through the mentor's internal (within the start-up) and external (within the ecosystem) position. They suggest that mentorship is a complex process composed of both altruistic and interest-based motivations and processes, represented along a continuum starting as part of the accelerator's educational program, and either ending with the end of the program or leading to a transformation to a partnership. Accelerators play an important role in recognizing mentors who are relevant to the ecosystem while providing mentors with opportunities to invest and learn about the ecosystem, enabling them to conduct informal due diligence prior to investing as business angels. They identify four distinct aspects that characterize the mentoring process: (1) setting up strategy and priorities, (2) revealing marketing opportunities, (3) structuring organizational processes, and (4) expanding ventures' social capital.

Chapter 5 by Michael Leatherbee and Juanita Gonzalez-Uribe addresses issues relating to the selection of entrepreneurs and their ventures for entry into accelerators. Commonly, accelerators select start-ups among a broader group of applicants. The assumption is that through the selection process, accelerators are able to discriminate between high- and low-potential start-ups. Thus, the expectation is that accelerators are an effective medium for capturing the upside potential of the select few start-ups that promise to deliver the highest value in the future. That upside potential may be materialized through attractive equity investments or increased socio-economic development, depending on the mission of the accelerator. Typically, the selection process relies on a set of objective criteria predetermined by the accelerator, which are applied by one or more entrepreneurship experts who act as judges or evaluators of the applicant pool. First the authors describe the different selection stages and methods typically managed by business accelerators. They then go on to explore the multiple important issues that must be taken into account when designing and managing selection processes. Comprehending these issues may help to understand the challenges and limitations of current selection methods, and to avoid potential pitfalls and unintended consequences.

Chapter 6 by Leatherbee and Gonzalez-Uribe examines KPIs in accelerators. KPIs can help gauge the health and progress of business accelerators. Their use is fundamental for learning how to improve organizational and programmatic effectiveness, and for building a data-driven shield from program skeptics. However, figuring out which indicators are best, how to develop them and what phenomenon they are actually reflecting is a nontrivial exercise. The authors provide an overview of different KPIs that can be used by accelerator stakeholders. By explaining their value, limitations, methods of construction and potential pitfalls, they aim to provide accelerator stakeholders with a toolkit for building an effective KPI dashboard.

Policymakers are one of the key stakeholders in the entrepreneurial ecosystem in which accelerators are embedded. We present two chapters covering policy issues. In Chapter 7, Iris Vanaelst, Jonas Van Hove and Mike Wright, after a brief review of US policy towards accelerators, focus on how EU policy engages with different stakeholders in order to support accelerator activity within the EU area. The EU interactions with accelerators are threefold: (1) the EU supports the setup of accelerator networks to create momentum for accelerators to meet and exchange experiences, expertise and knowledge (e.g. Accelerator Assembly); (2) the EU supports and funds accelerator programs (e.g. EU-XCEL-European Virtual Accelerator, IoT Accelerator Programme, Copernicus Accelerator Programme); and (3) accelerators serve as intermediaries between the EU and start-ups looking for funding (e.g. European Pioneers) in addition to the small and medium-sized enterprise (SME) funding instruments of the EU (e.g. SME Instrument). Interesting examples of each of these initiatives are discussed in more detail.

In Chapter 8, Van Hove, Vanaelst and Wright explore the differences across countries and regions in accelerator support programs in order to improve understanding of the continuously evolving accelerator landscape and concomitant activities by complementary actors within an ecosystem community. They emphasize the role of institutional intermediaries in shaping the ecosystem through the preservation of the aligned interests between policymakers and practitioners. Reviewing the evolution of the landscape of policy support for accelerators across national and regional levels, with particular emphasis on the UK context, they outline the challenges accelerators face and which policymakers need to take into account. They conclude with policy implications and recommendations focusing on how the ecosystem community can meet such challenges in order to spur ecosystem development and fuel the next generation of start-ups.

In Chapter 9, Martin Bliemel, Saskia de Klerk, Ricardo Flores and Morgan Miles review the historic context in which an accelerators industry emerged in Australia in parallel with policy development to indirectly support start-ups. Their study spans over three decades of policies aimed at supporting innovative high-growth ventures. Early attempts at stimulating an incubator industry failed. The authors focus on the most recent years, during which accelerators initially emerged in Australia in the absence of policy tailored to the accelerator business model, followed by the design and implementation of a A$23 million national Incubator Support Programme.

Finally, in Chapter 10, Massimo Colombo, Cristina Rossi-Lamastra and Mike Wright set out an agenda for future research on accelerators. They suggest that the agenda for future research is multi-leveled, involving the accelerators and their programs as well as the firms, entrepreneurs and mentors involved. As accelerators operate in a range of different contexts, a future research agenda needs to consider the dimensions of these contexts. As accelerators are a rapidly evolving phenomenon, there is also the imperative to consider the time dimension with respect to life-cycle issues.

CONCLUSIONS

In sum, accelerators serve as an organizational type that mobilizes both internal and external resources to enhance the innovation capabilities of start-ups and expose these innovations to markets and institutions. This mission of accelerators, of growing start-ups and fostering ecosystems of innovation, has placed them at the forefront of providing support for innovations in which new knowledge, products or services emanate from speculative ideas and entail risky execution. Studies on the innovation emerging from start-ups tend to focus either on the dynamics of creating innovation or on the constraints on innovation stemming from both organizational and market needs. However, the ability of start-ups to create innovations is dependent on ties and networks that connect communities of start-ups. Furthermore, most existing accounts of the emergence of innovation in start-ups provide little explanation about the actual process and how to enhance innovation through the creation of communities. This book seeks to fill the gap in understanding in how new innovative ecosystems emerge. We have compiled chapters on accelerators, organizational forms that serve as facilitators and brokers that shape the path and the pace of growing start-ups into viable organizations at the forefront of our rapidly changing society.

REFERENCES

Adkins, D. 2011. What are the new seed or venture accelerators? *NBIA Review*. Available at http://www.nbia.org/resource_library/review_archive/0611_01.php (accessed April 13, 2017).

Bakker, R.M., DeFilippi, R.J., Schwab, A. and Sydow, J. 2016. Temporary organizing: promises, processes, problems. *Organization Studies*, 37(12), 1703–1719.

Barbero, J.L., Casillas, J.C., Wright, M. and Garcia, A.R. 2014. Do different types of incubators produce different types of innovations? *Journal of Technology Transfer*, 39(2), 151–168.

Bone, J., Allen, O. and Haley, C. 2017. Business incubators and accelerators: the national picture. BEIS Research Paper #7. BEIS/Nesta.

Burke, C.M. and Morley, M.J. 2016. On temporary organizations: a review, synthesis and research agenda. *Human Relations*, 69(6), 1235–1258.

Clarysse, B., Wright, M. and Van Hove, J. 2015. *A Look Inside Accelerators*. London: Nesta.

Cohen, S. and Hochberg, Y. 2014. Accelerating startups: the seed accelerator phenomenon (March 30, 2014). Available at SSRN: https://ssrn.com/abstract=2418000 or http://dx.doi.org/10.2139/ssrn.2418000 (accessed November 9, 2016).

Dempwolf, C., Auer, J. and D'Ippolito, M. 2014. *Innovation Accelerators: Defining Characteristics among Startup Assistance Organizations*. Available at https://

www.sba.gov/sites/default/files/rs425-Innovation-Accelerators-Report-FINAL. pdf (accessed April 13, 2017).

Drori, I., Honig, B. and Wright, M. 2009. Transnational entrepreneurship: an emergent field of study. *Entrepreneurship Theory and Practice*, 33(5), 1001–1022.

Fishback, B., Gulbranson, C.A., Litan, R.E., Mitchell, L. and Porzig, M. 2007. Finding business 'idols': a new model to accelerate start-ups (July 2007). Available at SSRN: https://ssrn.com/abstract=1001926 or http://dx.doi. org/10.2139/ssrn.1001926 (accessed January 23, 2018).

Goswami, K., Mitchell, R. and Bhagavatula, S. 2018. Accelerator expertise: understanding the intermediary role of accelerators in the development of the Bangalore entrepreneurial ecosystem. *Strategic Entrepreneurship Journal*. DOI:10.1002/sej.1281.

Hathaway, I. 2016. Accelerating growth: startup accelerator programs in the United States. February 17, 2016. Washington, DC: The Brookings Institution. Available at: https://www.brookings.edu/research/accelerating-growth-startup-accelerator-programs-in-the-united-states/ (accessed January 10, 2018).

Hausberg, J.P. and Korreck, S. 2017. A systematic review and research agenda on incubators and accelerators (February 3, 2017). Paper to be presented at the Academy of Management Annual Meeting 2017, Atlanta (GA). Available at SSRN: https://ssrn.com/abstract=2919340 or http://dx.doi.org/10.2139/ssrn.291 9340 (accessed January 23, 2018).

Hochberg, Y. 2016. Accelerating entrepreneurs and ecosystems: the seed accelerator model. *Innovation Policy and the Economy*, 16, 25–51. DOI:10.1086/684985.

Hoffman, B. and Radojecich-Kelly, N. 2012. Analysis of accelerator companies: an exploratory case study of their programs, processes, and early results. *Small Business Institute® Journal*, 8(2), 54–70.

Isabelle, D. 2013. Key factors affecting a technology entrepreneur's choice of incubator or accelerator. *Technology Innovation Management Review*, February, 16–22. Available at http://www.timreview.ca/article/656 (accessed April 13, 2017).

Mian, S., Lamine, W. and Fayolle, A. 2016. Technology business incubation: an overview of the state of knowledge. *Technovation*, 50–51, 1–12.

Pauwels, C., Clarysse, B., Wright, M. and Van Hove, J. 2016. Understanding a new generation incubation model: the accelerator. *Technovation*, 13–24, 50–51.

Sparks, E. 2013. Top trends in state economic development. Washington, DC: National Governors Association. Available at http://www.nga.org/files/live/sites/ NGA/files/pdf/2013/1308TopTrendsinStateEconDevPaper.pdf (accessed April 13, 2017).

Vanaelst, I., Clarysse, B., Wright, M., Lockett, A. and Moray, N. 2006. Entrepreneurial team development in academic spinouts: an examination of team heterogeneity. *Entrepreneurship Theory and Practice*, 30(2), 249–271.

2. Acceleration as process: a strategy process perspective on startup acceleration

Matthias Wenzel and Jochen Koch

INTRODUCTION

Accelerators have become an important contemporary phenomenon. By helping (some) startups in the early stages of their life cycle "reach key success milestones" (Hallen, Bingham, and Cohen, 2014, p. 2), accelerators drive and shape the startup scene and, thus, essentially contribute to fostering innovation and economic growth. Therefore, scholars have become increasingly interested in the activities and practices of accelerators through which they accomplish these outcomes.

Given the economically important role of accelerators, scholars have begun to develop an understanding of *what* and *how* accelerators accelerate. This research mostly provides answers to these questions by capturing the unique characteristics of accelerators, such as their strategic focus, program duration, and funding structure (e.g., Cohen, 2013; Cohen and Hochberg, 2014; Clarysse, Wright, and Van Hove, 2016; Kohler, 2016; Pauwels, Clarysse, Wright, and Van Hove, 2016). These works have greatly contributed to highlighting the distinctive nature of accelerators, for instance, compared to incubators and angel investors. However, the *processes* through which accelerators foster the development of startups have yet to be described and explained. Exploring and conceptualizing these processes is important because "acceleration" is, after all, a processual phenomenon. In addition to the inherently processual nature of acceleration, examining acceleration as process allows scholars to unfold and explore the complexities of startup acceleration (e.g., Hallen et al., 2014; Seidel, Packalen, and O'Mahoney, 2016) in more depth (see Wenzel, Senf, and Koch, 2016). Therefore, we argue that, without a deeper understanding of these processes, it is difficult, if not impossible, to discern *what* accelerators accelerate and, even more importantly, *how* such acceleration occurs.

Given that the development of an early-stage startup is strategic in that already in its founding it involves making many decisions that have a lasting impact on the further development of the venture (e.g., Marquis and Tilcsik, 2013; Stinchcombe, 1965), we draw on the strategy process literature (e.g., Burgelman, 1983, 2002; Mintzberg and Waters, 1985; Mirabeau and Maguire, 2014; Regnér, 2003) to develop conceptual ideas on what accelerators accelerate and how such acceleration occurs. This literature is an important addition to our understanding of strategy content mainly because it draws attention to the processual patterns through which firms make strategy instead of predicting the effectiveness of a firm's strategy based on its characteristics (Mirabeau and Maguire, 2014). This focus allows us to conceptualize the object(s) of accelerators' acceleration activities as well as the processual patterns through which acceleration occurs.

Based on the strategy process literature, we make two key distinctions. First, we distinguish between the "strategic core" and the "strategic periphery" as the objects of acceleration. The strategic core, or the key aspect of strategy that influences the firm's trajectory, is often associated with the startup's product–market concept, whereas the strategic periphery relates to a startup's communicative packaging of the strategic core. Second, we distinguish between "forwarding" and "leaping" as two key ways in which acceleration can occur. Forwarding relates to supporting startups in making the transition of their strategic core or periphery to a new position within a shorter amount of time, whereas leaping refers to shifting a startup's strategic core or periphery to another state without the need for the startup to traverse this development itself. Based on these distinctions, we develop a typology (Cornelissen, 2017) based on which we argue that accelerators can "accelerate" the business development of startups in four different ways, targeting either the strategic core or periphery of a startup and occurring through either forwarding or leaping. As our conceptual ideas and examples indicate, these ways of acceleration are based on different assumptions, some of which coincide more with the realities of the startup landscape than others. These issues indicate that accelerators are particularly well suited to speed up the development of startups' strategic periphery through forwarding or leaping processes.

Our chapter makes two interrelated contributions to the emerging literature on accelerators. First, we highlight and explain the importance of examining startup acceleration as process and, in doing so, complement initial analyses that have provided insights into the (static) characteristics of accelerators. Second, we present conceptual ideas on *what* and *how* accelerators accelerate and, thus, provide a more specific and nuanced understanding of how startup acceleration occurs. Taken together, our chapter bolsters the nascent but growing literature on accelerators by promoting a process view on acceleration.

The remainder of this chapter is organized as follows. First, we provide a brief overview of prior literature on accelerators and explain why a process view on acceleration can add interesting insights to this literature. Second, we draw on the strategy process literature to develop a grid that helps us capture the ways in which acceleration can occur. Third, we discuss the extent to which these ways reflect the realities of the startup landscape. Fourth, we conclude this chapter by providing some directions for future research.

ACCELERATORS: TOWARD A PROCESS VIEW

Accelerators are a specific type of organization that foster the business development of startups especially in the early stage of these ventures' life cycles. Since the inception of the first accelerator—*Y Combinator*—in 2005 in Cambridge, MA, accelerators have rapidly become a global phenomenon (Pauwels et al., 2016). Accelerators can now be found in all parts of the world and in nearly all industrial segments. The phenomenon of accelerators has led to a revision of entrepreneurship education frameworks at universities and business schools, including studying hands-on mentoring and coaching that directly feeds into the business development of the new venture (see Chapter 4, Yitshaki and Drori, in this volume). However, Hallen et al. (2014) empirically showed that some accelerators are much more successful in helping new ventures develop their businesses than others. More specifically, they showed that while a few accelerators noticeably speed up the business development of startups, most accelerators have a low or even no such impact. Despite, or even because of, the study's inconclusiveness with regard to the underlying reasons, this finding suggests taking a more differentiated view on what and how accelerators accelerate the business development of startups.

Research has begun to develop a more differentiated perspective on accelerators by categorizing and examining their distinctive characteristics (e.g., Cohen, 2013; Cohen and Hochberg, 2014; Clarysse et al., 2016; Pauwels et al., 2016). For instance, Cohen and Hochberg (2014) describe accelerators in terms of program duration, cohorts, the business model, selection frequency, venture stage, type of education offered, venture location, and the degree of mentorship. Specifically, they argued that accelerators can be both profit-oriented and non-profit organizations that run a "*fixed-term* [about three months], *cohort-based* program [mostly for early-stage startups that are cyclically selected in a competitive process], including *mentorship and educational components* [especially seminars, usually on-site], that culminates in a public pitch event or *demo-day"* (Cohen and Hochberg, 2014, p. 4, emphasis in original). From this perspective, accelerators differ markedly from incubators and angel investors, which, among others differences, usually foster the business development of a loose portfolio of startups over a longer period of time and do not provide as much educational support (see also Cohen, 2013).

Pauwels et al. (2016) went even further by presenting another set of characteristics that describes differences between accelerators. Specifically, they argued that accelerators differ in terms of their strategic focus, program package, funding structure, selection process, and alumni relations. Based on these building blocks, Pauwels et al. (2016, p. 21) identified three design themes that characterize accelerators, namely, *ecosystem builders* that are "typically set up by corporate companies that wish to develop an ecosystem of customers and stakeholders around their company", *deal-flow makers* that "receive [. . .] funding from investors such as business angels, venture capital funds or corporate venture capital and ha[ve] the primary aim to identify promising investment opportunities for these investors", and *welfare stimulators* that "typically ha[ve] government agencies as a main stakeholder [and whose] primary objective [. . .] is to stimulate start-up activity and foster economic growth, either within a specific region or within a specific technological domain" (see also Clarysse et al., 2016). Kohler (2016) further specified the characteristics and dimensions along which ecosystem builders can vary, namely, the content of the program, the duration of the program, the people involved (managers of the accelerator, startup founders, mentors, etc.), and the place where the accelerator is hosted (e.g., on the campus of the sponsoring corporation or off-site).

Overall, prior research on accelerators has greatly contributed to teasing out and highlighting their distinctive natures. As these works demonstrate, gaining an understanding of how accelerators work based on insights on incubators and angel investors leads to partial conclusions at best, and drawing sweeping conclusions about what and how accelerators accelerate does not seem to reflect the specifics of different accelerators. These observations justify an examination of the inner workings of accelerators as a distinctive, contemporary, and complex phenomenon that plays an important role in the startup scene all over the world.

While these works have done accelerator scholars a great service by contributing to the establishment of a proprietary field of research on the accelerator phenomenon, they do not fully capture an important aspect of acceleration: its processual nature, that is, how it unfolds over time. More specifically, while the lists of characteristics and building blocks describe what accelerators are and what they do in a static way, acceleration occurs dynamically over time. For example, in physics, acceleration refers to change in velocity over time or the traveled distance divided by the squared elapsed time (e.g., Newton, 1729). From this perspective, it is impossible to think about acceleration without taking into account time elapsed: if time elapsed was set to zero, it would be impossible to calculate the acceleration of an object due to a division by zero. Therefore, we argue that acceleration cannot be fully understood without unfolding the processes through which it comes into being and, thus, with which it is inseparably intertwined.

In addition to the inherently processual nature of acceleration, we argue that examining acceleration as process helps scholars gain a complementary view of the complexities that it involves. More specifically, as shown above, prior research has countered its observation of the complex nature of and nuanced differences between accelerators by composing ever-more fine-grained lists of characteristics that describe these aspects. In contrast, taking a process view enables scholars to processually unfold this phenomenon and, in doing so, observe the actions that actors inside accelerators perform and reconstruct the underlying rationale in which these actions are embedded. This allows scholars to gain both a deep and holistic understanding of how and why this process occurs and what it targets (see Koch, Krämer, Reckwitz, and Wenzel, 2016, for a more comprehensive overview). Therefore, we argue that a process view on acceleration can add interesting insights to the nascent but growing literature on accelerators. In this vein, we define "acceleration" as the process of speeding up the business development of startups and, next, turn our attention to the strategy process literature, which provides helpful conceptual vocabulary for the development of conceptual ideas on what and how accelerators accelerate.

STARTUP ACCELERATION: A STRATEGY PROCESS PERSPECTIVE

To move toward an understanding of acceleration as process, we introduce the strategy process literature as a theoretical lens for the development of ideas on what and how accelerators accelerate. This literature is particularly well suited for this purpose because starting a new venture is essentially a strategic process (Hjorth, Holt, and Steyaert, 2015; McMullen and Dimov, 2013; Sarasvathy, 2001). The foundation of a new venture involves a stream of many (in part, seemingly small) decisions with a long-lasting impact on the further development of the business (e.g., Marquis and Tilcsik, 2013; Stinchcombe, 1965). As we explain next, this processual unfolding of strategy-making is at the heart of the literature on strategy process.

Strategy Process: A Synopsis

The literature on strategy process consists of different streams; these streams share that they are interested in the processes through which firms make strategy (Hutzschenreuter and Kleindienst, 2006). This aspect differentiates the literature on strategy process from prevalent research on strategy content, which is interested in exploring characteristics of strategies and predicting their performance implications (Mirabeau and Maguire, 2014). Thus, instead of describing and explaining strategy-making in terms of a list of characteristics, research on strategy process typically defines strategy-making as "a pattern in a stream of decisions" (Mintzberg, 1978, p. 934) and processually unfolds strategy-making to explore these patterns.

Interestingly, this processual understanding of strategy-making has already been developed and promoted by early research on strategy process (e.g., Burgelman, 1983; Mintzberg, 1978; Mintzberg and Waters, 1985). Yet, as Langley (2007, p. 272) explained, much of the subsequent literature on strategy process has made no difference to research on strategy content, given that "process is most often reduced to a variable" with entitative characteristics in this literature. More recently, however, strategy process scholars have rediscovered and reinvigorated the original strength of considering strategy as process (e.g., Balogun, Best, and Lê, 2015; Burgelman, 2002; Mirabeau and Maguire, 2014; Regnér, 2003; Rouleau and Balogun, 2011). Thus, this literature has restarted to explore patterns of strategy-making and how and why they occur.

The literature on strategy process provides at least two helpful conceptual distinctions that can be usefully translated into the context of startup acceleration. The first distinction relates to a firm's *strategic core* vs. *strategic periphery*, which can be described as the object of acceleration. The second distinction refers to *forwarding* vs. *leaping* as two distinct ways of accelerating the business development of startups. These two oppositional pairs help us cluster and describe four processes of startup acceleration along two dimensions that are of interest to this chapter, that is, *what* (object of acceleration) and *how* (patterns of acceleration) accelerators accelerate (see Figure 2.1), thus facilitating a more specific and nuanced conceptual understanding of the process(es) of startup acceleration. We now explain these conceptual distinctions in more detail.

Strategic Core vs. Strategic Periphery

A key strength of the literature on strategy process is that it provides a more specific and nuanced understanding of how firms make strategy. In this vein, Regnér (2003) showed empirically that firms do not make strategy in a unified way. Rather, actors at a firm's *core* make strategy in a deductive and exploitative way. In contrast, according to this study, actors at a firm's *periphery* enact an inductive and exploratory way of strategy-making.

In its early stages, a new venture usually does not consist of a large number of actors between which one can usefully distinguish in terms of core and periphery. Nevertheless, one can still leverage the strength of this distinction by translating it into and unfolding it as a content-based distinction (Luhmann, 1995), that is, as to whether acceleration affects the core or periphery of a startup's strategy—the object of acceleration.

From this perspective, the *strategic core* refers to the "product–market concept" (Burgelman, 1983) of a startup. It describes which kinds of products and services a startup aims to offer and which market segments it targets. The strategic core is aligned to a large extent with the idea of a business model (Massa, Tucci, and Afuah, 2017; Osterwalder and Pigneur, 2010; Zott, Amit, and Massa, 2011): it not only implicitly or explicitly defines the value proposition to consumers but also clarifies how the products and services are to be produced and how they are delivered to consumers.

In contrast, the *strategic periphery* relates to the communicative packaging (Dutton, Ashford, O'Neill, and Lawrence, 2001; Rouleau and Balogun, 2011) of the strategic core. It involves "selling" the strategic core to relevant external stakeholders, including investors and potential buyers, to nurture the growth of the new venture (van Werven, Bouwmeester, and Cornelissen, 2015). In the context of accelerators, such communicative packaging becomes especially manifest at the demo day, the final event at the end of the cyclical program at which the participating startups present their businesses to potential investors by means of a pitch. As such live presentations are "staged" events (Goffman, 1959) at which presenters package the strategic core of their new venture by means of oral communication, bodily movements, and the use of material artifacts (Wenzel and Koch, 2017), the strategic periphery involves the orchestration and coordination of discursive, bodily, and material resources (see Streeck, Goodwin, and LeBaron, 2011).

Forwarding vs. Leaping

Another prominent distinction in the literature on strategy process relates to the longitudinal patterns of how strategic change occurs. Specifically, this literature typically distinguishes between evolutionary and revolutionary change (Ansari, Garud, and Kumaraswamy, 2016; see also Amis, Slack, and Hinings, 2004; Tushman and Anderson, 1986). In this context, evolutionary change refers to a gradual and stepwise transition from one strategy to another. In contrast, revolutionary change relates to the radical and disruptive shift of a firm's strategy from one state to another.

Again, this distinction cannot be readily transferred to the context of startup acceleration. These categories usually refer to patterns of strategic change over longer periods of time. However, new ventures usually have a rather short and eventful history in which it is difficult to observe evolutionary strategic change, given that revolutionary strategic change is the norm rather than the exception. Nevertheless, if we consider "acceleration" as speeding up the development of a startup's strategic core and/or periphery, this distinction highlights two ways in which this can occur: as "forwarding" and as "leaping".

Forwarding refers to helping startups shift their strategic core or periphery within a shorter amount of time. For this, accelerators provide practical, hands-on knowledge by means of seminars, coaching, and mentorships that aim to directly feed into the business development of participating startups. Similar to firms' evolutionary strategic change, new ventures must traverse these processes themselves. However, in contrast to a "natural" strategic evolution outside of accelerators that is based on experiential learning, new ventures can potentially run through this gradual development faster, given that accelerators' semi-structured programs can provide learning short-cuts through the transfer of specialized knowledge, thus potentially helping startups avoid making common mistakes.

In contrast, *leaping* refers to shifting a startup's strategic core or periphery to another state without the need for the startup to traverse this development itself. Thus, through leaping, accelerators make essential resources for the growth of new ventures readily available, such as access to production networks, distribution nets, markets, and templates for the effective communication of the strategic core (presentation benchmarks, PowerPoint templates, etc.). Similar to firms' revolutionary strategic change, startups can make immediate use of these resources without having to accumulate them gradually over an extended period of time. Thus, accelerators can accelerate the business development of startups by making resources available that immediately change a new ventures' strategic core and/or periphery.

WHAT AND *HOW* ACCELERATORS ACCELERATE: A TYPOLOGY

The two distinctions that we drew based on the literature on strategy process now enable us to develop a 2×2 grid that sketches four ways in which accelerators can accelerate the business development of new

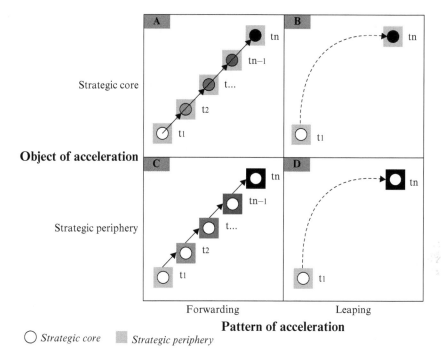

Figure 2.1   What and how accelerators accelerate

ventures: forwarding the strategic core, leaping the strategic core, forwarding the strategic periphery, and leaping the strategic periphery (see Figure 2.1). Thus, this typology provides a more nuanced understanding of the process of startup acceleration in terms of the targeted object (strategic core vs. strategic periphery) and pattern of acceleration (forwarding vs. leaping). We now discuss these four ways of accelerating with regard to the extent to which they can be enacted by accelerators.

Forwarding the Strategic Core

The first way of accelerating the business development of new ventures refers to forwarding the strategic core (see Figure 2.1, Field A). This way of accelerating relates to helping startups advance their product–market concept in a faster way, especially by offering specialized seminars and providing skilled mentors and coaches that transfer knowledge and skills that the startups would have to acquire through lengthy processes of experiential learning outside of accelerators. On the "product" side, it can include transferring relevant technological knowledge that helps startups improve the functionality and design of their product and/or service and increasing the efficiency of producing their offerings. On the "market" side, the strategic core can be forwarded by providing relevant knowledge that helps startups sharpen the targeted market segment(s) and improving the delivery of their products and/or services to the market.

This way of accelerating the business development of new ventures is based on the premise that accelerators have such knowledge readily available. Indeed, having such knowledge available may be one major reason why many accelerators match the selection of participating startups to their strategic focus (Pauwels et al., 2016), such as on digital health, food, and real estate. However, although the participating startups may aim to conduct their business within a similar strategic scope, the specific needs may vary strongly and, in part, be highly idiosyncratic (e.g., see Sarasvathy, 2001)—in fact, to be successful at some point in time, the development of the startups' strategic cores *must* be idiosyncratic (Barney, 1991). Therefore, Hallen et al. (2014) doubt that attempts to forward the strategic core significantly contribute to accelerating the business development of new ventures.

Leaping the Strategic Core

The second way of accelerating the business development of new ventures relates to leaping the strategic core (see Figure 2.1, Field B). Whereas forwarding the strategic core still requires startups to make the transition of their product–market concept themselves, leaping the strategic core refers to shifting the product–market concept to a new state without the need for new ventures to go through this transition. On the "product" side, this can include providing immediate access to relevant technologies and production networks. On the "market" side, the strategic core can be leaped by providing immediate access to relevant markets, for example, a large corporation that runs a "corporate accelerator" (Kohler, 2016) and buys out the products and/or services (or even the entire startup) that a participating new venture offers.

This way of accelerating the business development of new ventures is based on the assumption that access to relevant inputs to the "product" and/or "market" sides of the strategic core is readily available. In fact, it may be particularly well suited for the recognition or discovery of technological or market opportunities, and thus could potentially be practiced by accelerators. However, this way of accelerating essentially misses the transformational power of startups that may extend beyond what already exists in terms of products/services or markets (e.g., see Sarasvathy, 2001). For this, granting access to existing resources, knowledge, and skills can be important, but it does not allow new ventures to shift their strategic core from A to B without having to traverse this development; in the end, they must (gradually) shape technologies and markets themselves.

Forwarding the Strategic Periphery

The third way of accelerating the business development of new ventures relates to forwarding the strategic periphery (see Figure 2.1, Field C). This way of accelerating refers to helping startups improve the communicative packaging of their strategic core faster than experiential improvements outside of accelerators would allow. In practice, forwarding the strategic periphery can become manifest as seminars and coaching aimed at improving the founders' presentation skills to enable them to be more convincing during pitches for and discussions with investors and potential buyers. Given the embodied and material aspects of such interactions, training the founders' presentation skills may include the improvement of not only rhetorical skills but also the entire staged choreography.

Similar to forwarding the strategic core, this way of accelerating the business development of new ventures is based on the premise that the relevant knowledge and skills—here, presentation skills—are readily available, and indeed, the large number of presentation coaches indicates that accelerators do have such knowledge and skills available. Yet, whereas the development of the strategic core has to be idiosyncratic (Barney, 1991), the communicative packaging of the strategic core does not. Quite the contrary, there may even be value in standardizing communicative interactions with investors and potential buyers. On the one hand, using standard language as used in the startup scene signals being a (key) part of this landscape. On the other hand, given the complexity of evaluating the strategic core, this allows business partners to focus on key aspects in their evaluations instead of being distracted by a non-standard use of language (while still being able to communicatively conceal shortcomings of the strategic core).

Leaping the Strategic Periphery

The fourth way of accelerating the business development of new ventures relates to leaping the strategic periphery (see Figure 2.1, Field D). Whereas forwarding the strategic periphery still requires startups to shift the communicative packaging of the strategic core themselves, leaping the strategic periphery does not necessarily involve the need for new ventures to traverse this development. For example, startups may receive PowerPoint templates that provide guidance for the preparation of demo-day pitches without having to try out different ways of presenting the business model. Given the embodied and material aspects of pitches and other types of interactions with investors and potential buyers, startups may also be provided with benchmark videos of successful entrepreneurs who are renown for outstanding presentations.

Similar to leaping the strategic core, this way of accelerating the business development of new ventures is based on the assumption that accelerators can provide access to the templates and benchmarks for convincing in communicative interactions with investors and potential buyers. In fact, the high standardization of pitches indicates that accelerators do have such resources available. Consequently, it seems that accelerators largely forward or leap—either deliberately or unconsciously—the strategic periphery and play a lesser role in accelerating the development of the strategic core.

CONCLUSION

In this chapter, we set out to develop conceptual arguments on what and how accelerators accelerate. For this purpose, we drew on the literature on strategy process, which helped us make two distinctions—one relating to the object of acceleration (strategic core vs. strategic periphery) and another referring to patterns of acceleration (forwarding vs. leaping)— which results in four ways in which accelerators can accelerate the business development of new ventures. As we discussed, some ways of accelerating are more likely than others, given that they are based on assumptions that coincide with the realities of new ventures to varying extents. Specifically, as we argue, especially speeding up the development of the strategic periphery seems to play a preponderant role in accelerating the business development of new ventures.

Contributions and Implications

Our chapter makes two interrelated contributions to the emerging literature on accelerators. First, we highlight and explain the importance of examining startup acceleration as process. Whereas prior works have insightfully highlighted the distinct nature of accelerators by identifying their (static) characteristics (e.g., Cohen and Hochberg, 2014; Pauwels et al., 2016), our chapter specifies why it is interesting to unfold acceleration as process, explore the underlying patterns of this process, and explain how and why these patterns occur. As we argued, acceleration is inherently a processual phenomenon that requires a process perspective to be understood in more depth. Furthermore, we highlighted that examining acceleration as process also allows scholars to gain deeper insights into this phenomenon by processually unfolding its complexities.

Second, we present conceptual ideas on *what* and *how* accelerators accelerate. While mixed empirical evidence for the effectiveness of accelerators (e.g., Hallen et al., 2014) indicated the need for a more nuanced understanding of how startup acceleration occurs, our chapter draws on the literature on strategy process and specifies that there are different objects and patterns of acceleration that accelerators can leverage. As we explained, this leads to four different ways in which acceleration can occur—with an overall tendency toward accelerating the strategic periphery. In doing so, our chapter provides a more specific and nuanced understanding of how accelerators accelerate the business development of new ventures.

Directions for Future Research

Our conceptual ideas offer an initial impetus toward examining acceleration as process. Therefore, our chapter constitutes a starting point for future research that points in this direction.

Specifically, the ways in which accelerators accelerate the business development of new ventures is an empirical matter to a considerable extent; that is, the distinctions we drew are analytic in nature and may not become manifest in such a clear-cut way in empirical observations. Therefore, future research may provide further empirical insights into and details of what and how accelerators accelerate. For this, the presented grid may provide a useful heuristic for the analysis of empirical data. By using this grid, future research may gain insights into the underlying mechanisms in which the ways accelerators accelerate the development of new ventures are embedded. By doing so, future studies may explore empirically the conditions under which accelerators tilt to an emphasis on accelerating either the strategic core or the strategic periphery and on forwarding or leaping these objects of acceleration. Such studies may also observe the cohabitation of different ways of accelerating and how accelerators achieve it. In addition to the ambidextrous simultaneity of these processes, future research may also examine if, and if so, how, certain patterns and objects of acceleration might serve as necessary preconditions for other ways of acceleration. For instance, before leaping the strategic periphery, by providing a presentation template for investor pitches, it might be necessary to forward or leap the strategic core in order to be able to fill the blanks in the template with idiosyncratic information about the startup's product–market concept. In turn, forwarding the strategic periphery, for example, by educating founders in packaging the strategic core effectively, might contribute to advancing the startup's product–market concept by making founders repeatedly articulate their startups' strategic core and generating feedback in small training groups.

More generally, we encourage future research to consider and empirically examine acceleration more fully as process. In doing so, such works can explore and gain a more complete understanding of the complexities that are involved in accelerating the business development of new ventures and do justice to the inherently processual nature of "acceleration".

ACKNOWLEDGMENTS

We are grateful to Israel Drori and Mike Wright for inviting us to contribute to this edited collection and for their helpful comments and suggestions. Furthermore, we thank Thomas Andrae, Chief Strategist of the Berlin-based accelerator *AtomLeap*, Marius Sewing, CEO-in-Residence of the *Microsoft Ventures* accelerator in Berlin, and Robin Tech, Co-founder and Managing Director of *AtomLeap*, for inspirational chats and talks.

REFERENCES

Amis, J., Slack, T., and Hinings, C. R. (2004). The pace, sequence, and linearity of radical change. *Academy of Management Journal, 47*(1), 15–39.

Ansari, S., Garud, R., and Kumaraswamy, A. (2016). The disruptor's dilemma: TiVo and the U.S. television ecosystem. *Strategic Management Journal, 37*(9), 1829–1853.

Balogun, J., Best, K., and Lê, J. (2015). Selling the object of strategy: How frontline workers realize strategy through their daily work. *Organization Studies, 36*(10), 1285–1313.

Barney, J. B. (1991). Firm resources and competitive advantage. *Journal of Management, 17*(1), 99–120.

Burgelman, R. A. (1983). A model of the interaction of strategic behavior, corporate context, and the concept of strategy. *Academy of Management Review, 8*(1), 61–70.

Burgelman, R. A. (2002). Strategy as vector and the inertia of coevolutionary lock-in. *Administrative Science Quarterly, 47*(2), 325–357.

Clarysse, B., Wright, M., and Van Hove, J. (2016). A look inside accelerators in the United Kingdom: Building businesses. In P. Phan, S. Mian, and W. Lamine (eds), *Technology Entrepreneurship and Business Incubation: Theory, Practice, Lessons Learned* (pp. 57–86). London: Imperial College Press.

Cohen, S. L. (2013). What do accelerators do? Insights from incubators and angels. *Innovations, 8*(3/4), 19–25.

Cohen, S., and Hochberg, Y. (2014). Accelerating startups: The seed accelerator phenomenon. Working Paper. Available at http://seedrankings.com/pdf/seed-accelerator-phenomenon.pdf (accessed January 14, 2018).

Cornelissen, J. (2017). Developing propositions, a process model, or a typology?

Addressing the challenges of writing theory without a boilerplate. *Academy of Management Review, 42*(1), 1–9.

Dutton, J., Ashford, S., O'Neill, R., and Lawrence, K. (2001). Moves that matter: Issue selling and organizational change. *Academy of Management Journal, 44*(4), 716–736.

Goffman, E. (1959). *The Presentation of Self in Everyday Life.* New York: Doubleday.

Hallen, B. L., Bingham, C. B., and Cohen, S. L. (2014). Do accelerators accelerate? A study of venture accelerators as a path to success. *Academy of Management Proceedings, 2014*(1), 12955.

Hjorth, D., Holt, R., and Steyaert, C. (2015). Entrepreneurship and process studies. *International Small Business Journal, 33*(6), 599–611.

Hutzschenreuter, T., and Kleindienst, I. (2006). Strategy-process research: What have we learned and what is still to be explored. *Journal of Management, 32*(5), 673–720.

Koch, J., Krämer, H., Reckwitz, A., and Wenzel, M. (2016). Zum Umgang mit Zukunft in Organisationen—eine praxistheoretische Perspektive. *Managementforschung, 26*, 161–184.

Kohler, T. (2016). Corporate accelerators: Building bridges between corporations and startups. *Business Horizons, 59*, 347–357.

Langley, A. (2007). Process thinking in strategic organization. *Strategic Organization, 5*(3), 271–282.

Luhmann, N. (1995). *Social Systems.* Stanford, CA: Stanford University Press.

Marquis, C., and Tilcsik, A. (2013). Imprinting: Toward a multilevel theory. *Academy of Management Annals, 7*(1), 195–245.

Massa, L., Tucci, C. L., and Afuah, A. (2017). A critical assessment of business model research. *Academy of Management Annals, 11*(1), 73–104.

McMullen, J. S., and Dimov, D. (2013). Time and the entrepreneurial journey: The problems and promise of studying entrepreneurship as a process. *Journal of Management Studies, 50*(8), 1481–1512.

Mintzberg, H. (1978). Patterns in strategy formation. *Management Science, 24*(9), 934–948.

Mintzberg, H., and Waters, J. A. (1985). Of strategies, deliberate and emergent. *Strategic Management Journal, 6*(3), 257–272.

Mirabeau, L., and Maguire, S. (2014). From autonomous strategic behavior to emergent strategy. *Strategic Management Journal, 35*(8), 1202–1229.

Newton, I. (1729). *Mathematical Principles of Natural Philosophy.*

Osterwalder, A., and Pigneur, Y. (2010). *Business Model Generation: A Handbook for Visionaries, Game Changers, and Challengers.* Hoboken, NJ: John Wiley & Sons.

Pauwels, C., Clarysse, B., Wright, M., and Van Hove, J. (2016). Understanding a new generation incubation model: The accelerator. *Technovation, 50–51*, 13–24.

Regnér, P. (2003). Strategy creation in the periphery: Inductive versus deductive strategy-making. *Journal of Management Studies, 40*(1), 57–82.

Rouleau, L., and Balogun, J. (2011). Middle managers, strategic sensemaking, and discursive competence. *Journal of Management Studies, 48*(5), 953–983.

Sarasvathy, S. D. (2001). Causation and effectuation: Toward a theoretical shift from economic inevitability to entrepreneurial contingency. *Academy of Management Review, 26*(2), 243–263.

Seidel, V. P., Packalen, K. A., and O'Mahoney, S. (2016). Help me do it on my own:

How entrepreneurs manage autonomy and constraint within incubator organizations. *Research in the Sociology of Organizations, 47*, 275–307.

Stinchcombe, A. (1965). Social structures and organizations. In J. March (ed), *Handbook of Organizations* (pp. 142–193). Chicago: Rand McNally.

Streeck, J., Goodwin, C., and LeBaron, C. (2011). *Embodied Interaction: Language and Body in the Material World*. Cambridge: Cambridge University Press.

Tushman, M. L., and Anderson, P. (1986). Technological discontinuities and organizational environments. *Administrative Science Quarterly, 31*(3), 439–465.

van Werven, R., Bouwmeester, O., and Cornelissen, J. (2015). The power of arguments: How entrepreneurs convince stakeholders of the legitimate distinctiveness of their ventures. *Journal of Business Venturing, 30*(4), 616–631.

Wenzel, M., and Koch, J. (2017). Strategy as staged performance: A critical discursive analysis of keynote speeches as a staged genre of strategic communication. *Strategic Management Journal, 39*(3), 639–663.

Wenzel, M., Senf, N., and Koch, J. (2016). Exploring complex phenomena with qualitative research methods: An examination of strategic innovation trajectories in haute cuisine. In E. Berger, and A. Kuckertz (eds), *Complexity in Entrepreneurship, Innovation and Technology Research: Applications of Emergent and Neglected Methods* (pp. 163–182). Wiesbaden: Springer.

Zott, C., Amit, R., and Massa, L. (2011). The business model: Recent developments and future research. *Journal of Management, 37*(4), 1019–1042.

3. Business accelerator governance

Laurens Vandeweghe and Jyun-Ying (Trent) Fu

INTRODUCTION

Extant literature on the organizational aspects of business accelerators mostly focuses on the services accelerators perform for the accelerated companies or "portfolio companies", such as training, mentorship, networking and investment activities (Miller and Bound, 2011; Radojevich-Kelley and Hoffmann, 2012; Caley and Kula, 2013), and how this differs from incubators and angel investors (Cohen, 2013; Cohen and Hochberg, 2014; Bliemel and Flores, 2015). Further, accelerator literature has distinguished accelerator typologies based on their value proposition or the package of benefits and costs accelerators offer to start-ups (Dempwolf, Auer, and D'Ippolito, 2014) and their "business model elements" such as program package, strategic focus, selection process, funding structure and alumni relations (Pauwels, Clarysse, Wright, and Van Hove, 2016). While this research has been important in describing the functioning of (different models of) accelerators, it has taken a strong focus on accelerators' services as performed in relation to portfolio companies, rather than capturing all the different stakeholders involved. Although some recent studies have explored the relationships between accelerators and mentors (Bernthal, 2016, 2017), a holistic analysis of how accelerators interact with all their internal and external stakeholders is currently missing. Given the importance of stakeholder management within accelerators (Caley and Kula, 2013), there is a need for a comprehensive view of accelerator governance, that is, how accelerators build and manage relationships with internal and external stakeholders to effectively attain their organizational goals.

This chapter aims to fill this gap by identifying accelerators' main stakeholders and investigating accelerators' organizational and network governance mechanisms from a micro-perspective. Through a conceptual analysis, we distinguish three internal stakeholders – sponsors, directors and staff – and three external stakeholders – partners, investors and portfolio companies – and reveal the organizational and network governance mechanisms at play in their relations with accelerators. Furthermore, we look at corporate-backed, private-backed and public-backed accelerators and explore how these different types of accelerators govern their relationships with stakeholders. Three cases are used as examples to illustrate our notions: AppCampus, a corporate accelerator that ran between 2012 and 2015 and aimed at populating the Windows Phone platform; Techstars, a private accelerator that started in 2007 and currently runs over 28 programs worldwide, and Start-Up Chile, a public accelerator created by the Chilean government in 2010 to position Chile as a hub of innovation in South America.

This chapter contributes to the literature on accelerators and other business incubation models by providing an in-depth understanding of accelerators' stakeholders and governance mechanisms (Grimaldi and Grandi, 2005). As such, we introduce a stakeholder perspective (Freeman, 1984) and the notions of organizational governance and network governance (Jones, Hesterly, and Borgatti, 1997) into the literature on accelerators. In doing so, we contribute to the theoretical development of the accelerator concept which several researchers have recently called for (Kohler, 2016; Mian, Lamine, and Fayolle, 2016), and provide inspiration for the analysis of governance practices of other incubation models to which this approach may equally apply. Lastly, by looking at governance across different accelerator typologies, we respond to the call in extant literature to take the differences among accelerators into account (Hochberg, 2016; Pauwels et al., 2016) and contribute to further understanding this heterogeneity. The chapter is organized as follows. The next section presents a general review on accelerators and their stakeholders. This is followed by an analysis of accelerator organizational governance of internal stakeholders. Then we explore the accelerator network governance of external stakeholders and accelerator governance across different types. Following our empirical cases, we present the conclusion and implications.

ACCELERATOR STAKEHOLDERS

To effectively provide start-ups with time-limited, cohort-based mentoring and networking programs (Miller and Bound, 2011; Clarysse, Wright, and Van Hove, 2015), accelerators establish and manage relationships with internal and external stakeholders. A stakeholder is "any group or individual who can affect or is affected by the achievement of the organization's objectives" (Freeman, 1984: 46) and can be categorized into primary or secondary – depending on whether the stakeholder's participation is necessary or unnecessary for the survival of the focal organization (Clarkson, 1995) – and internal or external – depending on whether the stakeholder is situated within or outside of the boundaries of the focal organization (Freeman, 1984). In this chapter, we focus on the primary stakeholders (Freeman, 1984), as other accelerator literature has looked at secondary stakeholders who *indirectly* influence or are influenced by the accelerator, such as the local region (Fehder and Hochberg, 2014) or the business ecosystem (Thomas, Sharapov, and Autio, 2018; Sivonen, Borella, Thomas, and Sharapov, 2015).

Based on the extant literature (i.e. Caley and Kula, 2013; Bernthal, 2016), six different primary accelerator stakeholders can be distinguished of which three are internal – sponsors, directors and staff – and three are external – partners, investors and portfolio companies. Sponsors fund accelerators and could be corporations, private investors such as angel investors and venture capitalists (VCs) and public or semi-public organizations such as universities and government agencies (Pauwels et al., 2016). Directors are the general managers or executive directors responsible for the strategic decision-making and the management of the day-to-day operations while the accelerators' staff members (help) execute accelerators' day-to-day activities (Caley and Kula, 2013). Partners can be conceptualized as individuals or organizations that offer services and products to accelerators or their portfolio companies for free or at a discount (Caley and Kula, 2013). Typical partners would be mentors, professional services or technology companies, pre-accelerators and other incubation models, key customer networks and so on. Investors provide the follow-on funding for accelerated ventures and could be angel investors, VCs or large corporations (Miller and Bound, 2011). And last, portfolio companies relate to the new-venture teams that take part in accelerator programs or have ever graduated from them (Cohen and Hochberg, 2014).

We suggest that these six stakeholder groups are typically present in any accelerator, although the importance of each stakeholder and the boundaries between external and internal stakeholders might differ among different accelerators. Moreover, individuals or organizations may take up more than one stakeholder role simultaneously or change roles over time. In what follows, we outline the specificities of each stakeholder group, their interplay with accelerators and the formal and informal governance mechanisms that manage the stakeholder relationships. By governance mechanisms, we refer to those mechanisms that regulate the relationships between the accelerators and the stakeholder groups. More precisely, we distinguish between organizational governance mechanisms such as equity-based incentives or explicit contracts which apply to internal stakeholders (Jensen and Meckling, 1976), and network governance mechanisms such as norms of reciprocity (Bosse and Phillips, 2016), reputation and trust to make sure that external stakeholders "engage in collective and mutually supportive action, that conflict is addressed and that network resources are acquired and utilized efficiently and effectively" (Provan and Kenis, 2008: 231).

ACCELERATOR ORGANIZATIONAL GOVERNANCE OF INTERNAL STAKEHOLDERS

We adopt an organizational governance perspective to look at how accelerators govern relationships with internal stakeholders such as sponsors, directors and staff to ensure that they act in accordance to accelerators' goals.

Sponsors

To finance an accelerator, one or more accelerator sponsors would set up a fund to cover the accelerator operations and – if this is included in the offer of the accelerator – an initial investment in the portfolio companies (Nesta, 2014). This fund would typically cover the expenses and investments of an accelerator for a period of two to four years (Deloitte, 2015). The relationships between sponsors and accelerators are governed through formal mechanisms, such as monitoring, steering and control of the accelerators' managing directors through the board of directors or investment board and formal ownership of the accelerator organization (Bernthal, 2016).

Directors

Accelerators are typically managed by hands-on operators or managing directors (Caley and Kula, 2013; Bernthal, 2016), appointed by the sponsors and mainly responsible for co-developing the strategy with the sponsors and executing it accordingly. The managing directors of an accelerator would typically sit on a board of directors supplemented by non-executive directors. Often, the sponsors would be involved in the board of directors or in the advisory board to follow, steer and/or control the directors on a regular basis. To a certain extent, the directors possess great autonomy in their management of the accelerator, but important decisions such as venture selection would in some accelerators go through an investment board where the sponsors could be involved (Sharapov, Thomas, and Autio, 2013). Although most managing directors are governed through direct contracts, university accelerators are sometimes managed by student-volunteers (Adomdza, 2016).

Staff

Accelerators' managing directors are assisted by other staff who will be responsible for operations, marketing and external stakeholder management (Caley and Kula, 2013). These staff would normally be governed through organization–employee relationships but may also be working voluntarily and include entrepreneurs-in-residence (in between start-ups), technology experts, student interns and other staff (Bernthal, 2016). Although accelerators possess different internal structures, they are typically flat-structured, with relatively small numbers of staff, mainly focused on the executional activities of the accelerator (Caley and Kula, 2013; Cohen and Hochberg, 2014).

ACCELERATOR NETWORK GOVERNANCE OF EXTERNAL STAKEHOLDERS

Within their networks, accelerators manage relationships with external stakeholders such as partners, investors and portfolio companies to attract and allocate external resources (Figure 3.1). In doing so, they aim to satisfy the interests of the external actors while ensuring that their differing and sometimes conflicting objectives do not manifest themselves at the expense of attaining the accelerators' goals.

Partners

Accelerators have different kinds of partners of which the most important are mentors and service providers.

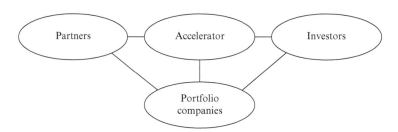

Figure 3.1   Accelerators' external stakeholders

Accelerators must organize mentors – usually in the form of technology or market experts, former entrepreneurs, private investors or corporate employees (Hochberg, 2016) – to provide the strategic assistance that portfolio companies require. Rather than hire in-house experts, or contract external experts, most accelerators assemble a volunteer network of experts to mentor portfolio companies using more implicit exchanges (Bernthal, 2016). While mentorship in a start-up market environment would mostly be governed by a dyadic exchange of cash or equity for expert services, in an accelerator environment, mentors typically do not secure cash or equity but instead contribute voluntarily (Bernthal, 2017). Informal governance mechanisms such as trust and indirect benefits such as reputation are at play between the mentors, the portfolio companies and the accelerators. As such, mentors trust they will get a future option to invest in the portfolio company or a future job opportunity as an employee or advisor, while portfolio companies trust that mentors will not behave opportunistically by using portfolio companies' sensitive information to their personal benefit (Bernthal, 2017). Mentors also receive indirect benefits by strengthening and broadening their relationships with other mentors in the entrepreneurial community, learning from novel technology and investment trends and increasing their reputation towards parties outside the network (Bernthal, 2017). Furthermore, some mentors commit because they want to "give back" to the start-up community after a successful entrepreneurial or investor trajectory (Miller and Bound, 2011; Nesta, 2014).

Besides mentors, accelerators also partner with professional services or technology companies. Some of them hold workshops in their area of expertise while others offer their services or products to the portfolio companies for free or at a discount (Caley and Kula, 2013). Similarly, the relationships between professional services or technology companies and portfolio companies are based on trust as most aim to convert the portfolio companies to customers after the acceleration program. Besides inroads to new start-ups, they may also seek engagement with the accelerators' mentors and investors (Miller and Bound, 2011). The networks of mentors and professional services or technology companies would in some accelerators be complemented with other partners such as key customer networks (Nesta, 2014) or other venture support organizations (Sharapov et al., 2013).

Investors

Accelerators play an important intermediary role between start-ups and potential investors. Specifically, accelerators aim to provide their portfolio companies with follow-on investment after the acceleration program by connecting them to more established investors such as angel investors, VCs, and corporate investment arms (Miller and Bound, 2011). Accelerators build and maintain strong relationships with these follow-on investors through informal mechanisms such as investor events and the related periodic source of deal flow (Bernthal, 2016) or – for accelerators that provide funding in return for equity – formal mechanisms such as common investments. Furthermore, the reputation of the accelerator and its portfolio companies plays an essential role in gaining visibility and credibility towards investors (Plummer, Allison and Connelly, 2016). A good and elaborate network of investors is not only necessary for potential follow-on investment but also for offering a unique source of advice and connections to the portfolio companies (Nesta, 2014).

Portfolio Companies

Most of the portfolio companies choose to be accelerated with the aim of expanding their network via mentors, gaining skills and receiving feedback on their business, benefitting from funding and co-working space (if applicable) and securing additional funding once the program is over (Christiansen, 2009; Birdsall, Jones, Lee, Somerset and Takaki, 2013). Both formal and informal governance mechanisms are used to govern portfolio companies. In exchange for the resources offered by the accelerator, such as financing or mentoring support, the ventures' founders often lose part of their equity to the accelerator. While this challenges the entrepreneurs' intention to retain full control of their new ventures (Wasserman, 2017), equity stakes provide a formal governance mechanism for accelerator organizations and help align the interests of accelerators with their portfolio companies. Besides equity, other formal governance mechanisms could be staged investments dependent on certain milestones or conditions (Sharapov et al., 2013; Gonzalez-Uribe and Leatherbee, 2016) and exclusivity agreements to tie portfolio companies' products to a certain platform in the case of corporate accelerators (Sharapov et al., 2013). An informal governance mechanism that is often used by accelerators is "accountability" (Caley and Kula, 2013; Gonzalez-Uribe and Leatherbee, 2016). This mechanism is executed through sessions where entrepreneurs go over the activities they had committed to undertake following the last accountability session and has been suggested to enhance portfolio companies' performance (Gonzalez-Uribe and Leatherbee, 2016). Other informal governance mechanisms are related to trust and social relationships nursed between company founders and directors, staff and mentors through coaching, workshops and frequent networking events during and often also after the acceleration program. The resulting social integration of the stakeholders within the network helps reduce opportunism (Bernthal, 2016).

ACCELERATOR GOVERNANCE ACROSS DIFFERENT TYPES

While accelerators have sprouted from a privately backed financial intermediary model with the sole purpose of offering deal flow to private investors, novel models have emerged from the 2010s onwards (Clarysse et al., 2015; Dempwolf et al., 2014; Pauwels et al., 2016). Accelerators now get their funding from three major sources: corporations, private investors and government schemes (Dempwolf et al., 2014). Although some accelerators receive their funding from a combination of these sources, there is often a primary institution that provides most of the funding and that will strongly impact the governance of the accelerator. Based on their sponsorship, three accelerator typologies can be distinguished: corporate accelerators, private accelerators and public accelerators. In what follows, we present the different types of accelerators and outline the differences in their organizational and network governance.

Corporate Accelerators

Corporate accelerators are funded by corporations that directly get reputational gains from the accelerators while they, in the long run, aim to insource external innovation through interaction with start-ups (Hochberg, 2016; Weiblen and Chesbrough, 2015), rejuvenate corporate culture and attract talent (Kohler, 2016) and contribute to the corporate's ecosystem of partners, users and customers (Dempwolf et al., 2014).

Corporate accelerators' organizational governance mechanisms depend on three organizational dimensions: their operational model, their connection to the sponsors and their leadership experience (Kanbach and Stubner, 2016). In terms of the operational model, corporate accelerators could be operated by an internal team hired by the organization or outsourced to an organization that provides such services, such as Techstars. Alternatively, companies could partner with others to establish a joint accelerator or join the sponsors of an existing accelerator (Hochberg, 2016). In terms of connection to the sponsors, a corporate accelerator may be run from an independent entity or from an organizational unit within the sponsor organization (Kanbach and Stubner, 2016). The leadership experience refers to the experience of the management team, that is, a corporate background from within the sponsor company or a background in the start-up world, which will reflect on the corporate accelerator's organizational practices (Souitaris, Zerbinati, and Liu, 2012).

Concerning their network governance, corporate accelerators typically offer the new ventures mentorship from a combination of internal "corporate coaches" and externals such as entrepreneurs and domain experts (Kohler, 2016). As corporate accelerators look for potential synergies between new ventures and their corporate sponsors, they may evoke a threat of misappropriation in potential accelerator applicants (Katila, Rosenberger and Eisenhardt, 2008). To avoid this, corporate accelerators typically do not take any equity (Clarysse et al., 2015). Examples of corporate accelerators include the Wayra Telefonica accelerators or the AppCampus[1] accelerator.

Private Accelerators

Private accelerators receive funding from private investors such as business angels and VCs with the primary aim to identify promising investment opportunities. They typically bridge the equity gap between early-stage projects and investable businesses and offer their sponsors a pipeline of investable companies, early market insights and, eventually, financial gains (Miller and Bound, 2011). Private accelerators' directors often have extensive experience as entrepreneurs or angel investors and adopt the organizational practices from these environments (Cohen and Hochberg, 2014).

As their main objective is return-on-investment, private accelerators are for-profit entities and tend to favor ventures that are in later stages of development (Clarysse et al., 2015). The mentors in these accelerators are often (former) business angels or (former) entrepreneurs who volunteer in return for reputation, social and human capital and future opportunities (Bernthal, 2017). In contrast to corporate and public accelerators, private accelerators typically provide money and services in exchange for equity stakes between 5 percent and 10 percent (or an equivalent convertible note) (Miller and Bound, 2011), which aids the alignment of interests between the portfolio companies and their accelerators. Y Combinator and Techstars[2] are the most popular examples of this type of accelerator.

Public Accelerators

Public accelerators have government agencies as their main sponsors, and their primary objective is often to stimulate start-up activity and foster economic growth within a specific geographic region or within a specific technological domain. They mainly receive funding from local, national and international government agencies and benefit the targeted regions or technological domains in terms of increased start-up activity and in attracting and deploying entrepreneurial talent (Pauwels et al., 2016). Public accelerators' managing directors may receive quite a bit of autonomy, which risks eroding board control and accountability (Malek, Maine, and McCarthy, 2014).

As opposed to corporate and private accelerators, mentorship in public accelerators is typically done by (former) entrepreneurs or business developers who provide hands-on guidance and advice on a paid basis (Pauwels et al., 2016). Hence, mentorship is governed by explicit contracts and not only by norms of reciprocity, reputation and trust. As these accelerators are non-profit organizations, they may offer stipends but typically do not request any equity in return (Pauwels et al., 2016). Start-Up Chile[3] or Climate-KIC are examples of such type of accelerator.

CASES

We illustrate the different governance aspects of each accelerator type (corporate, private, public) by using the examples of AppCampus, Techstars and Start-Up Chile. In doing so, we will use the framework as presented in this chapter and focus on the particularities of each case.

AppCampus (Corporate Accelerator)[4]

AppCampus was an accelerator that ran from spring 2012 till spring 2015. It was funded by two corporate sponsors, Microsoft and Nokia, and hosted by Aalto Center of Entrepreneurship (ACE), a unit within Aalto University that coordinated the activities related to technology transfer and start-up (Farny and Kyrö, 2015). AppCampus aimed to educate mobile application (app) developers about the Windows Phone platform and launch innovative apps on this platform. Overall, AppCampus accelerated 315 app developers and received more than 4,300 applications from over 100 countries. Its apps generated nearly seven times more downloads and twice more revenue than average in the Windows Phone Store.

AppCampus was open for everyone but highly selective, aiming for apps that were innovative, had a substantial potential and supported the key features of Nokia and Windows phones. Depending on the complexity of the app, the applicants could receive a €20,000, €50,000 or €70,000 investment without giving up intellectual property or equity. The only requirement was that the app, once developed, would be exclusively available on the Windows Phone Store for a period of – initially six and later – three months (Thomas et al., 2018). AppCampus' teams were invited to apply for a four-week training and mentorship program organized at Aalto University. The selection process for this camp was based on the added value it could provide to the applicants. The camp offered extensive one-on-one coaching and hands-on training in mobile branding and positioning, design, development, monetization, marketing, communications, pitching and so on. The teams also got networking opportunities with the corporate partners and potential follow-on investors (Sharapov, Thomas, and Autio, 2014). In what follows, we look at how AppCampus applied organizational and network governance mechanisms to manage its relationships with internal and external stakeholders.

Sponsors
AppCampus' investments were covered by Nokia and Microsoft who each put in €9 million, while the operational expenses of the accelerator such as personnel and office space were taken on by Aalto University (Sharapov et al., 2013). AppCampus' sponsors did not only provide financial support but also offered non-financial resources to portfolio companies. As such, Nokia and Microsoft provided members of the AppCampus portfolio with access to their corporate technological, marketing and merchandising expertise (Thomas et al., 2018) while ACE was strongly embedded in the entrepreneurial community and offered inroads to the VC community in Finland as well as internationally (Farny and Kyrö, 2015).

Directors and staff
To ensure that the strategy met the needs of Aalto University, Nokia and Microsoft, a steering board consisting of two members of staff from both Nokia and Microsoft, one member of staff from Aalto University and one independent member met monthly to evaluate AppCampus' performance and any required strategic changes (Sharapov et al., 2014). The steering board was responsible for appointing the head director and also decided upon the Key Performance Indicators, which were related to the number of AppCampus apps developed and their respective success on the platform in terms of downloads, revenue and user ratings (Sharapov et al., 2014). An investment board comprising two members of AppCampus and two members of ACE was established to select app ideas for funding (Sharapov et al., 2013).

Partners
AppCampus established partnerships to increase the magnitude and quality of the deal flow and attract expert resources to coach the teams.

As for the deal flow, AppCampus established partnerships with the sponsors' accelerators and camps such as Aalto University's Startup Sauna and Startup Bootcamp, Nokia's "Invent with Nokia" and Microsoft's BizSpark. Furthermore, AppCampus established partnerships with international accelerators such as Wayra Telefonica, GameFounders, The Founder Institute and the World Bank's Infodev program. These partnerships were geared to getting more and better teams into the program. Concerning the mentors, AppCademy attracted experts both from local start-ups or investment vehicles as well as from within the sponsors to provide mentorship and coaching on a variety of technical- and business-related subjects.

Investors

AppCampus teams were introduced to external VCs and angel investors to enable them to gain additional and/or follow-on funding. This opportunity was not only provided by the mentors but also built into the program as it organized demo days for investors and engaged the teams to participate in pitching competitions. Also, the partnerships with other accelerators served some companies in getting follow-on funding through referral.

Portfolio companies

AppCampus had a global remit, targeting mobile entrepreneurs around the world. By requiring the launched apps to be temporarily exclusive to the Windows Phone platform, Nokia and Microsoft tried to capture some of the value that was created by AppCampus through increased sales of apps and mobile phones. Furthermore, to ensure app quality, the investment was staged and contingent upon a successful launch of the app. As such, a team received only 30 percent of their grant upon acceptance of the app design while the remaining 70 percent was released upon launch and completion of the quality control stages (Sivonen et al., 2015).

Techstars (Private Accelerator)[5]

Techstars is a mentorship-driven private accelerator founded by one serial entrepreneur (David Cohen) and three angel investors (Brad Feld, David Brown and Jared Polis) in Boulder, Colorado in 2006. It accepted its first cohort of ten companies in a three-month mentoring program in 2007. Since 2007, Techstars has expanded its accelerator activities to other cities such as Boston in 2009, Seattle in 2010 and New York City in 2010. As of early 2017, Techstars has accepted around 895 companies into its mentoring program, and these ventures have raised $2.75 billion in funding, with a total of $7.5 billion market capitalization.

Admission to Techstars is quite competitive and jointly decided by directors inside Techstars, usually with a 1 percent acceptance rate. Once admitted, new-venture teams receive a $100,000 convertible note and $20,000 seed funding in exchange for a 6 percent equity stake. In addition to initial funding, Techstars provides other resources, such as access to investors, mentors, peers and so on. After a three-month mentorship program, new ventures have the opportunity to pitch to angel investors and VCs at the end of the program.

Furthermore, Techstars actively collaborates with big corporates to outsource its accelerator model, *"powered by Techstars"*. For example, since 2013, Techstars has collaborated with Kaplan to run an accelerator that focuses on new ventures at the nexus between education and technology, and since 2014, Techstars has managed the Barclay accelerator with a particular focus on fintech.[6] In what follows, we will focus on Techstars' private accelerators and analyze the governance mechanisms Techstars uses to manage its relationships with internal and external stakeholders.

Sponsors
The initial funding for Techstars came from 75 different VCs. After that initial funding, Techstars also raised several additional rounds of funding. For example, in 2011, Techstars raised $24 million of new funding from several VCs and some Techstars alumni. By raising funds from a broad range of investors, Techstars cannot only scale its model but can also offer its portfolio companies access to a larger investor community.

Directors and staff
The highest organizational layer in Techstars is the board of directors, currently consisting of 16 people ranging from CEO to senior executives. The next organizational layer includes the managing or operating managers for each accelerator program, usually industry experts or (former) entrepreneurs. Similar to other accelerators, Techstars features a relatively flat organization with few hierarchies.

Partners
Techstars boasts a global network of over 3,000 mentors, including some renowned entrepreneurs such as Tumblr CEO David Karp and HubSpot co-founder Dharmesh Shah.[7] Most mentors in Techstars are business angels, serial entrepreneurs or corporate partners. In addition to direct feedback, new ventures often have access to mentors' social networks of business angels and VCs. These mentors usually volunteer for mentorship support in return for reputational gains from participation in Techstars

and for gaining access to reputable mentors, investors or entrepreneurs. Techstars also partners up with government agencies and actively builds relationships with the government. As such, in 2011, Techstars collaborated with the White House to spur growth in entrepreneurship and is now part of the White House's Startup America Partnership initiative.

Investors

Techstars' network also features prestigious VCs and angel investors which are invited at demo days to attend the pitches or to be part of the panel. Due to its strict selection process, Techstars boasts that it provides investors first-hand access to those innovative start-ups and early-stage firms.

Portfolio companies

Like many other private accelerators, Techstars primarily funds technology-oriented companies (web-based, software or mobile-app sectors) with national or global reach in return for a share of their equity.

Start-Up Chile (Public Accelerator)[8]

Start-Up Chile (SUP) is a business accelerator based in Santiago founded by the Chilean Economic Development Agency (CORFO) in 2010. As of early 2017, CORFO has invested more than $40 million in 1,309 SUP ventures, which are estimated to be worth $1.4 billion. Interestingly, around 76 percent of founders are foreign from over 70 countries, while only 24 percent are Chilean. The program's end goal is to attract entrepreneurial talent from all over the world and transform Chile into the hub of innovation and entrepreneurship in Latin America.

Accepted teams receive $40,000 initial funding, a one-year working visa, and office space. The only requirement is that teams are expected to stay in Chile for around six months and actively engage in local entrepreneurial communities, such as attending workshops or lectures held by local entrepreneurs. Different from other accelerators such as Techstars, SUP provides seed funding but does not take any equity.

SUP's successful model has been replicated by a number of countries around the world. For example, Start-Up Brasil, Start-Up Perú and Malaysia's MaGIC have imitated the SUP model with the aim of boosting the local economy by promoting local entrepreneurial ecosystems.[9] In what follows, we identify the different internal and external stakeholders of SUP and the governance mechanisms at play in their relationship with SUP.

Sponsors

SUP is under the supervision of CORFO, Chile's development agency. The annual operating cost for SUP is around $15 million and is all supported by the Chilean government.

Directors and staff

The advisory board is the highest organization in SUP and consists of a group of professionals that provides advice or develops practices for SUP (Gonzalez-Uribe and Leatherbee, 2016). The board holds several meetings during the year and makes suggestions for changes to the implementation of the SUP program. The executive team is led by an executive director, accompanied by an accelerator program director, an operations director, a marketing and communications director and a community and network director.

Partners

SUP features a program that helps foreign entrepreneurs connect with local (aspiring) entrepreneurs (Melo, 2012). For example, SUP initiates the "internship" program that targets local undergraduate students, primarily from Santiago's universities. Once accepted, those undergraduate students work with SUP staff teams or SUP venture teams. SUP also sets up a website that helps SUPs' venture teams search for internships, hence stimulating the knowledge flow between the local community and the talented start-ups. Furthermore, SUP established the Godfathers ("Padrinos") program that assigns a local buddy (usually local entrepreneur) who helps acclimatize foreign SUP entrepreneurs to the new environment (Carmel and Richman, 2013). SUP matches the background of accepted foreign entrepreneurs with someone from the local business community, primarily based on language and interests. The matched local buddy then helps these participants with their daily basic needs, such as finding them flats, opening a bank account, getting a local mobile number or applying for their IDs. By providing those participants with such "soft landing" assistance, SUP creates links between the local business community and the foreign participants.

Investors

By leveraging the reputation of CORFO, venture teams at SUP have the opportunity to pitch in front of many prestigious national and foreign investors during the demo day or final pitching event upon graduation.

Portfolio companies

SUP typically accepts two cohorts of new ventures per year, with around 80 to 100 ventures per batch. SUP does not accept professional service firms such as consulting firms or export/import companies as these firms are not easily scalable. As SUP seeks to foster the entrepreneurial culture in Chile, their network governance primarily focuses on how to connect its local community and Chilean entrepreneurs more broadly with global talented entrepreneurs. Different from other accelerators, SUP does not aim to benefit from acquisitions or initial public offerings (IPOs). Instead, SUP views their portfolio companies as conduits that bring in entrepreneurial or innovation spirits from around the world (Carmel and Richman, 2013).

CONCLUSION

This study extends previous accelerator research by providing a holistic view on the micro-aspects of accelerator governance, encompassing its relationships with internal and external stakeholders and applying the resulting framework to the different types of accelerators. It contributes to practice and theory in the following ways.

Managerial and Policy Implications

While stakeholder management is an important activity within accelerators (Caley and Kula, 2013), a holistic framework for identifying, analyzing and managing stakeholder relationships has been largely missing. This chapter advances such a framework and suggests that it can be a useful tool for policy makers and practitioners to gain in-depth understanding of accelerators' governance mechanisms. It also complements the existing literature on how to design an accelerator (Deloitte, 2015; Christiansen, 2009; Kohler, 2016; Sivonen et al., 2015) and can be of additional value to practitioners and policy makers that intend to found accelerators. Moreover, although the framework has been derived from extensive analysis of the accelerator literature, it could also serve the analysis of governance practices of related business incubation models such as pre-accelerators and third generation incubators (Bruneel, Ratinho, Clarysse and Groen, 2012).

Theoretical Implications

Until now, little has been known about accelerators' primary internal and external stakeholders and their relationships with the accelerator. While some studies have looked at the relationship between accelerators and one of their stakeholders (Bernthal, 2016, 2017), a holistic analysis of accelerators' stakeholders has been largely missing. This chapter provides such analysis and sheds light on the governance mechanisms at play between accelerators and their main internal stakeholders – sponsors, directors and staff – and external stakeholders – partners, investors and portfolio companies. Second, it responds to the call in extant literature to take the heterogeneity among accelerators into account by looking into the differences in governance mechanisms across different accelerator sponsorship structures – corporate, private and public – and applying our framework to three different cases: (1) AppCampus, primarily sponsored by Microsoft and Nokia, (2) Techstars, sponsored by VCs and angel investors and (3) Start-Up Chile, sponsored by the Chilean agency for economic development. Third, by introducing the stakeholder perspective (Freeman, 1984) and the notions of organizational and network governance (Jones et al., 1997) into the literature on accelerators, the chapter responds to the call of accelerator researchers to further theoretical development of the accelerator concept (Kohler, 2016; Mian et al., 2016).

Limitations and Future Research

While this conceptual study of accelerator governance provided an in-depth holistic analysis of how accelerators manage stakeholder relationships, it did not specifically focus on stakeholders' conflicting interests. Nevertheless, this may be an important direction for future research as stakeholders' differing objectives, if any, may lead to interest conflicts and even harm an accelerator. Although some research has looked at how the problem of interest misalignment between accelerators and mentors could be alleviated (Bernthal, 2016, 2017), future research should explore how accelerators resolve conflicting interests from different stakeholder groups. Moreover, conflicting objectives may not only come from stakeholders' different interests but also from their different origins or institutional contexts. Accelerators operate in complex institutional environments and often have to manage demands from stakeholders coming from different institutional contexts, such as corporate sponsors and directors with VC experience in the case of many corporate accelerators (Souitaris et al., 2012). These different stakeholders hold different norms and practices and exert influence over accelerators to adopt these. The so-called institutional forces may not only be diverse but are often also competing. Hence, dealing with these competing institutional forces is a challenging task that has been largely overlooked by scholars and practitioners. More research is needed on how accelerators can resolve competing institutional forces while establishing or maintaining their legitimacy or the perception that their actions are desirable within each of these systems of norms (Suchman, 1995).

Besides the reconciliation of interest conflicts, we suggest that another interesting avenue for future research on accelerator governance relates to the differences across accelerators and their impact on portfolio companies' trajectories. As Gonzalez-Uribe and Leatherbee (2016) have suggested that governance mechanisms such as "accountability" are likely to influence portfolio companies' probability of raising seed and venture-capital funding, future research should delve deeper into the differences in governance across accelerators and their impact on portfolio companies' performance. This could be of importance to accelerators and other incubation models with comparable set-ups.

NOTES

1. For a description of AppCampus, see "Cases".
2. For a description of Techstars, see "Cases".
3. For a description of Start-Up Chile, see "Cases".
4. Source: Unless stated differently, the source for the information in this subsection comes from http://ace.aalto.fi/appcampus/ (last consulted 01/02/2017).
5. Source: Unless stated differently, the source for the information in this subsection comes from http://www.techstars.com/ (last consulted 01/02/2017).
6. Source: https://www.innovationleader.com/tracking-the-corporate-supported-startup-accelerators/ (last consulted 01/02/2017).
7. Source: http://www.cnbc.com/2013/11/21/whats-fueling-the-explosion-in-start-up-accelerators.html?view=story&%24DEVICE%24=native-android-mobile (last consulted 01/02/2017).
8. Source: Unless stated differently, the source for the information in this subsection comes from http://www.startupchile.org/ (last consulted 01/02/2017).
9. Source: https://techcrunch.com/2016/10/16/a-look-into-chiles-innovative-startup-government/ (last consulted 01/02/2017).

REFERENCES

Adomdza, G. K. (2016). Choosing between a student-run and professionally managed venture accelerator. *Entrepreneurship Theory and Practice*, 40(4), 943–956.

Bernthal, B. (2016). Investment accelerators. *Stanford Journal of Law, Business, and Finance*, 21(2), 139–191.

Bernthal, B. (2017). Who needs contracts? Generalized exchange within investment accelerators. *Marquette Law Review*, 100, 997–1061.

Birdsall, M., Jones, C., Lee, C., Somerset, C. and Takaki, S. (2013). Business accelerators: The evolution of a rapidly growing industry. University of Cambridge, Cambridge (MBA Dissertation at Judge Business School and Jesus College).

Bliemel, M. J. and Flores, R. G. (2015). Defining and differentiating accelerators: Insights from the Australian context. *Academy of Management Proceedings*, 2015(1), 14151.

Bosse, D. and Phillips, R. (2016). Agency theory and bounded self-interest. *Academy of Management Review*, 41(2), 276–297.

Bruneel, J., Ratinho, T., Clarysse, B. and Groen, A. (2012). The evolution of business incubators: Comparing demand and supply of business incubation services across different incubator generations. *Technovation*, 32(2), 110–121.

Caley, E. and Kula, H. (2013). *Seeding success: Canada's startup accelerators*. MaRS, Toronto, Canada.

Carmel, E. and Richman, J. (2013). Building international social capital at the Startup Chile accelerator. Working paper. Available at SSRN: https://papers.ssrn.com/sol3/papers.cfm?abstract_id=2326003 (last consulted 01/02/2017).

Christiansen, J. (2009). Copying Y Combinator: A framework for developing seed accelerator programmes. University of Cambridge, Cambridge (MBA Dissertation at Judge Business School and Jesus College).

Clarkson, M. E. (1995). A stakeholder framework for analyzing and evaluating corporate social performance. *Academy of Management Review*, 20(1), 92–117.

Clarysse, B., Wright, M. and Van Hove, J. (2015). *A Look Inside Accelerators*. London: Nesta.

Cohen, S. (2013). What do accelerators do? Insights from incubators and angels. *Innovations*, 8(3–4), 19–25.

Cohen, S. and Hochberg, Y. V. (2014). Accelerating startups: The seed accelerator phenomenon. Working paper. Available at SSRN: https://papers.ssrn.com/sol3/papers.cfm?abstract_id=2418000 (last consulted 01/02/2017).

Deloitte (2015). *Design Principles for Building a Succesfull Corporate Accelerator*. Available at: https://www2.deloitte.com/content/dam/Deloitte/de/Documents/technology/Corporate-Accelerator-EN.pdf (last consulted 01/02/2017).

Dempwolf, C. S., Auer, J. and D'Ippolito, M. (2014). *Innovation Accelerators: Defining Characteristics among Startup Assistance Organizations*. Small Business Administration. Available at: https://www.sba.gov/sites/default/files/rs425-Innovation-Accelerators-Report-FINAL.pdf (last consulted 01/02/2017).

Farny, S. and Kyrö, P. (2015). Entrepreneurial Aalto: Where science and art meet technology and business. In: Foss, L. and Gibson, D. (eds), *The Entrepreneurial University: Context and Institutional Change*, 150–166. New York: Routledge.

Fehder, D. C. and Hochberg, Y. V. (2014). Accelerators and the regional supply of venture capital investment. Working paper. Available at SSRN: https://papers.ssrn.com/sol3/papers.cfm?abstract_id=2518668 (last consulted 01/02/2017).

Freeman, R. E. (1984). *Strategic Management: A Stakeholder Approach*. Boston, MA: Pitman.

Gonzalez-Uribe, J. and Leatherbee, M. (2016). The effects of business accelerators on venture performance: Evidence from Start-Up Chile. Working paper. Available at SSRN: https://papers.ssrn.com/sol3/papers.cfm?abstract_id=2651158 (last consulted 01/02/2017).

Grimaldi, R. and Grandi, A. (2005). Business incubators and new venture creation: An assessment of incubating models. *Technovation*, 25(2), 111–121.

Hochberg, Y. V. (2016). Accelerating entrepreneurs and ecosystems: The seed accelerator model. *Innovation Policy and the Economy*, 16(1), 25–51.

Jensen, M. C. and Meckling, W. H. (1976). Theory of the firm: Managerial behavior, agency costs and ownership structure. *Journal of Financial Economics*, 3(4), 305–360.

Jones, C., Hesterly, W. S. and Borgatti, S. P. (1997). A general theory of network governance: Exchange conditions and social mechanisms. *Academy of Management Review*, 22(4), 911–945.

Kanbach, D. K. and Stubner, S. (2016). Corporate accelerators as recent form of startup engagement: The what, the why, and the how. *Journal of Applied Business Research (JABR)*, 32(6), 1761–1776.

Katila, R., Rosenberger, J. D. and Eisenhardt, K. M. (2008). Swimming with sharks: Technology ventures, defense mechanisms and corporate relationships. *Administrative Science Quarterly*, 53(2), 295–332.

Kohler, T. (2016). Corporate accelerators: Building bridges between corporations and startups. *Business Horizons*, 59(3), 347–357.

Malek, K., Maine, E. and McCarthy, I. P. (2014). A typology of clean technology commercialization accelerators. *Journal of Engineering and Technology Management*, 32, 26–39.

Melo, H. (2012). Prosperity through connectedness (Innovations Case Narrative: Start-Up Chile). *Innovations*, 7(2), 19–23.

Mian, S., Lamine, W. and Fayolle, A. (2016). Technology business incubation: An overview of the state of knowledge. *Technovation*, 50–51, 1–12.

Miller, P. and Bound, K. (2011). The startup factories: The rise of accelerator programmes to support new technology ventures. Nesta discussion paper. Available at https://www.nesta.org.uk/sites/default/files/the_startup_factories_0.pdf (last consulted 01/02/2017).

Nesta (2014). *Startup Accelerator Programmes: A Practice Guide*. Available at: http://www.nesta.org.uk/publications/startup-accelerator-programmes-practice-guide (last consulted 01/02/2017).

Pauwels, C., Clarysse, B., Wright, M. and Van Hove, J. (2016). Understanding a new generation incubation model: The accelerator. *Technovation*, 50–51, 13–24.

Plummer, L. A., Allison, T. H. and Connelly, B. L. (2016). Better together? Signaling interactions in new venture pursuit of initial external capital. *Academy of Management Journal*, 59(5), 1585–1604.

Provan, K. G. and Kenis, P. (2008). Modes of network governance: Structure, management, and effectiveness. *Journal of Public Administration Research and Theory*, 18(2), 229–252.

Radojevich-Kelley, N. and Hoffman, D. L. (2012). Analysis of accelerator companies: An exploratory case study of their programs, processes, and early results. *Small Business Institute® Journal*, 8(2), 54–70.

Sharapov, D., Thomas, L. D. W. and Autio, E. (2013). Building ecosystem momentum: The case of AppCampus. Paper presented at the 35th DRUID Celebration Conference, Barcelona, June 17–19.

Sharapov, D., Thomas, L. D. W. and Autio, E. (2014). AppCampus. In: Healy, A., Perkmann, M., Goddard, J. and Kempton, L. (eds.), *Measuring the Impact of University Business Cooperation (EAC/23/2012): Case Studies*, pp. 4–16. Luxembourg: Publications Office of the European Union.

Sivonen, P., Borella, P., Thomas, L. and Sharapov, D. (2015). How an accelerator can catalyze your ecosystem. *European Business Review*. September 17. Available at: http://www.europeanbusinessreview.com/how-an-accelerator-can-catalyse-your-ecosystem/ (last consulted 01/02/2017).

Souitaris, V., Zerbinati, S. and Liu, G. (2012). Which iron cage? Endo- and exoisomorphism in corporate venture capital programs. *Academy of Management Journal*, 55(2), 477–505.

Suchman, M. C. (1995). Managing legitimacy: Strategic and institutional approaches. *Academy of Management Review*, 20(3), 571–610.

Thomas, L. D., Sharapov, D. and Autio, E. (2018). Linking entrepreneurial and innovation ecosystems: The case of AppCampus. In: Alvarez, S., Carayannis, E. G., Dagnino, G. and Faraci, R. (eds), *Entrepreneurial Ecosystems and the Diffusion of Startups*. Cheltenham, UK and Northampton, MA, USA: Edward Elgar Publishing, forthcoming.

Wasserman, N. (2017). The throne vs. the kingdom: Founder control and value creation in startups. *Strategic Management Journal*, 38(2), 255–277.

Weiblen, T. and Chesbrough, H. W. (2015). Engaging with startups to enhance corporate innovation. *California Management Review*, 57(2), 66–90.

4. Understanding mentorship processes

Ronit Yitshaki and Israel Drori

INTRODUCTION

The objective of this chapter is to focus on one important aspect of accelerators' design structure and operation—mentoring. By mentoring we refer to the process of learning and coaching provided by the accelerator to its participating startups by a group of experts with knowledge and experience in founding and growing new ventures. We explore the mentoring process from the perspective of both mentors and mentees, with the aim of understanding the motivation behind mentoring as well as the dynamics and effectiveness of mentoring and the role it plays as part of the accelerator's program.

The study, carried out for Israeli accelerators, has two phases. The first focuses on mapping the field through scheduled interviews with 23 accelerator managers on various facets of the accelerators phenomenon within the Israeli ecosystem. The second phase consists of an in-depth ethnographic study of two different accelerators: corporation-owned and not-for-profit. At the two accelerators we carried out field research for the entire accelerating program (four and six months, respectively). The field studies include participant observation as well as interviews with the accelerator managers, startups' CEOs and mentors. In particular, we interviewed and shadowed 11 mentors and 37 mentees of the respective accelerators. We focus on the mentoring process, including issues such as the role of mentors, effective mentoring, motivation and interests, knowledge sharing and mentoring style. The chapter is organized as follows. The first section reviews the mentoring component of accelerators. This is followed by a brief review of accelerators in Israel. The third section presents our empirical findings and is divided into three main subjects: the mentoring phenomenon, the mentorship process and the effectiveness of mentorship processes. We conclude with a discussion and conclusions.

THE MENTORING COMPONENT OF ACCELERATORS

Accelerators aim at fostering entrepreneurial processes by providing mentoring that increases startups' knowledge-based resources and hence the likelihood of success. Knowledge-based resources are a bundle of resources that relates to the startup's technological, marketing and managerial capabilities (Wiklund and Shepherd, 2003). Entrepreneurs have to make key decisions in the early stages, facing the challenge of leveraging the knowledge-based resources in parallel to the launching stages. Specifically, after making the entry decision and choosing the accelerator path (Smith and Hannigan, 2015), entrepreneurs face the challenge of how best to exploit the opportunity identified (Shepherd, Williams and Patzelt, 2015) and overcome heuristics and biases in decision making (Hayward, Shepherd and Griffin, 2006).

Mentoring is considered to be one of the building blocks of accelerators' educational programs (Cohen and Hochberg, 2014; Pauwels et al., 2016) contributing to knowledge-based resources, which are constantly accumulated and evolve. Mentors thus play an important role in the following educational tasks: (1) sharing knowledge and experiences related to their field of expertise, (2) providing advice on recurring dilemmas and strategies that require knowledgeable understanding of the issues involved and (3) exposing mentees to the social networks of mentors.

Usually mentors have extensive experience in the relevant industry, either as former successful entrepreneurs, or as specialist investors who are well informed about the needs of new ventures and the stakes involved. The mentorship idea is based on the assumption that startups often lack knowledge and resources and may benefit from mentors' experiences in strategic planning, marketing, technological development and financing. Mentors provide external resources and act as a bridge between startups and different actors in the ecosystem (Chandler, Kram and Yip, 2011), thus helping startups to overcome the liability of newness (Stinchcombe, 1965; McKevitt and Marshall, 2015). Mentors also provide entrepreneurs with tacit knowledge, thus serve as active actors that contribute to the diffusion of knowledge (Gaba and Meyer, 2008). In addition, mentors' tasks are associated with accelerating entrepreneurs' learning processes and professional and personal identity growth as well as expanding entrepreneurs' access to social networks (Haggard et al., 2011), which are valuable in a startup's early stages (Elfring and Hulsink, 2007; Vissa and Bhagavatula, 2012).

Most mentoring-related research (Haggard et al., 2011) has focused on the mentees perspective, while mentors' motivations have remained under-researched. In this chapter, we examine the interaction between mentors and their mentees. Given the limited amount empirical study on accelerators' mentoring processes, we based our chapter on an exploratory study of the Israeli accelerators' ecosystem.

ACCELERATORS IN ISRAEL

The robustness of the Israeli high-tech innovation ecosystem is well documented and attributed to several factors including effective government policies, a meaningful venture capital industry with strong global linkages, strong network ties, human and social capital that provide strong support for the enhancement of innovation, and an entrepreneurial culture (de Fontenay and Carmel, 2004; Breznitz, 2007; Senor and Singer, 2009; Drori, Ellis and Shapira, 2013). The Israeli high-tech cluster, which, relatively speaking, has been a highly stable sector of the economy, exhibits high performance in relation to major economic criteria such as investment, employment, contribution to the country's gross domestic product (GDP) and the steadily growing number of startups and exits. Several studies (de Fontenay and Carmel, 2004; Breznitz, 2007; Senor and Singer 2009; Ellis et al., 2017) claim that Israel's historical legacy of survival and lack of tangible resources has led to a unique configuration of institutional arrangements and the emergence of an entrepreneurial culture that together harness and mobilize the country's resources for the promotion of innovation. In particular, a strong higher education sector, the military, waves of immigration, and those engineers, scientists and entrepreneurs who have returned to Israel, particularly from the US, play a crucial role in the development of a dynamic, innovative and globally oriented high-tech sector. These antecedents are backed by high national expenditure on research and development (R&D), second to the US and China in companies listed in NASDAQ, and the highest level of venture capital in relation to the GDP. In 2015 the number of new startups in Israel was estimated to be 1,400, of which 373 companies raised approximately $3.58 billion and 69 companies were acquired for a total of $5.41 billion (Korbet, Feldman and Ravon, 2015). The growth in startup numbers corresponded with an unprecedented growth of accelerators. As noted in Chapter 1, a conservative estimation claims that currently there are around 90 active accelerators, including social, public (government, municipality, academic or kibbutzim affiliation), non-governmental and venture capital affiliated accelerators.

It is important to note that the different types of accelerators present a different mission and objectives, which influence respectively their selection of startups and key performance indicators. For example, Microsoft's accelerator is operated on the premise that the startups participating in its program could be part of Microsoft's innovative ecosystem and will use its cloud technology. The Microsoft accelerator also links the startups to its networks and provides access to Microsoft itself. An example of a notable not-for-profit accelerator is EISP, an accelerator founded by the alumni of a renowned technological Israeli Defense Force unit, which it considers to be a hotbed of entrepreneurship, using the network of its alumni as the key resource for growing entrepreneurs from all fields. EISP's stated mission is to encourage startups at the very early stage and emphasize the diversity of its selection in terms of the startups' ideas and sectors. Accordingly, its accelerating program is focused on providing startups with basic entrepreneurial-related skills, mentoring and networking. EISP is considered a successful program. By 2015, graduating 5 cohorts, the program accelerated approximately 80 startups that in total raised more than $250 million, while 4 startups were acquired. Other examples include mixed social and business accelerators, such as those affiliated with universities or hospitals, which accelerate startups that have dual social and economic missions and objectives (such as in the field of health, energy or transportation). The Israeli accelerator ecosystem is also notable for its social accelerators (approximately 33 percent of the total). These accelerators engage in a wide range of social and community activities with a purpose of, for example, promoting economic development, clean energy and solutions for public transportation; encouraging the founding of small businesses by minority entrepreneurs; absorbing immigrants, refugees and asylum seekers; encouraging minority women to participate in the labor market; or providing solutions and products to individuals with disabilities.

In sum, the Israeli accelerator ecosystem is characterized by a relatively high number of diverse accelerators which cater for the varied needs of startups. Israeli accelerators are diverse in terms of both type and category. First, there is a wide range of accelerators, including those that are social, hybrid or economic in orientation. Second, the wide range of accelerators, both specialized and general in scope, attract startups from numerous industrial and social sectors, including ecommerce, the internet, health, energy, fin-tech, cybersecurity or the internet of things. Third, Israeli accelerators are attractive for startups in different stages of their life cycle and with different levels of funding, thus attracting both nascent and mature startups. Fourth, the organizing principles of Israeli accelerators in terms of their educational programs, mentoring and the final outcomes (demo day) are relatively similar, while there are differences in terms of participation. For-profit accelerators usually provide seed money (up to $50,000) for equity, while some nonprofit accelerators only charge a "symbolic" fee for participation, and rely on sponsorship to generate operating funds.

The accelerator seems to be an emergent organizational form in the Israeli ecosystem. As part of the startup-nation ideology (Senor and Singer, 2009), accelerators' aim is to accelerate ventures in the startup stage. The various types of accelerators, such as high-tech, corporate, municipal, academic and venture capital, aim to accelerate different types of startups. Some of them are vertical, focusing on a specific area of interest, while others are horizontal, focusing on a variety of different startups.

Within the Israeli entrepreneurship context, accelerators play a role in validating those who are best placed to grow the most. By selecting the most promising startups, accelerators provide a signal of legitimization and an indicator of a startup's potential. The validation processes are oriented to the local ecosystem. However, as many Israeli startups are "global born", validation processes are also oriented toward the global ecosystem, especially in the case of high-tech firms.

Accelerator managers mentioned a few reasons for the rapid proliferation of accelerators in Israel, including the lack of a funding platform for early-stage startups, a desire to be part of the innovation community and a desire to create a wider entrepreneurial ecosystem and to help startups to overcome the "liability of newness" with regard to the global market (Stinchcombe, 1965). An example is given by *GBA* (*high-tech accelerator manager*), who indicated that "we help startups to become unicorns . . . we connect nascent Israeli entrepreneurs to the US market".

Corporate accelerator managers provided a different point of view related to the challenge corporates face to enhance innovation. Corporate accelerator managers indicated that by establishing accelerators programs corporates are able to better compete and generate innovation: "it is hard to generate innovation in corporates. Often, the firms tend to focus and underinvest in ideas that don't fit their core activities" (*DL, corporate accelerator manager*). Another accelerator manager stated that "we find innovations before our competitors" (*A*). As part of the ecosystem, corporates also seek to enhance innovations that connect internal and external actors in the ecosystem:

> Our model is both internal and external. We seek to position the accelerator not only as relevant to our niche, but also as a meaningful worldwide accelerator that creates breakthroughs. Exposing the startups to the environment enables them to become innovative actors . . . it is a coopetition model. I believe that developing good startups will serve to bridge between *C* [the corporate] and the whole ecosystem . . . The startups are viewed as having complementarities rather as competitors. Successful startups are (a) exposed to the internal innovative ecosystem of the corporate and (b) exposed to the entire environment.

Our aim is to improve startups so that our accelerator will be considered superior and therefore will be attractive to good startups. (*G, corporate accelerator manager*)

Within a developed entrepreneurial context such as Israel, accelerators are seen as part of a constant search for institutional mechanisms that could effectively identify and promote nascent entrepreneurs. Furthermore, the proliferation of accelerators in Israel reiterates the idea that enhancing innovation through startup activities requires a specific organization that has two objectives: to identify and select high potential startups and provide them with a tangible head start through an educational and mentoring program, and to eventually introduce them to the investors' community.

EMPIRICAL FINDINGS

The Mentoring Phenomenon

Mentors within accelerators
Accelerators face a challenge in trying to attract the best mentors. The list of mentors is usually considered as an indication of accelerator credibility and quality. One of the mentors testified, "a successful accelerator is one that is attractive to the best mentors and therefore can create a successful ecosystem that is composed of investors and business partners" (*HF*). Accelerator managers related to the mutual interdependence between accelerators and mentors. One stated, "mentors are considered as valuable resource in each accelerator . . . they define the accelerator's value" (*O, local accelerator*). Mentors help the accelerator to generate deal flow. As explained by *AR* (*private accelerator*):

Our target is to reach the best firms. We are doing that by bringing the best mentors who have extensive social networks . . . the more you invest in expanding your mentors' circles and the more professional they are, the more influence they have on the number of firms you can attract in the future.

However, it was mentioned that due to the growing number of accelerators in Israel, "the best mentors get many requests" (*AC, private accelerator*). It should be noted that startup quality is an incentive for the best mentors to participate: "if you select unqualified entrepreneurs, mentors will not be willing to participate" (*T, municipal accelerator*).

Many of the mentors are former serial entrepreneurs who have made one or more successful exits and who are currently active as venture

capitalists or angel investors. These mentors experienced different managerial roles within startups. For example, "*E* is a high-tech industry executive, a seasoned entrepreneur and an investor in early stage startups. His
current investments are in the areas of Enterprise Software, Data Analysis,
Internet, Social Gaming and Mobile apps. Currently he serves as the CEO
of . . . a global leader in innovative Business Intelligence systems" (*corporate accelerator mentors' booklet*).[1]

In addition, mentors have different types of social capital based on the
above-mentioned experiences. As an example, the following description
relates to *ZA*, who is a co-founder of a mobile app venture that is listed as
a Deloitte Fast 50 company: "The company serves top comScore 100 pub-
lishers and works closely with the world's largest demand side platforms,
ad networks, ad agencies and Fortune 500 brands . . . *ZA* has over 13 years
of experience in managing large organizations and has vast experience in
entrepreneurship, general management, marketing, business development
and sales" (*corporate accelerator mentors' booklet*).

The mentors' booklet also presents business mentors, experts in marketing such as *TS*: "A veteran in the mobile industry with vast experience in
marketing, *biz dev* and sales both to end users and to mobile operators . . .
I've worked with app developers to build Go-to-Market plans and monetization strategies . . . Vis-à-vis mobile operators . . . [I have an experience]
in long and complex sales processes." Mentors indicated that they were
invited by the accelerator managers to serve as mentors: "the manager of
the accelerator has known me for many years . . . I worked in the Silicon
Valley for many years. I was asked to be mentor when I returned to Israel"
(*MA, an experienced mentor*).

Overall, mentors have various managerial experiences that are relevant
to startups, with deep connections to the Israeli and the international ecosystems. As mentioned by *RS*:

> Our mission is to provide an understanding based on our experiences and help
> startups to grow as fast as they can . . . I was a CEO of C (a big international
> corporation) . . . I have been involved since the first batch. I was working with
> internal investors, American corporate clients and made some investments in
> ventures within the accelerator.

Thus, mentors are usually experienced entrepreneurs who link startups to
the ecosystem through their knowledge and familiarity with the different
aspects of growing a business. By being willing to serve as mentors, these
entrepreneurs recognize the need to share their expertise, connections and
knowledge with those "nascent entrepreneurs who walk the walk" (*RZ, an
experienced mentor*).

How do mentors perceive their role?

A key insight of our findings is that most mentors refer to the mentoring process as multifaceted, which implies taking multiple roles. For example, mentors see themselves as educators: "[We] seek to help and share our experiences. To help other entrepreneurs and to serve as a kind of educator" (*AF*). Furthermore, mentors indicated that their role is to create value by serving as a "sanity check, reflecting the real story to entrepreneurs and validating their ideas" (*HF*). Or, mentors are those "who give advice based on their experiences but don't make decisions" (*NO*).

Mentors emphasized they have an advantage as external actors. In this sense, they function as a consultant:

> As a mentor, I can analyze the venture from an objective rather than emotional perspective, thinking through business lens. I ask questions such as why would somebody spend his money on your product? What kind of return on investment are you providing to your customers? Asking these types of questions forces entrepreneurs to think strategically and more objectively . . . mentors are free from the day-to-day intensive entrepreneurial processes and therefore they are able to ask questions and confront the entrepreneur with tough questions about his or her products or services . . . you have a limited amount of responsibility unlike those who are active in the venture. It is like with grandchildren. You finish playing with them and then return them to their parents who are responsible for changing their diapers. (*BD*)

Consistent with the consultancy process, mentors indicated that their task is to intensify processes and to shake entrepreneurs out of their "comfort zone":

> To put a mirror that reflects what could be going wrong. If you can, generate an understanding that without such a reflection the startup would fail. Sometimes your task is to wake them up and keep them from making mistakes. Eventually your task is also to make them believe they can do it, that they are heading in the right direction. (*RS*)

Thus, mentors see themselves as following and shaping a process through their coaching of the startups and assessing and advising on their value offering. The end of the process is a distinct event, as noted by one of the mentors: "we accomplish our mission when the venture is ready to raise funds and approach the market" (*RS*).

Selection and matching processes

In recognition of the importance of matching the startups to the right mentor, accelerators sometimes assign several mentors to a single startup. However, the involvement of several mentors in advising the same startup, although on different topics, leads to confusion, as testified by one of the mentors: "the startups didn't understand the role of mentors. Entrepreneurs expected mentors to manage their firms. This was further complicated when a single startup had several mentors. Entrepreneurs got different advice and got confused and couldn't decide on the best decision or practice."

Mentors indicated that the challenge is to match mentors to mentees according to a venture's stage of development: "it is a challenge to help firms to shift from the pre-seed and the seed stages. Similarly, it is a challenge to help ventures at the execution stage ... it means that you need different mentors with different skills" (*HF*).

The process of matching mentors to mentees is built upon a formal introduction and assessment of the startups needs and the respective expertise of the potential mentor. The accelerator's management decide on the actual matching, attempting to follow principles of the business needs and personal fit. Mentors indicated that the actual process begins before the formal introduction. Mentors are searching for startups based on the information provided by the accelerator. One of the mentors stated:

> As a mentor I look at the ventures accepted to the batch and am looking for those within the field of my expertise. I am looking for those who are making something interesting, different, and innovative with potential ... usually I mark 3 or 4 firms that I think will value my mentorship. At the matching gathering I have an opportunity to get more information and an impression based on the entrepreneurs' presentations. (*BD*)

Mentors indicated that during the formal introduction they are trying to get an impression of the interaction with the entrepreneurial team. For example, *RS* indicated that he is "looking for a responsive team, that is open to getting feedback and is willing to work hard". Similarly, *BD* indicated "I am trying to speak with one of the team members to get a better understanding about the venture. In this conversation, I get an impression about the chemistry and interaction we have with each other" (*BD*).

Mentors mentioned that they get requests to be mentored by entrepreneurs prior to the matching meeting. Mentors indicated that in choosing mentors, the entrepreneurial teams are looking for someone that has a relevant background. For example, *NO* indicated "actually they approached me. They heard that I worked in Google. They wanted someone with international experience in commercial advertising."

The dual purposes of mentors' motivations

The mentors interviewed stress the fact that the mentoring involves hybrid objectives. On the one hand, mentors mentioned an altruistic motivation to help entrepreneurs to accelerate. On the other hand, mentors indicated that they have business motivations. Thus, during the mentorship processes, mentors seem to manage two kinds of dualities regarding their motivations. The first refers to the *give and take* duality. The second refers to their *mentorship role* duality.

Give and take duality   Mentors stated that one of the main reasons for becoming a mentor is their wish to help other entrepreneurs. In their narratives, mentors referred to their desire to "give back" to the ecosystem, helping the community and assisting entrepreneurs to be part of the startup's community. Mentors stated that they have a desire to share their accumulated tacit knowledge and familiarity with the ecosystem with other entrepreneurs. As one of the mentors *(PG)* stated: "it is an altruistic activity . . . I don't want the knowledge to remain stuck in my brain." Similarly, *HF* explained:

> Part of our job is a contribution to the ecosystem: experience and learning. During the mentorship, you learn about the intellectual challenges of entrepreneurs and transfer your knowledge forward. There is no other meaning for such an investment but the contentment you get from knowledge sharing and helping people to get answers.

In a broad sense, mentors referred to their role in helping startups to grow and create more jobs. Mentors also framed the meaning of being a mentor as a matter of "give and take", as explained by *RZ*:

> There are two big benefits from being a mentor. The first is giving and taking back in its pure meaning. The second is that I get a chance to help to create a new startup . . . I don't think that there is anybody who will refuse to be involved to some degree in startups.

Mentors indicated that they gain from being selected to be mentors. Mentors mentioned that the meaning of being mentors is a kind of recognition by both the accelerators' managers and startups for their relevance to the startups' "conversation". As one of the mentors stressed: "being selected to be a mentor by this specific accelerator [*a corporate accelerator*] elevates you up; it introduces you to a selected team and exposes you to other investors" (*NO*). Mentors mentioned that being part of the accelerator enables them to be exposed to the ecosystem, as explained by *HF*: "I am exposed to new ventures, entrepreneurs, other mentors and other related networks that are part of the ecosystem."

All mentors agreed that mentorship provides an opportunity for them to be updated about new technologies and to learn about new ideas and trends. *RS*, for example, said: "I am highly involved in the high-tech industry. However, there are always new things. If you don't learn you are not staying at the same place, you are moving backwards. I am learning about new trends and technologies." *BD* also indicated that

> I am motivated by altruistic concerns but also want to be updated. Entrepreneurs are brilliant . . . entrepreneurs are investing much time to become experts . . .. I learn about new areas and expand my education as well . . . I don't have the same responsibilities and concerns as entrepreneurs and at the same time it provides me with an intellectual stimulation and I enjoy it.

Mentors indicated that they implement the new information they learn during mentorship in their other activities: "this accumulated knowledge about new markets and technologies such as big data, influence my ability to make different connections. It is like every bit of knowledge that I have learned in my life so far. I can implement the knowledge when I am working with other firms" (*RZ*). Similarly, *AL* indicated that "I transfer my learning as a mentor to other ventures that I am involved in. I update them about new tools or models that I have been exposed to."

Mentorship role duality
Mentors specify that their motivations relate to their other roles as investors and business managers. Explicitly, mentors indicated that they agreed to mentor regardless of the payback they can get. However, implicitly they also specified what kind of outcomes they gain from being mentors. *AL* indicated that "my sense is that most mentors are oriented to help entrepreneurs; however, from time to time you can discover an investment opportunity, but this is not the prime motivation to be part of the accelerator".

A few mentors referred to their motivations in terms of the future payback they can get. *RF* delineated a connection between his efforts as a mentor and the payback he expects to get:

> Mentorship does not remain at the voluntary dimension . . . it is an interesting opportunity for us . . . especially as we have economic returns. Following my experience, if you generate value, startup will offer you options and a role in their advisory board . . . you are exposed to startups that after the program ask you to proceed . . . when I get options, then helping the venture is in my self-interest because at the same time I am helping myself.

This kind of duality is also demonstrated by *HF*, who related to the challenge of the mentorship processes:

I have two hats: one as a mentor and one as an investor. If there is a company that is interesting for me as an investor, it is a good opportunity to carry out due diligence. However, at first I am positioning myself as a mentor and not as an investor . . . it is confusing because you are coming as someone who wants to help and you also have another interest . . . it can be somewhat unethical to use this platform to screen investments.

Similar insight is provided by *AL*, who connected between his role as an investor and outcomes he gains from being a mentor: "I arranged an investment in a venture together with a group of investors that previously invested in companies in this accelerator. Usually, entrepreneurs keep in touch with me after finishing the accelerator program."

The Mentorship Process

Structuring the mentorship process

Mentorship processes seem to be unstructured, and each mentor has his/ her own methodology for how to mentor entrepreneurs. Mentors indicated that they have freedom to develop their own mentorship methodology. Therefore, each develops his/her own approach based on previous experiences and independent learning. For example, *HF* indicated: "I have an experience of 20 years. I gained a general understanding from 'Y Combinator' and 'Techstars' who developed an ethical code . . . here in the accelerator we didn't get any training or best practices expectations. I read about the topic before starting."

The process of mentorship is voluntary and based on mutual understanding about the process and its outcomes. From the mentors' point of view, often mentorship processes are dependent on entrepreneurs'/ CEOs' presumptions about the learning processes and what they would like to get from mentorship. Usually, mentors meet CEOs once a week or every two weeks, depending on the dynamics and the interaction between them.

A few mentors mentioned that they build up a structured process:

The meaning of the first meetings is to get to know each other and see if there is chemistry. Then I start from the very basics to see if the venture is established appropriately, that there is IP [intellectual property]. I try to understand the technology and the product and analyze the market . . . we always find some issues that they didn't think about. We then plan what are the key issues that we want to address during the process . . . we then define missions and priorities that have to be done before our next meeting. (*AL*)

Another approach is demonstrated by *HF*: "I let them reach conclusions in accordance to the homework I give them from week to week such as marketing plan, vision, priorities and things they have to accomplish before the demo day."

In other cases, the mentorship process was less structured:

> We conducted two-hour meetings. At the end of these meetings I suggested that the CEO think ahead about the issues he wants to discuss next time but it didn't work . . . sometimes I suggest the topic. Overall, as the process was not structured I attended the meeting without preparing ahead . . . the process of mentorship was unstructured. It was like a timely conversation in which I tried to suggest some ideas . . . sometimes I joined them in meetings. (*NO*)

It should be noted that the above-mentioned challenges vary across the ventures' stages of development. One of the mentors explained:

> In young companies the challenges relate to basic issues such as how to hire and fire and how to raise seed funds . . .. In later stages such as in DC [*a startup name*] which is in a more mature stage with a mature team, we tried to find out how I can help and we have decided that we will focus on long term strategy and in preparing the venture to raise round A funds. (*HF*)

Startups' needs

Mentorship processes were viewed by mentors in light of the venture's needs. Mentors indicated that usually entrepreneurs have good insights about technical issues but have "blind spots" regarding other issues. Mentors addressed some key issues/challenges for which entrepreneurs need help. These include over-optimism and "naivety" about market barriers and the business model; commercialization of the product and targeting a large market; marketing and dealing with global markets; and lack of managerial experience and difficulties in managing scaling-up processes.

Mentors agreed that one of the most important challenges for startups is searching for "product–market fit". *AL* explained:

> I think that each venture has different needs but overall they have something in common. They have technology and an idea that needs to be reshaped. There is a lot in the technological part but less in the business part. They need help to formulate the technology for a product and get an understanding about how to approach the market.

Similarly, *BD* indicated:

> There is a misconception about marketing among startups . . . marketing starts at the ideation stage. You can develop a very interesting technology but without a market you can't create a positive business model . . . even if there is a defined market, new ventures get lost in trying to explain their product and how it

differs from other products that exist in the market place . . .. It is very interesting to help entrepreneurs to resolve this puzzle. Sometimes they are close to the core story but they need help in taking two steps back and rephrasing the story in terms that the rest of the world can understand.

Another issue that emerged is that nascent CEOs need help in managing startups in the early stages:

> CEOs are sometimes lonely without an ability to consult with others while having to make important decisions . . . wise entrepreneurs build an advisory board; however, they still need to be aware of the different interests of their partners . . .. Mentors can provide advice based on their accumulated knowledge that entrepreneurs can trust. The aim of mentorship is to lead new ventures to success; to build them up and bring them into focus. (*AF*)

Mentors' perceptions of mentorship processes were influenced by the above-mentioned challenges. When asked about the mentorship process with respect to a specific venture, mentors related to four kinds of processes that were involved: (1) *setting up strategy and priorities*, (2) *revealing marketing opportunities*, (3) *structuring organizational processes* and (4) *expanding ventures' social capital*.

Setting up strategy and priorities   One of the main challenges mentioned by mentors referred to how ventures can leverage their technology to markets that can maximize value for its investors. The initial question that was addressed by mentors is:

> What are the venture's resources and to what extent are the resources sufficient for approaching the target markets? . . . usually we start with a definition of the challenge and with an analysis of the market's key actors and potential customers. Then we consider 2–3 alternatives from which we could start working . . . it is hard to understand the size of the potential market because it doesn't exist yet. (*HF*)

In another case, mentorship was mentioned as being associated with a "restructuring of the product. I sent the team to talk with their customers. We discovered that the customers are looking for something different . . . then we restated the vision to create a fit between the product and market needs" (*RS*). When referring to another venture, *RS* explained that "the process was focused on refining the product and its added value and gaining an understanding of how to sell the product, what are the venture's key performance indicators and building a working plan".

Mentors emphasized their advantage as external advisors in setting up priorities and drawing road maps, as stated by one of the mentors:

> I realized that many CEOs need an external point of view from somebody who can look at the long term rather than the "day to day" point of view. It helps them to get another perspective . . . most of the time I helped them to formulate a business model and define priorities. Sometimes I helped them to set up priorities for the short term to ensure they don't get confused. (*AL*)

Revealing marketing opportunities   Mentors indicated that they help entrepreneurs by asking questions about market needs and potential customers:

> I don't fully understand the technology of the "internet of things" as the CEO of PX [*a startup name*]; however, mentors help by asking relevant questions. Why is your solution unique? How are you different from your competitors? Why would a customer use your product? If there are between 200 and 300 competitors it is important for them to redefine their market segment and focus on potential customers that may need their technology as well as building up product messaging. (*BD*)

Similarly, *RZ* gave an example of mentorship processes in a venture that operated in the advertising technology: "we analyzed the product capabilities and advantages and reanalyzed a much wider market segment . . . we changed the target market from a mobile application to a data processing platform for big retailing corporations such as 'Tesco'. . . the startup's capability to raise funds is now much better."

Another marketing challenge mentioned was pricing. For example, one of the mentors testified: "commercialization is one of the startups weaknesses. I had a conversation with the CEO about pricing. If they demand 30 dollars at the beginning, they wouldn't be able to ask for 500 dollars later; they understood that the pricing delays them" (*NO*).

Structuring organizational processes   Mentors referred to their involvement in advising entrepreneurs how to build organizational processes. Mentors provided suggestions about how to build a global venture based on their experiences. In addition, they related to their involvement in team building, especially in cases in which the team's previous experience didn't fit the venture expertise. *RS*, an experienced mentor, indicated that his interaction with the founder led to "the replacement of the marketing VP due to changes he suggested to make in the product and market".

Mentors indicated that in some cases they were involved in major organizational change including team building and managing intercultural conflicts:

> We took a venture that almost collapsed and we ensured that they will go on . . . mentorship in startups focuses first on the most painful issues . . . they had an

American CEO who understood the business but had no idea about the technology and Israeli entrepreneurs who had no understanding about the business. They faced some intercultural and managerial conflicts . . . the value we brought together with the accelerator manager was psychological . . . the mentorship processes focused first on "inside out" processes of building a managerial team and trust between each other and then on issues such as raising funds and ways to approach the market. (*AF*)

Expanding ventures' social capital   Mentors mentioned their contribution to entrepreneurs' social capital: "I connect ventures in the accelerators with other portfolio companies I have. Making connections is an important part of mentor's tool box" (*HF*). *RS* mentioned that he connected ventures he mentored to potential customers and investors. In addition, he mentioned that "investors often ask my opinion about a startup". *AL*, a former serial entrepreneur, indicated that "from time to time I try to connect between firms that I am involved in . . . usually when I am engaged with a venture after the acceleration period, I become a board member and then I try to connect them with my business network abroad."

Effectiveness of Mentorship Processes

The effectiveness of mentorship processes was mentioned to be associated with two main aspects: (1) the interaction and commitment to mentorship processes and (2) team learning orientation.

Interaction and commitment to mentorship processes

While mentors indicated that their assistance is valuable to every startup, they sometimes face a challenge to create trust and working relations with CEOs: "working with mentors is like mentorship by investors facing the same kinds of challenges: how much to share? What kinds of details are relevant and what kinds of processes to practice?" (*HF*).

Mentorship was described as a reciprocal process with feedback loops between mentors and entrepreneurs. *BD* indicated that the mentorship process is "creative because you provide some ideas and feedback to entrepreneurs. Then, they check those ideas and return with their understanding. You can see how the process evolves. You can see how you add value and how they make an advancement." However, mentorship cannot be enforced, and therefore mentors agreed that the effectiveness of mentorship is dependent on a mutual commitment and entrepreneurs' understanding of the benefits that can be gained through such processes. When referring to the willingness of entrepreneurs to be mentored, *AL* indicated: "I wish I had mentors in startups that I have led in the past . . . in that sense I think that the accelerator provides a fascinating service to entrepreneurs; however, I think that some entrepreneurs understand it and some don't."

It was mentioned that in some cases the interaction between mentors and entrepreneurs doesn't work: "sometimes it didn't work because we didn't have interpersonal chemistry" (*AL*). Another example is given by *BD*:

> Mentorship efforts didn't work . . . in the last batch we have decided to have three meetings with a CEO . . . the meetings were ok but didn't lead to any significant processes . . . we got an impression that mentorship was not within their priorities. They seem to be less interested . . . maybe they are working with other mentors and there is no match between us.

Thus, the issue of fit between the mentors and the startup is not only based on professional expertise and synergy, but also on personal interaction and empathy, including achieving an understanding and consent for the mentoring process.

Team learning orientation

Mentors indicated that their ability to add value depends on the desire of CEOs to be mentored. In addition, it was also indicated that team learning is related to the gains startups can get from the accelerator program: "Those who are more coachable gain more from the accelerator" (*BD*).

Mentors indicated that, overall, entrepreneurs are ready to be mentored, as explained by *AL*:

> Overall most of the people who were selected to the accelerator are willing to listen and get advice. Those who think they know everything will not attend or will not be selected . . . I can see that there is a willingness to learn. That entrepreneurs see value in my mentorship . . . part of the process is that CEOs should understand where they need help. I am trying to understand what kind of learning they need. Is there anything they didn't do either because they didn't think about it or they don't know or something else.

At the same time, team learning is considered to be dependent on the CEO attitudes: "the desire of the CEO to be mentored is crucial especially in the Israeli culture in which most people think that they know best" (*NO*). It was mentioned that when CEOs think that they have the best understanding, the mentorship processes are limited to 2–3 meetings and a general tendency of the CEO to get some advice. In such cases the CEOs "just wanted to see if we can add something to the venture and didn't come with a coachable attitude" (*BD*).

Mentors indicated that teams' coachability can be identified relatively quickly. As one of the mentors explains:

Coachability is a soft skill that you discover through the initial interaction . . . you can identify if the CEO is coachable in a minute. You can identify whether the CEO comes with an attitude that he knows everything and he tries to understand what you can do for him or whether he comes with an understanding that he is looking for answers that he wants to get. (*BD*)

A different example was given by *RZ*, who indicated that, overall, entrepreneurs "have learning capabilities at the technological level. I can tell you that most of them are less familiar with marketing . . . they seek to acquire practical and simplistic knowledge" (*RZ*). *RZ* indicated that the learning processes with regard to marketing would be longer when the entrepreneurial team had just technological background.

Mentors indicated that mentorship processes are dynamic and reciprocal: "You can't dictate and force your opinion. I am not in their shoes and there are things that I don't know" (*BD*). *BD* indicated that team learning is dependent on entrepreneurs' understanding about their disadvantages. When relating to a specific example, he indicated:

It was clear to Y [*a CEO*] what are his disadvantages and what are the problems . . . I think that the CEO understands what kind of mentorship he needs at the individual level and what kind of solution they are looking for at the firm level. That's why they gained much from participating in the accelerator program.

The learning challenges during the accelerator program seem to depend on the stage of the startups and their CEOs' previous experiences. When relating to a specific venture, *NO* indicated that "they made nice progress. There are things that cannot be . . . changed entirely . . . but overall the CEO understood that he has to be focused on finding investors rather on sales."

Contribution to acceleration

Accelerator programs provide startups with different ways to accelerate: "The acceleration program is very structured. Eventually the accelerator provides startups with connections, mentorship and training that leads to changes in startups and to their acceleration" (*RS*). However, there is a general understanding that measuring the contribution of mentorship to the acceleration is complicated. *HF*, an experienced mentor, comments: "There is a question around how to support mentors, how to guide them, what issues are important . . . 4 months is a short time and there is an issue of how you define mentors' contribution to the venture's success . . . it is a challenge for other accelerators such as 'Techstart' as well." The effectiveness of mentorship processes is mentioned to be "contingent upon each venture situation . . . sometimes the effectiveness of a mentorship process is demonstrated by leading to a venture closure and preventing subsequent losses" (*RS*).

Overall, mentors indicated that during the acceleration program they had an opportunity to influence the evolution of startups: "the accelerators can accelerate processes that usually would take a startup much more time, due to the help of mentors" (*RZ*). Mentors view their main contribution to learning processes to be time saving. Mentors indicated that mentorship processes enhance entrepreneurial learning. One mentor stated:

> My impression is that ventures' experience during the acceleration program is positive. They acquire meaningful assets and knowledge to start with ... we bring life experience and the result of the acceleration can lead to changes in ventures' directions and even to their termination ... at the same time we also provide them an understanding of how investors think and reach decisions. (*HF*)

Mentors indicated that they contribute to the prevention of mistakes:

> The processes of market understanding take much time. Regardless of the price of the mistakes you can make if you are heading in the wrong direction ... if you are developing the wrong product it is even worse. We don't have a magic formula. As mentors we can bring our prior experiences, understanding and objectivity to try to avoid mistakes that without mentorship would be costly in terms of time and money and opportunity loss. This is a contribution to the acceleration process. (*BD*)

Mentors emphasized their ability to contribute to the acceleration based on their knowledge and experiences: "mentors bring with them experience because they have done the same kind of processes before. Their advice can save much time because they can direct entrepreneurs how to manage processes in a way that saves them many iterations. I think that in that sense we save new ventures much time" (*BD*).

Thus, mentors help new ventures to accelerate by helping them to be more focused and understand what is most important: "in a relatively short time they are able to shape the product and to create connections with a client and hence to learn from the market. In several months, the venture can be heading in the right direction with the right product." Founders indicated that with the assistance of mentors, technological, marketing and financial processes are clearer. RZ, a founder, summarizes: "A mentor's knowledge contributes to the understanding of how to do things right" (*RZ*).

DISCUSSION AND CONCLUSIONS

By relying on thick data based on interviews and observations, we provide several insights at the nexus of the relationship between accelerators, mentors and startups. We claim that the mentoring process provides a bridge between the accelerator, the startup and the ecosystem through the mentor's internal (within the startup) and external (within the ecosystem) position. We also suggest that mentorship is a complex process composed of both altruistic and interest-based motivations and processes. These two aspects represent a continuum. The mentoring process starts as part of the accelerator's educational program, and it can end with it or, alternatively, it could lead to a transformation of the relationship of the mentor and mentee to a partnership.

Our suggested overall framework of accelerators' internal and external ecosystem (summarized in Figure 4.1) indicates that accelerators play an important role in recognizing mentors who are relevant to the ecosystem. Accelerators also provide mentors with opportunities to invest and learn about the ecosystem, enabling mentors who serve as angel investors to conduct an informal due diligence.

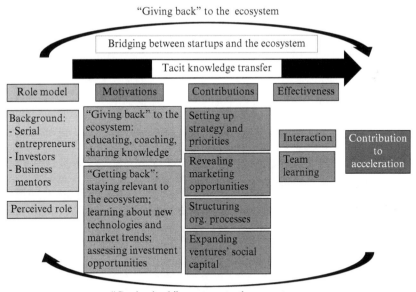

Figure 4.1   Findings summary

Our findings add to the literature on mentorship, suggesting that mentors provide entrepreneurs with tacit knowledge that is relevant to their role identity by sharing their experiences as former entrepreneurs, investors or business mentors. By doing so, mentors serve as role models through which nascent entrepreneurs learn how to think and act and how to confront unexpected issues and dilemmas that stem for the "liability of newness" (Watson, 2009).

Our findings also shed light on mentors' motivations. Mentors face somewhat contradictory motivations based on a "give and take" rationale. On the explicit level of analysis, mentors' motivations are based on their desire to "give back" to the ecosystem. However, our analysis reveals that mentors' motivations are also related to the possibility of being embedded in the startup ecosystem and understanding its dynamics. In addition, mentors also gain accessibility to investment opportunities in promising startups and have an opportunity to be updated about new technologies and market trends. As can be seen in Figure 4.1, though mentors mentioned their advantage as external "objective" advisors, their contributions depend upon the interaction between them and the entrepreneurial team. Different from other mentorship settings, our findings indicate that the team learning orientation plays a major role in the effectiveness of mentorship processes. These findings add to the understanding that within the accelerator context, mentors and mentees relations are recursive, providing both mentors and entrepreneurs with different types of learning possibilities and added value (Haggard et al., 2011).

Overall, our findings identified four different aspects that characterize the mentoring process: (1) *setting up strategy and priorities*, (2) *revealing marketing opportunities*, (3) *structuring organizational processes* and (4) *expanding ventures' social capital*.

Mentors commit themselves to a work process with startups which is based on ad hoc needs. This implies that the mentors are adjusting to the educational program of the accelerators by becoming an integral part of it, but not much beyond. Regardless of the style or content, structured or less structured meetings, the mentoring process is often detached from the startup's real position within its ecosystem, but converges by adopting the style and content of the accelerators' general educational program. In this sense, mentors are providing added value mainly as educators or coaches, but not necessarily as real promoters of startup growth beyond the accelerators' boundaries.

From the mentor's point of view, the main thrust of their relationship with startups is reciprocity. Although mentors recognize their potential contribution based on their experience and expertise, being exposed to new startups' ideas and creativity seems to invigorate and sustain the mentors' links to the ecosystem. There is high premium with the interaction with the startups in terms of give and take, particularly in cases where mentors are able to move from a position of mentorship to one of a business partner. Thus, the mentorship process as part of the accelerator's educational program is also a prerequisite for mentorship as a mechanism of identifying business opportunities.

From the accelerator's perspective, mentoring provides legitimacy and validation for the accelerator's program and position. A mentor's identity and experience is superimposed on the accelerator's position and reputation. Accelerators see the mentoring process as complementary to their educational program and link to the ecosystem. In this sense, mentors bridge between the accelerator and the ecosystem by bridging between startups and other stakeholders (investors, market). This bridge is considered to be imperative to startups' success once they have graduated following the demo day. Thus, the mentors are a kind of extension of the accelerator's program. If the relationship between the mentor and the startup continues beyond the official period of the accelerating program, it implies that a business relationship has been formed and the stake of the mentor has increased and changed. The mentor role in such a process evolves from coach to full participant/member of the startup team.

As noted in our findings, the logic of mentorship is holistic in the sense that the mentor's personal history, experience and expertise places him/her in the best position to understand the startup from both behavioral and organizational perspectives. Revealing the mentoring processes contributes to our understanding of the mentoring phenomenon as embedded in the emergence of the venture and context, and adds to the basic notion of mentoring as a process of coaching.

NOTE

1. A corporate accelerator mentors' booklet is usually distributed by the accelerators management to the cohort participants. It is an informal document which specifies the mentors' expertise and experience and aims at helping the startup to choose the best mentor for their needs.

REFERENCES

Breznitz, D. (2007). *Innovation and the state: Political choice and strategies for growth in Israel, Taiwan, and Ireland.* New Haven, CT: Yale University Press.
Chandler, D. E., Kram, K. E. and Yip, J. (2011). An ecological systems perspective

on mentoring at work: A review and future prospects. *Academy of Management Annals*, 5(1), 519–570.

Cohen, S. and Hochberg, Y. V. (2014). Accelerating startups: The seed accelerator phenomenon. Available at http://papers.ssrn.com/sol3/papers.cfm?abstract_id=2418000 (accessed January 24, 2018).

de Fontenay, C. and Carmel, E. (2004). Israel's Silicon Wadi: The forces behind cluster formation. SIEPR Policy Paper No. 00-040.

Drori, I., Ellis, S. and Shapira, Z. (2013). *The evolution of a new industry: A genealogical approach*. Stanford, CA: Stanford University Press.

Elfring, T. and Hulsink, W. (2007). Networking by entrepreneurs: Patterns of tie—formation in emerging organizations. *Organization Studies*, 28(12), 1849–1872.

Ellis, S., Aharonson, B., Drori, I. and Shapira, Z. (2017). Imprinting through inheritance: A multi-genealogical study of entrepreneurial proclivity. *Academy of Management Journal*, 60(2), 500–522.

Gaba, V. and Meyer, A. D. (2008). Crossing the organizational species barrier: How venture capital practices infiltrated the information technology sector. *Academy of Management Journal*, 51(5), 976–998.

Haggard, D. L., Dougherty, T. W., Turban, D. B. and Wilbanks, J. E. (2011). Who is a mentor? A review of evolving definitions and implications for research. *Journal of Management*, 37(1), 280–304.

Hayward, M. L., Shepherd, D. A. and Griffin, D. (2006). A hubris theory of entrepreneurship. *Management Science*, 52, 160–172.

Korbet, R., Feldman, Y. and Ravon, A. (2015). *Annual Report 2015: Startups and venture capital in Israel*. Available at http://www.geektime.com/2016/01/11/annual-report-2015-startups-and-venture-capital-in-israel/ (accessed January 24, 2018).

McKevitt, D. and Marshall, D. (2015). The legitimacy of entrepreneurial mentoring. *International Journal of Entrepreneurial Behavior and Research*, 21(2), 263–280.

Pauwels, C., Clarysse, B., Wright, M. and Van Hove, J. (2016). Understanding a new generation incubation model: The accelerator. *Technovation*, 50–51, 13–24.

Senor, D. and Singer, S. (2009). *Start-up nation: The story of Israel's economic miracle*. Toronto: McClelland & Stewart.

Shepherd, D. A., Williams, T. A. and Patzelt, H. (2015). Thinking about entrepreneurial decision making: Review and research agenda. *Journal of Management*, 41(1), 11–46.

Smith, S. W. and Hannigan, T. J. (2015). Swinging for the fences: How do top accelerators impact the trajectories of new ventures? Paper to be presented at DRUID15, Rome, June 2015.

Stinchcombe, A. L. (1965). Social structure and organizations. In: March, J. G. (Ed.), *Handbook of organizations* (pp. 142–193). Chicago, IL: Rand McNally.

Vissa, B. and Bhagavatula, S. (2012). The causes and consequences of churn in entrepreneurs' personal networks. *Strategic Entrepreneurship Journal*, 6(3), 273–289.

Watson, T. J. (2009). Entrepreneurial action, identity work and the use of multiple discursive resources: The case of a rapidly changing family business. *International Small Business Journal*, 27(3), 251–274.

Wiklund, J. and Shepherd, D. (2003). Knowledge-based resources, entrepreneurial orientation, and the performance of small and medium-sized businesses. *Strategic Management Journal*, 24(13), 1307–1314.

5. Selection issues

Michael Leatherbee and
Juanita Gonzalez-Uribe

INTRODUCTION

Because the performance (and sustainability) of accelerators depends heavily on the ability to attract and choose the best startups, selecting startups is a key aspect for the survival of business accelerators. As discussed in the key performance indicators chapter in this book (Chapter 6), accelerators strive to attract, select, and (sometimes) invest in the highest-potential startups. Doing so effectively provides accelerators with valuable pecuniary and non-pecuniary resources. For example, having an equity stake in a profitable startup (or one that gets acquired or goes public) certainly helps fill the accelerator's coffers, which is useful to sustain the operation and keep accelerator sponsors happy. Selecting high-potential startups also increases the chances of having high-profile startup alumni. This aspect is valuable because it provides accelerators with legitimacy, which in turn helps attract other high-potential applicants. Business schools know about this virtuous cycle all too well. Being able to attach an institution's name to high-profile alumni certainly helps increase the institution's media exposure and the subsequent desire of new applicants to be part of that institution. According to the authorities of some of the world's leading universities, the quality of an institution's alumni is, to a large degree, a result of the quality of an institution's pool of applicants. Thus, choosing the best applicants can be an effective way to improve an institution's alumni pool.

Having capable and successful alumni can also be useful for developing other non-pecuniary resources, such as a mentor support platform for accelerator participants and graduates. Much like the top business schools have sophisticated alumni network platforms, managing an alumni network of successful entrepreneurs can help incoming accelerator entrepreneurs tap into the social resources implicit in the accelerator's alumni network (e.g., advice, ideas, and contacts with potential investors, partners, customers, and employees). Thus, selecting the right startups (and entrepreneurs) is key for accelerators because it could provide them with cash (from investment in successful startups), media coverage, and a valuable social network.

SELECTION STAGES

Business accelerators typically manage three key selection stages: *application*, *special services*, and *cohort champions*. The application stage entails the evaluation of startup applicants who wish to become accepted into the accelerator. Depending on the number of applicants, the selection process can take different forms (as discussed further below). For example, Y Combinator, Techstars, and Start-Up Chile receive approximately 1,000 applicants each application cycle and have an acceptance rate of roughly 5 percent to 10 percent. Thus, a poor application selection process has a very high chance of leaving some of the highest-potential applicants in the rejection pool, which can have significant consequences for the performance and sustainability of accelerators.

The special-services stage corresponds to a selection process that occurs at some point during participants' tenure in the program, typically before the halfway point. The purpose of this stage is to select participants that may benefit the most from the special services provided.[1] This stage can take the form of a competition between accelerator participants, among which the winners receive additional benefits unavailable to all participants. For example, Start-Up Chile runs a voluntary "pitch-day" competition two months into the six-month program. Most participants opt-in to compete, because winners receive attractive perks such as a visit to Silicon Valley, media coverage, or access to high-profile mentors.[2] Because these special services are limited to only a few, the selection process plays the key role of identifying those startups that will benefit the most from the additional resources. Thus, again, a poor selection process could waste an opportunity to improve the performance of those startups that would benefit the most from the special services.

The cohort-champions stage entails the attempt to select the best (highest-potential) startups of a given cohort at the end of the program. This selection process typically involves a pitching competition, whereby competing startups make a short (e.g., five-minute) investor-focused presentation of their venture. The audience may vary from a select group of privately invited competition judges to an open admission of members in the community. The former is common in investor-led accelerators who aim to capture the potential upside of the new ventures, whereas the latter is consistent with the philosophy of ecosystem accelerators who aim to spur entrepreneurial activity in the community.[3] At this stage, being effective at selecting the highest-potential entrepreneurs from the rest is not very critical for ecosystem accelerators, because the competition is mostly symbolic. That is, ecosystem accelerators do not typically take an equity stake (e.g., stock ownership) in the business. Rather, ecosystem accelerators indirectly benefit from the success of their alumni pool more broadly. However, selecting the right startups at the cohort-champions stage can be critical for (investor-led) accelerators that base their investment decisions on the outcome of this competition. Therefore, if the selection process is not effective, it will have direct consequences on the cash-generating capabilities of the accelerator and, consequently, on its sustainability.

SELECTION METHODS

The selection method can differ at the different stages depending on the number of applicants to be evaluated and the programmatic design of the accelerator. If large numbers of applicants must be evaluated in a short time period (as is common with the most popular programs), business accelerators tend to outsource their application process to external companies—such as YouNoodle in the case of Start-Up Chile. These companies typically manage an internet-based platform that receives submissions from applicants on the one hand, and on the other hand provides access to judges who review the applications. Thus, once the request for applications is closed, these companies assign the applications to a corps of judges committed to review them, who in turn score the assigned applications. In the case of YouNoodle, three independent judges review each application, and each judge reviews roughly ten applications. At the end of the assessment process, scores are averaged and applications are ranked according to the averaged score. The results and applications are then provided to the business accelerator.

Volunteers, who are deemed to have some expertise in entrepreneurship, typically compose the pool of judges. Thus, the pool includes entrepreneurs, investors, academics, and industry experts. Frequently, business accelerators rely heavily on their alumni to act as judges. This reliance could potentially lead to another virtuous (or vicious) cycle. Assuming the application-stage selection process is able to pick skilled entrepreneurs who end up becoming accelerator alumni judges, a positively reinforcing virtuous cycle is created. That is, skilled applicants become skilled alumni who in turn become skilled judges who are able to identify skilled applicants. However, business accelerators are also at risk of falling into a vicious cycle where the opposite is true. Thus, the selection process can be a critical aspect in the sustainability and success of accelerators.

Usually, once the external application-process company provides the results to the business accelerator staff, a second-stage evaluation process is activated. This second stage consists of having a panel of internal evaluators review the top-ranked applications for a final decision. Thus, if the cohort capacity were 100 startups, this panel of internal evaluators may limit their analysis to the top 200 ranking applications resulting from the external application process (from a total of, say, 1,000). In this case, internal evaluators can decide whether they wish to divide their limited time into reviewing all 200 cases superficially, or reviewing, for example, applications ranking 50 through 150 more thoroughly. This latter decision relies on the assumption that the external application process is able to effectively identify the top 50 applicants, which would not require a second assessment by internal evaluators. We will come back to this assumption later in the chapter.

Once the final selection decision is made at the application stage and the new cohort gets installed into the accelerator, some accelerators move on to the special-services selection stage. In this stage, because the volume of applicants can be significantly smaller than at the application stage, the selection method can differ. For example, the selection can take the form of a pitching competition (which may take more than a day to conduct), whereby contestants (typically fewer than 100) have a limited time (five minutes) to present (or "pitch") their business ideas to a panel of expert judges. This panel can consist of accelerator staff and entrepreneurship experts from the community in which the accelerator is located. The judging criteria are tailored to the special services provided by the accelerator, and scores are typically pooled among judges. The top-scoring contestants are then awarded a slot in the special-services program.

An important issue at this selection stage is the alignment of the selection criteria with the rate of contribution of the special services to the awarded startups. That is, the ideal scenario would be that the startups selected to receive the special services are, in fact, the startups that would benefit the most from the special services—in accordance with the goals of the accelerator. For example, if the goal of the accelerator was to identify the best startups in which to invest (as is the case for investor-led accelerators), the selection criteria should be based on the candidate's potential to provide a high return on investment for new investors. If, on the contrary, the goal was to help those startups that need the most help (as might be the case of some ecosystem accelerators), then the selection criteria should be aligned with this goal. In other words, judges should not score pitch competitors based on the potential rate of return for stockholders (as typically done), but rather on how much the startup could improve if it received the special services. In this case, the "best" contestants from the perspective of a potential investor may actually not win the competition, because these contestants may well be successful regardless of the services.

In this latter case—where the awarded startups are not necessarily the most attractive from the perspective of a potential investor, but rather those that could benefit the most from the special services—the accelerator may have to deal with potential "gaming." For example, contestants may feign weaknesses in order to convince judges about the startup's (fictitious) needs for the special services, thus increasing their chances of winning the competition. Of course, conventional business-plan competitions are also not absent feigning. Contestants may feign strengths in order to convince judges of the startup's (fictitious) potential to provide future investors with attractive returns. However, in this latter case, over time, judges may have become more sensitized to this potential feigning, as opposed to the feigning of weaknesses.

The final selection stage that characterizes business accelerators is the cohort-champions stage. The goal of this stage is to select the most promising startups of the cohort. To do so, accelerators organize a business-plan pitching competition, commonly dubbed the "demo day." This competition may be completely open to the community in which the accelerator is immersed, or it may be a private event closed to all but the competition's judges. The former is more common in ecosystem accelerators, which aim at increasing public spillovers within the community. The latter, by contrast, is typical of investor-led accelerators, which prefer to have more exclusive information that will provide an advantage when investing in promising startups.

The judges of this stage are typically high-profile investors or entrepreneurship experts from the community, who score contestants' pitches according to a rubric predefined by the accelerator. Contestants typically have limited time (e.g., ten minutes) to explain the achievements and business potential of their startups, and may have the opportunity to fend off questions from the judges. One after the other, contestants go on stage to pitch their startup and are scored by the judges. After the end of the competition, judges average the individual scores assigned to each contestant and (may) deliberate about the potential winners. Lastly, the judges inform the contestants of the final selection.

One of the challenges of trying to identify the highest-potential startups in a given cohort using external judges is the limited information these judges have to make an informed decision. Regardless of how skillful these judges may be at discriminating between high- and low-potential startups, these judges rarely make their own personal investment decisions based on a short business-plan presentation. They may use the presentation as a stepping-stone to make a decision about initiating a due diligence of the startup, but they are unlikely to make an investment decision without the due diligence. The due diligence is the process that provides potential investors with enough information to commit to an investment (or non-investment) decision. Deals commonly fall through during the due-diligence phase, which suggests a pitch competition does not provide enough information to make a serious decision about a startup's potential.

Some accelerators, such as Village Capital, have developed a strategy to address the challenge of assessing startup potential with the limited information provided by the business-plan pitching competition. Instead of relying on external judges that are not able to spend much time on assessing each contestant, Village Capital relies on the startups' peers. That is, the accelerator's cohort members collectively identify (e.g., through a voting system) the highest-potential startups. This approach relies on the principle that peers—who have spent several months working in close proximity to each other—have more accurate information about the potential of the startup as a whole than judges who have a few minutes to observe a pitch presentation. That is, peers are able to observe not only the logical potential of the idea (i.e., the business model), but also the *behaviors* of the founding team throughout the length of the program. A similar phenomenon occurs in business schools. Classmates typically know much more about a given student than a single professor does.

Although whether an investment strategy that relies on the wisdom of the crowd (the cohort participants) is more effective than relying on a panel of external judges is still in question, it is certainly an interesting idea to follow closely. For example, Village Capital's strategy for sustainability relies on investing in the cohort champions identified through a peer selection process. An interesting experiment would compare the post-accelerator-participation performance of winners of a business-plan pitching competition selected by external judges, against the performance of winners based on peer selection.

In some cases, accelerators take advantage of the selection processes to provide contestants with feedback based on the opinions of judges. The principle behind this idea is that potential value is created as a consequence of the evaluation by third parties, which could be used to improve entrepreneurial performance. That is, the impressions of external parties could potentially improve the performance of contesting startups, and making the extra effort to provide contestants with evaluators' feedback can provide an opportunity to benefit those startups. For example, Valid Eval developed a startup evaluation software that helps judges register their assessment of each contestant and facilitates the process of providing feedback. In essence, this tool reduces the cost of providing and managing the feedback.

Is going through the effort of providing feedback actually useful? Recent scientific research has aimed at answering this question. For example, Wagner (2016) conducted a randomized control trial using Start-Up Chile applicants with the support of YouNoodle. The treatment group received feedback from judges about their applications, whereas the control group received none. By looking at the startups' performance a few years later, Wagner found that those who received the feedback were doing significantly better than those who did not. Thus, going the extra mile to provide feedback appears to be useful for entrepreneurs, although not necessarily for accelerators. Whereas the goals of ecosystem accelerators are aligned with the way spillovers may benefit the community (but not directly benefit the accelerator), investor-led accelerators are more focused on making sure they achieve a high return on investment. For the latter, any expense that creates value that is not captured by the accelerator may be considered a source of inefficiency that must be corrected.

Another example of the effects of feedback on startup performance is a study conducted by Howell (2017). She found that informing rejected applicants about how poorly they fared relative to their peers increases the likelihood of abandoning the startup by 12 percent. This finding suggests that, if the aim is to induce entrepreneurs to persist with their startups, providing a rejection letter without informing them of the relative judging scores is probably better.

However, whether providing this negative feedback to entrepreneurs is actually detrimental for them in the end is unclear. Entrepreneurs may, when facing the harsh reality of pursuing a low-potential opportunity, abandon their startups only to start searching for better opportunities. In this case, providing (realistically) negative feedback may encourage entrepreneurs to explore (and subsequently capture) better opportunities they would not have considered had they not received the feedback.[4] As a white paper by the Evidence-based Policy and Innovation Research Lab suggests,[5] entrepreneurs can be quite resilient in their search for better opportunities, especially when leveraging useful feedback about their startups.

SELECTION ISSUES

Because the selection process can have such a significant impact on an accelerator's outcome, designing effective selection methods is key for performance and sustainability. Nevertheless, this exercise is non-trivial. It is fundamental to understand the potential pitfalls, limitations, challenges, and unintended consequences of the different selection approaches, lest one were indifferent to setting the accelerator on a trajectory that would lead to a substandard (and potentially terminal) outcome.

For example, take the case of the selection process in an investor-led accelerator. If the process were not able to pick out the best applicants, such an accelerator would not capture all of the potential value implicit in the applicant pool. Leaving untapped value in the ecosystem opens the possibility for a competing accelerator to capture such value, thus eroding the competitive advantage of the focal accelerator. In other words, the long-term sustainability of investor-led accelerators relies heavily on the ability to ride the curve of maximum potential performance. One important activity in riding this curve is the capture of the best possible startups within a given applicant pool. Of course, as discussed previously, an alternative (indirect) approach to improving the output of the selection process would be to improve the average quality of the applicant pool. Thus, despite an ineffective selection process, an accelerator's cohort quality may increase (and the accelerator's subsequent performance) simply because the average quality of the applicant pool has increased. In other words, better results can be produced from a random selection of items in a given pool simply by improving the quality of the items in that pool.

When "Best" Is Not "Right"

In the case of ecosystem accelerators, because their goals are more oriented toward building a vibrant entrepreneurial ecosystem, the criteria of what constitutes the "right" applicant are likely to differ from investor-led accelerators. For example, if an ecosystem accelerator's goal was to have the largest possible effect on an entrepreneur's performance trajectory, selecting anyone but those applicants who would benefit the most from the accelerator experience would be an inefficient use of resources. That is, selecting an applicant who would perform just as well without the acceleration experience, at the cost of selecting an applicant who would benefit significantly from the experience, would be a wasted opportunity to have a positive effect on the latter.

This tension between selecting the highest-potential applicant and the applicant most in need of support may seem evident in hindsight, but rarely do accelerators keep this in mind when designing their selection processes. Some entrepreneurs who get accepted into the accelerator might not improve as a consequence and would have done just as well in the absence of the accelerator experience. That is, the highest-potential startups (those that would provide the best profitability to investor-led accelerators) might *not* also be those that benefit the most from the accelerator experience *treatment*. If we assume accelerators provide certain services that help a certain type of startup more than others (e.g., perhaps those startups that are weak in social capital), and if we assume startups high in social capital are *ex ante* the highest in potential, it would behoove investor-led accelerators to select the startup high in social capital (to ensure the highest potential for performance), whereas it would behoove the ecosystem accelerator to select the startup that could improve the most in social capital as a consequence of having the accelerator treatment.

For example, Table 5.1 illustrates how accelerators (specifically the entrepreneurship schooling component of accelerators) can have heterogeneous treatment effects on different types of entrepreneurs. The entrepreneurship school provided by the Start-Up Chile ecosystem accelerator is much like a business school, but for entrepreneurs. It is a competitive program that provides participants with certification (from being accepted into a prestigious program), education (through workshops), mentorship, access to valuable social networks, exposure to the market and potential investors, accountability structures for making progress toward key milestones, and a boost in entrepreneurial self-efficacy.[6] From a sample of Start-Up Chile participants, entrepreneurship schooling appears to have a particularly strong effect on the amount of capital raised for Chilean (domestic) and South American (regional) entrepreneurs (columns 1 and 3). In terms of market traction, the effect is particularly strong for foreign (non-South American) and regional (Latin American excluding Chilean) entrepreneurs (columns 6 and 7). Thus, in designing and managing business accelerator programs, we must keep in mind that not everyone will respond in the same way to participating in an accelerator.

(In)ability of Expert Judges

The most common approach for evaluating applicants is to rely on expert judges. These individuals typically review an application and provide a qualification score that is used as an input for the selection decision. These evaluation approaches rely on the assumption that expert judgment is the most effective tool to gauge future performance. However, some evaluation strategies appear to be relying too heavily on this assumption. Although reliance on expert judges does seem to be effective in some cases, it certainly has limitations that warrant a greater level of skepticism.

For example, Gonzalez-Uribe and Leatherbee (2018) found that selection processes that rely on expert judges do appear to discriminate between low- and high-potential-performance startups. However, the effectiveness of this discrimination is limited. From a sample of over 3,000 startups applying to Start-Up Chile, applicants judged to be among the top 10 percent (roughly, those accepted into the accelerator) were, on average,

Table 5.1 Heterogeneous effects of entrepreneurship schooling on the amount of capital raised and market traction

Variables	Capital raised				Market traction			
	(1) Domestic	(2) Foreign	(3) Regional	(4) Non-regional	(5) Domestic	(6) Foreign	(7) Regional	(8) Non-regional
Entrepreneurship schooling	7.601*	2.540	5.673*	1.523	0.827	0.175*	0.600**	0.054
	(3.941)	(1.597)	(3.060)	(1.608)	(0.679)	(0.093)	(0.299)	(0.056)
Constant	0.785	0.850	0.825	1.010*	0.019	0.012	0.011	0.031
	(0.916)	(0.560)	(0.772)	(0.597)	(0.070)	(0.029)	(0.055)	(0.019)
Observations	58	218	108	168	58	218	108	168
R-squared	0.251	0.150	0.077	0.217		0.342	0.008	0.341
t-stat differences		1.65		1.60		1.19		2.23

Note: This table compares the effect of entrepreneurship schooling among Start-Up Chile participants of different regional origins. Domestic (Regional) refers to Start-Up Chile participants originating in Chile (South America). Foreign refers to Start-Up Chile participants originating outside of South America. The sample includes all applicants to the entrepreneurship school in Start-Up Chile during the 4th and until the 7th generation of the program (from 2012 to 2014). All regressions include generation fixed effects and control for fundraising prior to participation in the program. Capital raised corresponds to the natural logarithm of funds raised within four years of participation in Start-Up Chile (source: CB Insights). Market traction corresponds to the logarithm of the number of Facebook likes in the participant startup's webpage, within four years of participation in Start-Up Chile. T-statistics of the differences in effects across different regions are presented in the last row. The t-statistics in columns 2, 4, 6, and 8 compares the coefficients in columns 1 and 2, 3 and 4, 5 and 6, and 7 and 8, respectively. Standard errors are robust and presented in parentheses, *** p<0.01, ** p<0.05, * p<0.1. The effect of entrepreneurship schooling is estimated using a regressions discontinuity approach that exploits discontinuities in the selection rule to the entrepreneurship school of the program. For more details, see Gonzalez-Uribe and Leatherbee (2017).

only about 6 percent more likely to raise capital within the four years following the assessment than those judged to be among the lower 90 percent. This difference is not very big. In fact, for an average cohort of 1,000 applicants, about 8 accepted applicants reported raising capital, and 13 rejected applicants reported raising capital. In other words, for every cohort, the selection process was able to select only 8 out of the 21 applicants that had the potential to raise capital within four years after the application (i.e., a success rate of 38 percent). This comparison is even starker if we assume that the 8 selected applicants might have improved their likelihood of raising capital as a consequence of being accepted into the accelerator.

We recognize that this analysis is naïve and does not accurately reflect the ability (or inability) of selection processes based on expert judges. The purpose of our example is to illustrate that selection processes typically used by accelerators are far less effective than probably assumed. That is, although large-scale judging processes appear able to produce a pool of selected applicants that is *on average* slightly better than the pool of rejected applicants, such processes are far from perfect.

Supporting the notion that the judging process of discriminating between high- and low-potential applicants has important limitations, we conducted an analysis of the Start-Up Chile judging process. Table 5.2 shows the predictive capability of the pooled judges' scores (Applications Scores) and investment potential (Investment Recommendation) on the later performance of the judged startups for all accelerator participants (i.e., conditional on being ranked among the high-potential-performance applicants). Performance measures include whether the teams are selected to compete in the demo day, the amount of private capital raised, cumulative sales, previous year's sales, valuation, and number of employees. The application scores are effective at predicting whether participants were selected during the pitch competition to participate in the demo day (column 1). That is, startups that received high scores at the application stage also received high scores at the special-services stage, despite the fact that judges and the judging criteria in both stages are different. Surprisingly, however, the judging scores are not predictive of other, more objective measures of startup performance (columns 2–5).

Why are application-stage scores correlated with special-services-stage scores but not with other more objective measures of performance? One plausible explanation is that some entrepreneurs have a special knack for convincing judges they are a high-potential startup, and that—above a certain threshold—this unique skill is not strongly correlated with actual startup performance. In this case, business accelerators should try to figure out ways to distinguish the ability to persuade potential investors from the ability to build profitable ventures.

*Table 5.2   Capacity of judging process to predict later entrepreneurial
          performance*

Variables	Demo day	Private capital	Cumulative sales	Sales last year	Valuation	Employees
Application score	0.531***	244,327	124,277	−867.6	3.045e+06	0.757
	(0.000)	(0.136)	(0.213)	(0.987)	(0.161)	(0.588)
Investment recommendation	0.288***	−31,984	51,880	25,637	−292,881	0.154
	(0.004)	(0.367)	(0.327)	(0.449)	(0.433)	(0.799)
Observations	1,114	527	514	508	227	578

Note: This table shows the relation between pooled judging scores (Application score is the result of the application criteria, and Investment Recommendation is the self-reported likelihood of judges to recommend the startup to an investor) and different performance measures. Demo day is a binary variable that represents whether the startup was selected during the special-services selection stage (the pitch-day competition) to be part of Start-Up Chile's special services. Private capital represents the amount the startup raised in USD. Cumulative sales and sales last year represent sales in USD. The valuation of the startup is based on a significant transaction or, in its absence, the entrepreneur's self-assessment. Demo day is estimated with a probit model. All other models are OLS. Standard errors are robust. P-values are presented in parentheses, and *** $p<0.01$, ** $p<0.05$, * $p<0.1$.

One plausible explanation for the imperfect expert judgment is that judges are capable of discriminating between the obviously good applicants and the obviously bad applicants, but they are not as good at discriminating between applicants that are neither obviously good nor obviously bad. The inability of selection processes using expert judges to discriminate among projects that are not blatantly bad or good is not too surprising if we look at the way applicants get assigned their scores. To start with, judges differ in their expertise and are susceptible to subjective and boundedly rational decision-making. Therefore, even if judges were identical and graded a given startup in the same way, their ability to predict the future performance of *different* startups would depend on the alignment between the features of the startup and the expertise of the judges. That is, one might easily imagine how an expert in biotech could more accurately predict the performance of a biotech startup than an e-commerce startup. Therefore, misalignment between startup characteristics and a judge's expertise can be an important source of ineffectiveness.

One way that accelerators have attempted to address the misalignment problem is to rely on a panel of judges, who together offer a broader range of different criteria and expertise. However, a broader range of judges' expertise may inadvertently decrease the power of selection processes if the assignment of judges to startups is not judicious. For example, if judges' skill is sector specific and assignment is not sector-based, then the noise to quality ratio of judges' average scores may increase with the number of judges in the panel. That is, an averaged score is not necessarily an accurate reflection of potential. On the one hand, a first judge may have just the right knowledge to accurately assess the potential of a given startup and give it a high score, whereas on the other hand, a second judge may happen to not have the adequate knowledge for that given startup and give it a low score. Thus, the final, averaged score on which the decision is based will be confounded by both a precise and an imprecise assessment of future success. As a result, the average score would be lower than the score the startup should have objectively received.

Because matching the characteristics of a cadre of applicants to the expertise of a panel of judges is virtually impossible, the selection process inevitably will have a lot of noise (or imprecision). Simply by chance, a lower-potential startup with a favorable match between its characteristics and the panel's expertise may receive a higher score than a higher-potential startup with an unfavorable match between its characteristics and the panel's expertise.

Another major challenge associated with judging processes is the limited time judges are able to spend assessing the potential of a given applicant or contestant. For large-scale application processes (such as Start-Up Chile), a large number of judges are typically summoned. These judges generally participate on a voluntary basis and are required to evaluate multiple applications during a relatively tight time frame. Thus, the amount of information they are able to gather to make an informed decision is not comprehensive (and certainly far from that acquired during a typical due diligence conducted by a venture capitalist). Moreover, judges are not usually allowed to contact applicants to clarify issues in their application that may be critical for the judges' expert assessment of the applicant.

In the case of business-plan or "pitch" competitions, time restrictions are even greater. Expert judges are required to make informed decisions about multiple startups (a typical competition may have 10–15 contestants) based on presentations of roughly ten minutes each. Judgments are typically required shortly after the end of the competition, by which time judges must try to make sense of the relative future potential of each contestant in order to identify the competition "winners." Again, because these competitions rely on a panel of judges, the same issues discussed previously (averaging the opinions of multiple judges) arise. Moreover, group-decision biases may further add to the noise of the selection process, as judges discuss (and potentially negotiate) their assessments prior to making a final decision about who they believe are the highest-potential contestants. Thus, non-rational aspects may severely taint the final decisions made by a group.

A further challenge in the judging process is the difficulty in separating the potential of the business idea or opportunity from the entrepreneur's potential to discover high-value opportunities in the near future. Essentially, the motor of entrepreneurial success is not the "opportunity" per se, but rather the entrepreneur driving the opportunity discovery process. Rarely do successful entrepreneurs understand the definitive business model that would lead to their success during the early stages of their entrepreneurial process. Rather, as they make progress toward their initial vision, they gather information that enables them to discover a better business opportunity. For example, Airbnb engaged in more than a year of business-model refinements, from the moment they first thought about renting out their air mattresses until they managed to understand the business model that would lead them to success. Thus, much of the information about the potential of a given application resides in the characteristics of the entrepreneur and how these characteristics interact with the initial opportunity.

In other words, an entrepreneur's application may describe a low-potential opportunity during the application stage (Airbnb founders were rejected by prominent venture capitalists early on), yet the entrepreneur may have the potential to discover a superb idea during his or her subsequent entrepreneurial efforts. Thus, for a process of identification (and selection) of future performance to be effective, it must somehow recognize the potential of the individual entrepreneur to discover a high-potential opportunity. However, this ability is non-trivial. Essentially, aside from using proxies for the potential of the entrepreneur (e.g., his or her educational background or experience), one approach to identify potential is to spend enough time with that person to become familiar with his or her unique abilities (and aspirations) to explore, test, persist, and learn.

One accelerator that exploits this mechanism is Village Capital. As described previously, Village Capital relies on the cohort peers to select the highest-potential-performing startups. Thus, at the end of the program, cohort peers vote for the best startups. This approach relies on the principle that peers spend a considerable amount of time with, learning from, and learning about each other. This intense exposure provides peers with information that goes beyond the opportunity per se, allowing them to observe the individual characteristics that may be key for identifying future performance.

Gaming the Application

Gaming occurs when entrepreneurs tailor their application to increase their chances of being accepted, without changing their underlying opportunity.

For example, two identical startups using different presentation strategies will most likely be judged differently. This phenomenon was recognized in SRI International as it realized some of its most interesting technological inventions were not getting funded due to an unconvincing presentation method (Carlson and Wilmot, 2006). Therefore, whether business-plan-competition winners are actually the startups with the highest-potential return on investment, or simply those teams that provide the best "show" onstage, is unclear. Without further due diligence, differentiating between high future potential and a compelling presentation is difficult. Although this issue is most prevalent in business-plan pitching competitions (e.g., during the special-services and cohort-champion stages), it can also be present at the application stage. If applicants are privy to the unique selection criteria of the accelerator, by emphasizing one aspect over others, judges will be more or less willing to score the application highly—again with no change in the underlying value of the opportunity. For example, The S Factory is an accelerator that aims at supporting female-led start-ups. Thus, by simply stating during the application stage that the lead co-founder is a woman (when perhaps three coequal co-founders exist, one of which is a woman), the applicants will improve their chances of being accepted, irrespective of their underlying potential.

Of course, entrepreneurs frequently adjust their rhetoric to achieve their goals. Thus, entrepreneurs will naturally tailor their application process (and pitch-competition presentations) to match their audiences' expectations. However, if judges assume all entrepreneurs are tailoring their applications perfectly to the selection processes' expectations, and make an assessment of the applicants' comparative future potential based on this assumption, the selection will most likely fail to select the right applicants. Essentially, the "right" candidate is not necessarily the applicant that is best at tailoring the application to the selection processes' expectations. Thus, the selection process may be prone to errors if it is not able to account for the heterogeneous "gaming" conducted by applicants.

Inducing the Opportunity

Because incentives and rules influence behaviors, the selection methods and rules at the different selection stages may drive the opportunities the applicants and participants eventually pursue. For example, a given accelerator may indicate a preference for funding startups with a business-to-business business model. This explicit expectation of the selection process will certainly attract those startups that are implicitly of the business-to-business type. However, it will also have an effect on founders who are in the process of creating their business models. A given entrepreneur might have discovered an opportunity that is more suited to a business-to-consumer business model, but to improve his or her chances of getting into the accelerator, he or she begins imagining and creating ways to turn the idea into a business-to-business business model. In other words, the selection criteria and processes may drive the types of entrepreneurial opportunities applicants pursue.

This issue is important to keep in mind, especially for ecosystem accelerators. Because their goal is to spur the entrepreneurial ecosystem, by inducing the types of business models the entrepreneurs in the ecosystem imagine and craft, these accelerators might see an unintended crowding out of opportunities the entrepreneurs would have otherwise imagined and created absent this exogenous and opportunity-unrelated factor. Therefore, if the application rules effectively distract entrepreneurs from pursuing opportunities that have a better product–market fit, and induce them to pursue opportunities that have a better fit to the application (at the expense of a better product–market fit), this opportunity-inducing mechanism may actually play against the goals pursued by the ecosystem accelerator in the first place. Essentially, anything that draws entrepreneurs away from pursuing higher-potential opportunities is detrimental to the purposes of creating socioeconomic value.

A second way selection stages can potentially affect entrepreneurial progress is by shifting entrepreneurs' focus from creating a viable business model to creating a compelling pitch. When accelerators place too much emphasis on the pitch competition, entrepreneurs may naturally tend to spend their efforts on improving the "delivery" of their pitch as opposed to improving the value provided to potential customers. This issue is important because if the accelerator's main goal is to help participants raise capital by perfecting their pitch, then its structural elements must differ from those of other programs whose main goal is to help participants create value for customers. In the former case, the emphasis would be on training for the pitch, whereas in the latter, the emphasis would be on creating a viable business model and validating the product–market fit. Thus, the selection method plays a relevant role, because it will condition the behavior of participants. If the institutionalized goal (and corresponding selection method) is to win a pitch competition, participants will likely behave differently than in a context in which the institutionalized goal is to close a deal with a paying customer. Business accelerators must make a conscious effort to align their programmatic milestones, competitions, and selection methods with their desired outcomes. Misalignment on this issue may have a negative effect on accelerators' key performance indicators, and accelerate their demise.

Selection Speed, a Double-Edged Sword

As emphasized previously, the more time spent on evaluating the performance potential of a given startup, the more likely the judgment will be accurate, which is why early-stage investors rely on due diligences before investing. From this perspective, one may prematurely conclude that longer selection processes are better than shorter ones. The key issue with taking too long to make a selection decision is that high-potential startups will likely find other paths that are not compatible with going through the business accelerator once the accelerator's mind is made up.

For example, take the case of an application selection process that receives applications for a period of three months. Once the application period closes, the accelerator takes another two months to evaluate each application and make a final decision about accepted and rejected applicants. While the accelerator is deliberating, applicants (particularly the high-potential ones) are also searching for alternatives, either by applying to other accelerators or meeting with early-stage investors. The higher-potential startups (the ones the accelerator may want to select) are more likely than the lower-potential startups to receive offers from other accelerators or investors. Therefore, by the time the business accelerator has reached its final verdict, those applicants to whom it sends acceptance letters might already have committed to irreversible decisions that are incompatible with participating in the accelerator. In the case of Start-Up Chile, roughly 15 percent of accepted applicants decline to participate, presumably because they have committed to other options. Essentially, the longer accelerators take to make a decision about applicants, the higher the likelihood that the higher-potential applicants self-remove from the applicant pool.

Managing the tradeoff between carefully reviewing applications and making a quick decision is not trivial. One way would be to spend greater resources by increasing the number of expert judges. However, this approach may lead to a greater variability in the judging criteria, which may increase the noise of the selection process. An alternative way currently being explored by Leatherbee and del Sol (2016) is the reliance on rational heuristics, which constitute a series of simple rules or cognitive shortcuts organizations can use to make quick decisions in uncertain environments. Theory states that organizations can effectively develop a series of simple rules that can help them outperform other organizations when competitiveness relies on making fast decisions with limited information. Preliminary evidence suggests accelerators can rely on the construction of simple rules to select applicants, and these selection mechanisms are significantly more effective at identifying high-performance applicants than the traditional method of relying on a pool of expert judges. Most importantly, however, using a method such as the one explored by Leatherbee and del Sol may effectively decrease the length of the decision-making process to only a few days.

CONCLUSION

Selecting the right startups is a key aspect in the success of business accelerators, in a similar way that selecting the right students is key for the success of business schools. However, the effective selection of applicants is a non-trivial activity. It requires a clear understanding about the accelerator's goals (e.g., to invest in the highest-performing startups, or support the entrepreneurs who could benefit the most from the acceleration experience), because the selection criterion can (willingly or unwillingly) filter out applicants with specific characteristics that may be useful for achieving the aforementioned goals.

Business accelerator managers must be aware of the many potential pitfalls and unintended consequences. For example, spending a lot of time evaluating applications may increase the accuracy of the selection process at the expense of losing good candidates that are not willing to wait for a decision from the accelerator. Furthermore, the business accelerator's judging criteria may have an effect on the types of business models pursued by the stock of entrepreneurs in the ecosystem. Thus, selection processes may have the unintended consequence of biasing the types of opportunities pursued in the local ecosystem.

Importantly, one must recognize that current selection methods are far from accurate. Even the most intensive evaluation processes are limited in their ability to separate the right from the wrong candidates. Such limitation means many right candidates are being left out of the accelerator simply because of the weaknesses of the selection process. It also means room remains for improvement. Thus, accelerators that work hard on improving their selection processes are likely to significantly increase their competitive advantage or impact.

NOTES

1. For an example of the effects of entrepreneurship schooling as a special service, see Gonzalez-Uribe and Leatherbee (2018).
2. Accelerators are constantly experimenting with different processes and methods, thus changing their programs and benefits.
3. For a more detailed explanation of the different types of business accelerators, see

Clarysse, Wright, and Van Hove (2015). To better understand the effects of having more open-access competitions, see Fehder and Hochberg (2014).
4. For a better understanding of the opportunity discovery refinement process entrepreneurs undergo as a consequence of market feedback, see Leatherbee and Katila (2016).
5. EPIC Lab white paper available at http://epiclab.uc.cl/wp-content/uploads/2016/11/False-positive-negative-white-paper-2-EPIC-Lab-EN.pdf (accessed May 2017).
6. For more information about the effects of entrepreneurship schooling on new venture performance, see Gonzalez-Uribe and Leatherbee (2018).

REFERENCES

Carlson CR, Wilmot WW. 2006. *Innovation: The Five Disciplines for Creating What Customers Want*, 1st ed., Crown Business, New York.

Clarysse B, Wright M, Van Hove J. 2015. *A Look Inside Accelerators: Building Businesses*, Nesta, London, February.

Fehder DC, Hochberg YV. 2014. Accelerators and the Regional Supply of Venture Capital Investment. Available at SSRN: https://ssrn.com/abstract=2518668 (accessed May 2017).

Gonzalez-Uribe J, Leatherbee M. 2017. The Effects of Business Accelerators on Venture Performance: Evidence from Start-Up Chile. *The Review of Financial Studies* 31(4): 1566–1603. https://doi.org/10.1093/rfs/hhx103.

Howell ST. 2017. Learning from Feedback: Evidence from New Ventures. Working Paper. Available at: http://web.business.queensu.ca/faculty/jdebettignies/Docs/Howell_Learning_from_Feedback_June8_2017.pdf (accessed June 2017).

Leatherbee M, del Sol P. 2016. Predicting Entrepreneurial Performance: Simple Rules versus Expert Judgment. Working Paper. Available at: http://ctie.econo mia.cl/wp-content/uploads/2017/07/Predicting-Entrepreneurial-Performance-Si mple-Rules-2016.pdf (accessed May 2017).

Leatherbee M, Katila R. 2016. Stay the Course or Pivot? Antecedents of Cognitive Refinements of Business Models in Young Firms. Working Paper. Available at SSRN: https://ssrn.com/abstract=2902869 (accessed May 2017).

Wagner RA. 2016. Does Feedback to Business-Plans Impact New Ventures? Evidence from a Field Experiment. Working Paper. Available at SSRN: https://ssrn.com/abstract=2766566 (accessed May 2017).

6. Key performance indicators

Michael Leatherbee and Juanita Gonzalez-Uribe

INTRODUCTION

Business accelerators have the potential to influence entrepreneurial eco-systems and socioeconomic development in multiple ways, well beyond the direct effects they may have on the startups they sponsor. Accelerators can influence the rate of new-business creation (Table 6.1), early-stage venture investment activity (Fehder and Hochberg, 2014), the flow of foreign entrepreneurial human capital (Leatherbee and Eesley, 2014), the legitimacy of entrepreneurship as a career path, and entrepreneurs' assimilation of valuable entrepreneurial knowledge (Hallen, Bingham, and Cohen, 2016). Because the dimensions of an accelerator's potential impact can be highly orthogonal and the spillover effects can reach far beyond an accelerator's boundaries, figuring out how and what to measure to determine whether an accelerator is making effective headway can be a non-trivial exercise.

Selecting the proper set of key performance indicators (KPIs) is important for assessing the progress of a business accelerator. By keeping a close eye on KPIs, program managers (and sponsors) can gauge the health of their accelerators as they move toward their predefined goals. Selecting and monitoring KPIs is useful because it offers managers the opportunity to learn from failures and successes, and provides the justification to implement organizational or programmatic changes (Locke et al., 1981). However, setting and measuring KPIs can be a double-edged sword. Much like the way pilots rely on the instruments distributed on an airplane's dashboard, focusing on the wrong KPIs can lead managers to incorrectly interpret the state of the accelerator. Analogously, although gauging the outside air temperature can be particularly important for pilots, this knowledge is only secondary to knowing the relative airspeed of the plane. Thus, focusing only on the thermometer at the expense of the airspeed indicator can be potentially disastrous. Such a pilot may easily run the plane aground without even realizing his or her mistake until it is too late.

In addition to *knowing* which KPIs are useful for tracking an accelerator's trajectory toward its specific goals, *measuring* KPIs properly is also important. False readings can misrepresent the state of the accelerator and cause incorrect (or insufficient) adjustments. Tragic airplane accidents have been caused because ground crew failed to advert to the fact that the static pressure port had been taped over for a paint job and therefore failed to provide the pilot with the correct altitude reading. Thus, ensuring the information needed to build a given KPI is accurate is a key part of developing an effective KPI dashboard.

Managing a large number of KPIs is not necessarily a good thing. Having too many can be detrimental because individuals (and organizations) are limited in their ability to process information (Simon, 1991). Too many indicators can draw attention away from the key ones, crowding out thoughtful and useful discussions about the accelerator's progress or need for change. Moreover, gathering the information needed to build KPIs requires time and resources. Thus, accelerator managers should be careful to find the right cost/benefit balance. After a certain threshold, incorporating additional KPIs provides decreasing marginal returns, and the marginal benefit of developing and managing an additional KPI may be lower than its marginal cost.

This chapter provides a stockpile of KPIs from which business accelerator stakeholders can draw. It was developed over more than three years of in-depth research of the Start-Up Chile business accelerator program, and supplemented through interviews with multiple business accelerator managers. Moreover, we conducted an extensive review of the finance and entrepreneurship literatures focused on business accelerators, from which we drew several of the KPIs listed here.

Many of the KPIs discussed in this chapter may seem irrelevant to some accelerator stakeholders, because specific goals can be quite orthogonal depending on the accelerator type. Two different accelerators may benefit from two different sets of KPIs. For example, ecosystem accelerators may be interested in gauging spillover KPIs, because their main goal is to spur the domestic entrepreneurship ecosystem. By contrast, investor-led accelerators may be interested in gauging the growth or market-traction KPI of their portfolio startups in an effort to identify high-potential startups early on.

The KPIs listed in this chapter are by no means exhaustive, because business accelerator objectives can vary widely. We may have overlooked some unique goals of specific programs, for which unlisted KPIs could be developed. Our hope is that this chapter provides inspiration to business accelerator stakeholders as they identify and craft their unique dashboard of KPIs, and to researchers as they explore the phenomena underlying business accelerators.

SHOW ME WHO FUNDS YOU AND I WILL TELL YOU WHAT YOUR GOALS ARE

KPIs are intended to reflect, on a regular basis, an organization's progress toward a set of predefined goals. They are useful for guiding behaviors and effort aimed at reaching those goals (Locke, 1996). Thus, when thinking about accelerator KPIs, recognizing that not all accelerators are created equal is important. For example, some accelerators are aimed at spurring socioeconomic development, whereas others are created with the goal of yielding an attractive return on investment for the accelerator's sponsor.

Accelerators can be classified into three broad categories: investor-led, ecosystem, and matchmaker (Clarysse, Wright, and Van Hove, 2015). Investor-led accelerators (e.g., Y Combinator, Techstars) are typically aimed at discovering investment opportunities. That is, they have a competitive application process through which they screen startups and select those that appear to offer the most promising investment prospects. Because investor-led accelerators typically take equity stakes in their sponsored startups, a key goal for their portfolio of startups is the achievement of significant transactions that provide positive returns on their investments (Cohen and Hochberg, 2014). Therefore, once accepted into the accelerator, startups are encouraged to focus wholeheartedly on growth. For example, Y Combinator expects their participant startups to grow at a rate of 7 percent per week.[1]

By contrast, ecosystem accelerators (e.g., Start-Up Chile, Village Capital, and Parallel 18) are typically sponsored by government agencies or nonprofit organizations. These accelerators also have a competitive application process but do not require an equity stake in the startups they sponsor. Their aim is to stimulate startup activity in their focal regions, under the expectation that it will spur socioeconomic development. They do so by supporting large numbers of startups (sometimes providing grants) and fostering interaction between the sponsored startups and the surrounding community. Thus, they expect their startups to grow their businesses *and* spend time on community-related activities. For example, Start-Up Chile requires that participants complete a minimum number of return value agenda (RVA) points during their tenure in the accelerator.[2] For each specific activity, such as mentoring a local entrepreneur or giving a lecture at a school or university, participants earn RVA points. In contrast to investor-led accelerators, ecosystem accelerators have a much broader range of specific goals (e.g., job creation, early-stage investment activity, community engagement). However, unintended effects also arise that accelerator managers do not yet seem to fully understand. We will explore these effects further below.

Finally, large corporations sponsor matchmaker-type accelerators (e.g., Microsoft Ventures Accelerator, Google Launchpad Accelerator). They are typically associated with a corporation's investment arms and are aimed at matching the corporation's customers with potential new service providers (i.e., the startups). Matchmaker accelerators do not typically take equity stakes in the businesses they support, and sometimes provide seed capital. Because of the accelerator's incentive to grow the corporation's business and the technological support network the startups are connected into once accepted into the program, startups typically build their businesses on top of the corporation's existing technological platforms and customer networks. Thus, the goals of matchmaker accelerators include growing the sponsor corporation's business and establishing tighter ties with existing customers through the development of new products or services that use the corporation's existing solutions.

TYPICALLY USED KPIs

To gauge performance, we can classify accelerators' focus of attention into three dimensions: recruitment, acceleration, and spillovers. The *recruitment* dimension encompasses activities associated with the attraction and evaluation of applicants, with the goal of picking high-potential startups. The *acceleration* dimension entails the programmatic activities and resources available to the accelerator with the expectation of improving the performance trajectory of participating startups. The *spillovers* dimension corresponds to the broader effects the activities organized or induced by the accelerator have on stakeholders within the accelerator's ecosystem. Frequently, these spillovers have positive indirect effects on accelerators, as we discuss further below.

Recruitment KPIs

Having an effective recruitment process is key for accelerator performance and sustainability. "Quality in, quality out" is a principle accelerator managers, computer scientists, and university admissions offices understand well. The better the applicant pool, the more likely the graduates will be high performing. Venture capitalists operate by this same logic. Being able to attract high-potential applicants and associate the accelerator with high-performing graduates is fundamental at two levels: resources and legitimacy. For investor-led accelerators, having early successful exits can increase the perception by outsiders that the accelerator is effective at improving participant performance, as well as fuel the operation of the accelerator with new funds to invest in new applicants. For example, Techstars accelerator achieved the sale (through acquisitions) of 20 percent of its portfolio of startups within a year of becoming established. In addition to providing fresh capital, this achievement also provided validation for its model and much-needed public attention (further helping to attract more high-potential applicants). In the case of ecosystem accelerators, having successful graduates is particularly useful for legitimizing the accelerator's existence in the face of sponsors (governments or non-profit organizations), thus encouraging further financial support to cover the accelerator's operational expenses. Moreover, accelerators can leverage the success cases of their graduates to promote themselves publicly and further attract high-potential applicants, thus pushing the accelerator into a virtuous cycle of attracting and graduating high-performance entrepreneurs.

Recruitment KPIs can be separated into *outreach* and *intake*. Outreach encompasses measures of all activities associated with capturing public attention, with the goal of increasing the number of high-potential applicants. Intake encompasses measures of the application process. Outreach and intake are highly related, because successful outreach efforts will likely improve the intake indicators.

Many of these recruitment KPIs reflect the intensity of the activities conducted by accelerator staff. Because these activities can ultimately affect other relevant KPIs, accelerator stakeholders should keep an eye on these indicators. Moreover, exploring relationships between outreach KPIs and intake KPIs can help guide accelerator managers regarding the effectiveness of specific activities. For example, to what extent does *social networking activity* (an outreach KPI) cause an increase in *participant quality* (an intake KPI)? And how does *participant quality* (an intake KPI) relate to company *valuation* (an acceleration KPI)? Thus, because activities are sometimes easier to measure than outcomes, and to the extent that certain activities are related to performance, accelerator managers might want to consider including these KPIs in their dashboard.

Examples of outreach KPIs

Promotional gatherings   Corresponds to the number of meetings held to promote the accelerator among prospective applicants. These meetings may be organized and held by the accelerator staff, accelerator participants (who, in the case of Start-Up Chile, get awarded RVA points), or accelerator alumni. These gatherings may be timed around the corresponding cohort application deadline, with the aim of increasing the applicant pool. Depending on the international orientation of the accelerator, this KPI can be classified into foreign or domestic. Moreover, it can be further dissected to achieve greater granularity by focusing on the average number of attendees per gathering. Some accelerators may further include in this KPI the number of visiting delegations to the accelerator premises.

Media coverage   Corresponds to the number of appearances in the media. This KPI is an important indicator because public attention in general (and a positive public opinion in particular) is likely to increase the number of high-potential applicants. Media coverage can be further dissected into foreign and domestic, and positive and negative.

Social network activity   Corresponds to the measure of presence in social network platforms such as Facebook, Twitter, YouTube, Instagram, and LinkedIn. The intensity of social network activity is likely to influence application rates in a similar way as media coverage, and can be further dissected in the same way.

Examples of intake KPIs
Applicant count   An important indicator commonly used by accelerator managers. The volume of applicants reflects the general appeal of the accelerator from the perspective of entrepreneurs. In principle, the larger the applicant pool, the higher the likelihood of identifying high-potential entrepreneurs. However, this indicator alone can be misleading if not complemented by others that proxy for the quality of the applicant pool. For example, an increase in the number of applicants may reflect a specific outreach activity in a new market (e.g., press coverage in a specific country); however, applicant entrepreneurs may not necessarily be higher in potential performance.

Acceptance rate   Reflects the ratio of accepted to all applicants. Depending on whether the accelerator has a fixed budget constraint (and hence the number of potential participants is also fixed for each cohort), this KPI can substitute for the Applicant Count KPI. However, sometimes accelerators select based on budget availability or on the perceived quality of applicants, funding as many applicants as they deem surpass a given quality threshold.

Development stage   Corresponds to the level of maturity of applicant startups. For example, Start-Up Chile classifies applicants from *concept* (founders are at a very early stage) to *scaling sales* (the startup is in the growth stage). Because having more validated startups decreases the risk of portfolio failure, one might naturally expect accelerators to push to increase their development-stage KPI. Figure 6.1 shows how Start-Up Chile tracks both Applicant Count and Development Stage KPIs. The

START-UP CHILE

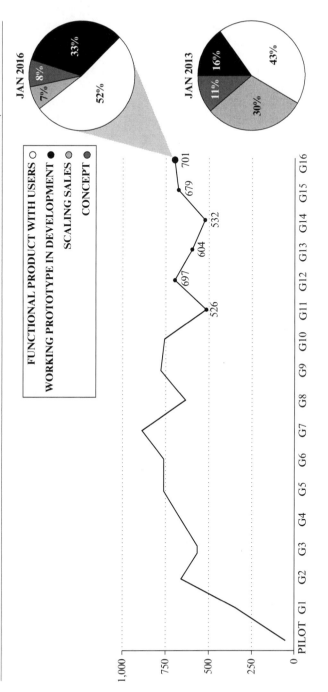

Note: Special attention is given to the change in the stage of applicants. In this example, applicants with a functional product grew from 30 percent to 52 percent from 2015 to 2016.

Figure 6.1   Evolution of valid applicants to Start-Up Chile for the first 17 cohorts

graph suggests an evolution in the applicant pool between 2015 and 2016 toward a higher development stage.

Participant quality   Corresponds to the quality of the individual participants. It is an important indicator because it directly influences the acceleration and spillover goals of accelerators. The higher the quality of participants, the higher the likelihood of having successful alumni who will contribute either directly with resources (as in the case of an exit event for investor-led accelerators) or with legitimacy (by which accelerators leverage the success and media coverage of their alumni). Quality can be gauged by comparing the judging scores between one application process and another. Although this measure is not exact or precise (because judges may be different at each application process, and scores may carry significant levels of subjectivity), the indicator can be complemented by other proxies. For example, participant quality can be estimated using the university rankings where they studied, their level of education, or prior work experience.

International Representation   Refers to the proportion of foreign applicants. This indicator is particularly useful for those programs that aim at attracting entrepreneurs to their regions. Assuming the judging criterion is country-agnostic, comparing the distribution of applicants against the distribution of participants can be useful in identifying the countries from which high-potential entrepreneurs are coming. Moreover, a low representation of a specific country in the participants list may reflect an ineffective outreach strategy.

Industry distribution   Refers to the types of industries represented in the application pool. Some accelerators are industry focused, in which case this KPI can help to indicate whether the outreach efforts are targeting the industries of greatest interest.

Demographic distribution   Some accelerators are driven by the goal of positive action in their selection process. Thus, demographic-distribution KPIs (e.g., gender, ethnicity, or locality) are useful in supervising the achievement of this goal.

Processing time   Corresponds to the time it takes to process applications. Accelerators typically take about two months between the application deadline and the acceptance decision, which can be a long time for fledgling startups. The problem from the accelerator's perspective is the potential loss of high-quality startups. High-quality startups are very likely to find funding elsewhere within the two months accelerators take to make a decision. Thus, when the final verdict is made about who is be selected, a non-trivial proportion of the selected applicants reject the offer because they have already found funding elsewhere. A long processing time can jeopardize the quality of the incoming cohort, because the best startups may be lost to other accelerators or investors.

Acceleration KPIs

New-venture-performance *acceleration* is the key promise of business accelerators. This promise is important because it is one of the main reasons entrepreneurs compete to be accepted into these programs. Thus far, accelerators have typically used the performance metrics of their alumni as KPIs that indicate actual acceleration effects. They promote this information in an effort to attract better applicants. Moreover, many accelerators even argue the success of their alumni is proof that they are successfully delivering on the promise of acceleration. In turn, this message sometimes induces the press and potential applicants to become excited by the apparent prospects of acceleration. However, concluding that a given accelerator indeed provides an acceleration effect by looking exclusively at the performance of alumni can be very misleading.

Whether business accelerators indeed accelerate and *how* acceleration occurs are non-trivial questions.[3] How can we know accelerator alumni are doing well because they participated in a given accelerator and not because they were going to do just as well on their own (in the absence of the accelerator)? Without a valid counterfactual for accelerator alumni (i.e., a control group), knowing what would have happened in a parallel universe where those same alumni did not have the business accelerator experience is impossible. Moreover, assuming accelerators do add value to participants, how exactly does this happen? Do they have better mentors, supervisory processes, workshops, and participants, or are they simply better connected to value-adding financiers?

Answering these questions for each specific accelerator is very important for accelerator managers, sponsors, and applicants. Even though the acceleration conundrum (whether an accelerator accelerates) may be less important today for investor-led accelerators (because one of their key goals is to attract and identify good investment opportunities, regardless of whether they actually accelerate *because* of the accelerator), it should become very relevant as more information becomes publicly available about the real (causal) effects of each business accelerator. For instance, we could imagine a near future in which causal estimates of the acceleration effects of different business accelerators are publicly known, enabling applicants to select accelerators based on their *real* promise of acceleration, and not on the performance reports of their alumni. Once robust evidence of the acceleration effects for specific accelerators emerges, accelerator managers will have to strive to improve (or fix) their programmatic interventions in order to remain an attractive option to potential applicants. For example, a recent study on the effects of Start-Up Chile on new-venture performance found that specific programmatic aspects of the accelerator caused an improvement in startup performance by 20 percent to 40 percent (Gonzalez-Uribe and Leatherbee, 2018). As a result, Start-Up Chile's managers refocused their efforts on the aspects that were proven to work effectively, further extending their service to all accelerator participants (as opposed to the select few for which the service was originally designed).

In the case of ecosystem accelerator sponsors (particularly for non-profit sponsors who do not take equity stakes in participants' startups), knowing whether the accelerator actually has an effect (on whatever goal the sponsors are interested in) is especially important. As any sensible person would be, accelerator sponsors are interested in knowing whether the resources they are giving away indeed serve the purpose of reaching the goal(s) they are trying to achieve. For example, ecosystem accelerator sponsors may be interested in encouraging job creation, in which case they would want to know whether participating in the accelerator has a causal effect on the employee count of startups. By focusing exclusively on the employee count KPI of alumni startups (without comparing that count to a valid counterfactual), sponsors will never know whether the startups they supported would have created as many jobs had they not consumed sponsor resources.[4]

For applicant entrepreneurs, understanding the difference between the real acceleration effects from a given accelerator and the innate performance abilities of the accelerator's alumni is also very important. Accelerator applicants believe getting into the right accelerator is important for their startup trajectory, in the same way that business school applicants believe getting into the right business school can improve their professional prospects. However, most of the existing information on the supposed acceleration effects does not help accelerator applicants make an informed decision. If anything, the information can be potentially misleading, because interpreting alumni performance as a signal that a given service will deliver on a performance-enhancing promise is not a robust interpretation. Thus, in the absence of evidence about real acceleration effects, entrepreneurs cannot be sure that participating in that specific accelerator would actually benefit them.

We know that business accelerators, in general, can positively influence new-venture performance by improving the entrepreneurial capital of participants through entrepreneurship schooling (Gonzalez-Uribe and Leatherbee, 2018). However, the specific dimension in which a given accelerator can have an effect on a specific population will most likely depend on the context and programmatic elements of that accelerator. For example, some accelerators may be best at helping participants secure follow-on funding, others may be best at scaling participants' market traction, and others may be best at fostering employee growth. Given the proper evaluation procedures and metrics, accelerators could not only know whether they are helping their participants, but also in which dimensions they are particularly good at doing so. Moreover, by making this information public, applicants could make more informed decisions about which accelerators they need in order to achieve their goals. Thus, we could imagine that applicants who wish to secure venture capital would prefer those accelerators that are best at securing follow-on funding to accelerators that are best at helping entrepreneurs build market traction. If a particular entrepreneur were not keen on raising venture capital (perhaps because she prefers an organic growth strategy), she should probably steer her startup away from accelerators that are effective at getting her funded by venture capitalists. Of course, sometimes these different dimensions (market growth and follow-on funding) go hand in hand—but not always.

In principle, a greater focus on estimating real acceleration effects (as opposed to the delusion of acceleration) should also improve the system-wide impact of accelerators more broadly. In the same way that transparency and a focus on robust and meaningful KPIs improve decision-making in other social settings, this approach could help accelerator managers, sponsors, and applicants. Making an effort to increase their ability to determine the real effects of each accelerator program would behoove business accelerator stakeholders. This effort would improve decision-making, programmatic design, accountability in the face of sponsors, and ultimately socioeconomic development.

Setting up the capability to determine the real acceleration effects of accelerators can be quite simple and straightforward, barring a few key (and relatively trivial) restrictions that must be put in place. For example, the *Capital Semilla* (Seed Capital) business incubator program of Chile's Ministry of Economy recently implemented the structural elements in its selection process that will allow them to determine the real effects of the program. The program did this by establishing a few rules in its selection criteria and relying on a regression discontinuity design (cf. Leatherbee, Frias, and Gonzalez, 2016).

Business accelerators commonly use acceleration KPIs to gauge alumni performance. Thus, accelerators are well on their way to being able to establish the structural and methodological elements that will allow them to determine their real effects on participant acceleration. However, one must keep in mind that even though accelerators may use the following acceleration KPIs, if they do not compare them against a valid counterfactual, these KPIs should not be interpreted as real acceleration effects. At most, they can be interpreted as a measure of the quality of their participants and alumni.

Examples of acceleration KPIs

Market traction Corresponds to the indicator of the appeal of the product or service developed by the startup, combined with the ability of the startup to reach the target market. If the value proposition of the startup is theoretically appealing, but the founding team is not competent at reaching potential customers, the market-traction KPI may remain low. The opposite is also potentially possible. For example, by using "growth-hacking" techniques, startups can gain much social network activity (e.g., Twitter mentions). However, if the product or service is not appealing enough, growth will eventually tail off. Typical measures for this KPI include the number of registered users, Facebook likes, website visits, Twitter mentions, and sales.

Of course, the relevance of these measures depends on the startup's business model. For example, business-to-consumer startups may have higher measures for registered users and Facebook likes than business-to-business startups, simply because the volume of consumers is greater than that of businesses. Therefore, a comparison between different startups in the same cohort must be conducted with care. By contrast, a comparison of the *average* of any of these measures between the participants (or alumni) and a valid counterfactual group can be quite informative, because it will reflect the real acceleration effects for the market-traction KPI.

Employees Corresponds to the number of employees working for a given startup. This KPI can be dissected into measures of full-time and part-time employees. Because job creation does not necessarily indicate profitability or return on investment, this indicator is less relevant for investor-led and matchmaker accelerators. However, it is typically a very relevant KPI for ecosystem accelerators because job creation is commonly equated with socioeconomic development (a key goal for these programs).

Fundraising Corresponds to the act of securing follow-on, third-party investment by startups. Raising capital has been commonly viewed as a measure of success, because it indicates a third-party opinion that the startup has upside potential. However, it is important to keep in mind that raising capital is not the only path to success. Many successful startups have grown organically by capitalizing on sales. Thus, a low fundraising KPI may be a reflection of the startup's ability to postpone fundraising (thus increasing its pre-capital valuation) or of the founders' preference to keep a greater percentage of ownership in the hands of the founding team.

Understanding that fundraising is partly a strategic choice made by the founding team (i.e., not necessarily a measure of success), one must be careful in comparing accelerator alumni against a counterfactual group. A higher average fundraising KPI may simply be an indication that the accelerator experience influences the strategic choice of founders (to search for fundraising), and not necessarily an indication of the measured startups' higher potential for success.

Typical measures used for this KPI are the indicator of the fundraising milestone (i.e., whether a relevant transaction was completed) and the amount raised. For example, Gonzalez-Uribe and Leatherbee (2018) found that participation in Start-Up Chile's entrepreneurship school increased a startup's likelihood of fundraising (as a relevant transaction milestone) by 21 percent. They also found that startups participating in the entrepreneurship school saw a threefold to sixfold increase in the amount of capital raised.

Valuation Corresponds to the pre-money valuation of the startups in the face of a relevant transaction. Post-money valuation can be used as an alternative measure, but care must be applied when gathering and analyzing data to avoid confusion between pre-money and post-money measures. For example, the estimated effect of participation in Start-Up Chile's entrepreneurship school was a fivefold increase in pre-money valuation (Gonzalez-Uribe and Leatherbee, 2018).

The more objective source of this measure is typically captured by a relevant transaction (e.g., fundraising). However, the same fundraising KPI caveat applies here. To the extent that accelerator participation influences the founders' capitalization strategy, biases may exist when comparing participants against their counterfactual. That is, the inexistence of a relevant transaction must not be equated with a low valuation. Therefore, an alternative approach could be to ask founders directly what their self-assessed valuation is. Although this measure may be inflated by respondents' over-optimism, this bias is likely to be similar for accelerator participants and their control group.

Profits Corresponds to the measure of a startup's profits for a predefined period (e.g., the last 6 to 12 months). The founding team typically self-reports this measure. Although profits (as opposed to losses) are certainly a reflection of the financial health of a startup, they are not a perfect measure of future potential. Many times, founding teams may systematically reinvest their monthly profit margins into growth opportunities (e.g., new employees or marketing), which would be reflected in a temporary decrease in the profits KPI.

Survival Corresponds to the startup's state of operation. This KPI is typically quantified as a binary variable, where being "alive" is codified as 1 and "shut down" is codified as 0. For example, Yu (2016) found investor-led accelerator startups are less likely to remain alive than non-accelerated (comparable) startups. By contrast, Gonzalez-Uribe and Leatherbee (2018) found no evidence that ecosystem accelerators affect startup survival *on average*. However, they did find the performance KPIs for accelerator participants appear more disperse than for non-participants. Together, these studies suggest accelerators may be actually accelerating the death of low-potential startups, while simultaneously accelerating the growth of high-potential startups.

Whether participating startups survive can be particularly relevant for investor-led accelerators, because these accelerator sponsors have equity stakes in the startups they support. However, survival rates may be less relevant for ecosystem accelerators, because their main goal is the promotion of socioeconomic development through entrepreneurship, and therefore the level of analysis that matters most is the founder, not the startup. Ultimately, the source of value creation is the founder, who in turn must have the drive and skills to create a startup that will eventually contribute to socioeconomic development.

For example, a given low-potential startup may fail faster as a consequence of participating in the accelerator, as suggested by the findings of Yu (2016) and Gonzalez-Uribe and Leatherbee (2018). This outcome can be positive, because productive factors (i.e., the entrepreneur) will be removed from a low-productive activity (i.e., running a low-potential startup). At the same time, the accelerator experience may teach participants how to discover higher upside-potential opportunities and build better startups, as suggested by the findings of Hallen, Bingham, and Cohen (2016), Wagner (2016), and Leatherbee and Eesley (2014). Thus, by accelerating the demise of low-potential startups, the corresponding founders become free to leverage their newly acquired skills and knowledge to create a higher-potential startup.

Although this reasoning is still mostly theoretical, findings by Gonzalez-Uribe and Leatherbee (2018) provide suggestive evidence that the accelerator experience induces founders to persist in their careers as entrepreneurs. That is, although the average failure rate between accelerated and non-accelerated startups in ecosystem accelerators is similar, the rate of individuals who continue to be entrepreneurs several years after participating in the accelerator is higher. Essentially, founders of failed startups who go through the accelerator experience are more likely to try to build new startups vis-à-vis non-accelerated founders. Therefore, the use of survival as a KPI must be interpreted with care, and should be dissected into two complementary measures: the survival of the startup and the persistence of the individual as an entrepreneur.

Growth rate   Corresponds to the period-over-period growth rate of any given measure that is relevant for the specific startup. For example, some investor-led accelerators register week-over-week growth rate, and argue that anything below a 7 percent growth rate is underperforming. Measures can include Facebook likes, sales, registered users, website visits, application downloads, and number of customer reviews (e.g., for apps). The growth-rate KPI as an extrinsic motivator can be potentially useful for founders, because it provides quick performance feedback and can help keep founding teams under constant pressure to outperform (Latham and Locke, 2006).

However, using this KPI as a comparison between startups can be challenging. The relevant measures can differ for different business models, thus rendering comparability between startups more challenging. For example, one of Instagram's growth-rate KPIs was user subscription. However, before being purchased by Facebook for roughly one billion dollars, Instagram had no sales to report. Thus, comparing *comparable* startups is key for gaining reasonable insights from this KPI.

Assessing the effect of a given accelerator on the average startup growth rate can be particularly useful. As has been emphasized previously, the key to successful assessment is the construction of a valid counterfactual group that can be systematically monitored in the same way as the accelerated group. Insights on the growth-rate effect may serve as a means by which accelerator managers can test which programmatic interventions work best, and promote their growth-acceleration capabilities (if any) to attract higher-quality applicants.

Spillover KPIs

Spillovers are particularly relevant for ecosystem accelerators, whose key goal is to spur domestic socioeconomic development. However, they are also relevant (although more indirectly so) for investor-led and matchmaker accelerators. Essentially, a healthy entrepreneurial ecosystem is like a rising tide that raises all boats. For example, the prestige of Techstars in Boulder, Colorado, or Start-Up Chile in Santiago has driven many entrepreneurs to migrate to these locations, despite not being selected into the accelerators. These migration forces increase the supply of business opportunities and human capital, as well as knowledge and access to new networks potentially useful to domestic entrepreneurs. Such changes are advantageous for early-stage investors, because investors benefit from the availability of greater numbers of higher-quality entrepreneurs. Moreover, a migration of entrepreneurs increases market competition, which helps to erode potential monopolistic features in the economy that typically preclude the creation of new value from reaching the broader population of consumers. Therefore, keeping a close eye on the effects accelerators have beyond their organizational boundaries is of great importance.

Spillover KPIs are less trivial to pin down than acceleration KPIs, because the former are typically non-obvious and unexpected. For example, Fehder and Hochberg (2014) found the establishment of an accelerator in a given location considerably increased early-stage investment activity in startups, many of which were *not affiliated* with the accelerator. Moreover, findings by Leatherbee and Eesley (2014) suggest domestic entrepreneurs can learn skills and knowledge that is not readily available in the local ecosystem, as a consequence of interacting with foreign entrepreneurs who bring unique skills and knowledge from abroad. These unexpected skills and knowledge may grant domestic entrepreneurs a greater toolbox from which to build higher-performing startups.

Examples of spillover KPIs

Relocation　Corresponds to the indicator of entrepreneurial immigrants who remain in the host region. For example, one of Start-Up Chile's goals is to attract (and retain) high-potential entrepreneurs from overseas with the aim of contributing to domestic socioeconomic development. The relocation KPI can be counted as the number (or proportion) of participant foreign startups that remain in the domestic locality after a given time period. However, because founders typically outlast startups, a potentially better measure is the number of foreign *entrepreneurs* who remain in the domestic region (regardless of whether the original startups remain in existence).

One of the challenges of this KPI (and spillover KPIs in general) is the identification of the source of the effect. That is, relocation may not just be a consequence of *participating* in the accelerator: it may also be a consequence of the outreach activities abroad that may help paint an attractive picture for immigrant entrepreneurs, regardless of their participation in the accelerator. Thus, counting only the number of foreign participants who decide to relocate to the host locality may be an incomplete measure for this KPI. To learn about this secondary effect, accelerators could work with immigration offices to identify the source that motivated the relocation (which may have been the accelerator's prestige abroad or its outreach efforts).

Vicarious founding   Corresponds to the number of startups created in the locality of the accelerator that did not directly participate in the accelerator. For example, Table 6.1 shows the results of a difference-in-differences methodology that compares business-creation rates before and after the inception of the Start-Up Chile program. After Start-Up Chile was created, 6 percent more companies registered in the localities around (and

Table 6.1   Regional effects: new-business registration rates

	(1) Number	(2) Number	(3) Log.	(4) Log.
Post 2010 × contiguous	0.314*** (0.097)		0.024*** (0.005)	
Post 2010 × contiguous × venture		0.483** (0.213)		0.060*** (0.022)
Observations	426,180	426,180	426,180	426,180
R-squared	0.043	0.900	0.062	0.783
Comuna FE	Yes		Yes	
Year FE	Yes		Yes	
Industry × year FE		Yes		Yes
Industry × comuna FE		Yes		Yes
Comuna × year FE		Yes		Yes

Note: This table reports the regional effects of the program on new-business registration rates. Estimates in columns (1) and (3) are based on the regression New Business$_{cit}$ = $\gamma_t + \gamma_c$+ Post_2010$_t$ × Contiguous$_c$+ ε_{cit}, where New Business$_{cit}$ corresponds to the number and logarithm of new businesses registered in comuna c, industry i, and time t, respectively, and Post_2010 is a dummy that equals 1 after 2010 (i.e., the inception year of the program) and Contiguous$_c$ equals 1 if the comuna neighbors the comuna where the program is headquartered. In detail, the contiguous comunas correspond to Independencia, Providencia, Nunoa, San Joaquin, San Miguel, Pedro Aguirre Cerda, Estacion Central, Quinta Normal, and Santiago Central. Estimates in columns (2) and (4) are based on the regression New Business$_{cit}$ = $\gamma_{it} + \gamma_{ic} + \gamma_{cy}$ + Post_2010$_t$ × Contiguous$_c$ × Venture$_i$ + ε_{cit}, where Venture$_{iv}$ equals 1 for all those industries similar to the industries of the program's participants (i.e., venture industries): activities of experimental research and development, auxiliary transport activities, business-to-business services, information services, other types of financial intermediation, and retail trade not realized in shops, telecommunications, and travel agencies. Robust standard errors are presented in parentheses. *, **, and *** indicate statistical significance at the 10%, 5%, and 1% levels, respectively. Models include or exclude fixed effects (FE) for comuna, year, and corresponding interactions.

in the industries akin to) Start-Up Chile, compared to localities and industries unrelated to Start-Up Chile (column 4).

Domestic jobs Corresponds to the jobs created *domestically* by the participating startups. The distinction between domestic and non-domestic jobs created is important given that many participating startups may open offices abroad, and foreign startups may return to their localities of origin. As with the relocation KPI, identifying whether the accelerator's existence is causing foreign non-participants to relocate to the host locality, subsequently creating startups and new jobs, is not trivial. This measure can be further complemented by the salary of the jobs created and the demographics of the employees. As would be expected, higher-paying jobs likely reflects the greater value-creation capability of the corresponding startup.

Venture investments Corresponds to the early-stage investment activity occurring in the accelerator's region of interest. A direct measure of this KPI can be obtained by following accelerator alumni. However, as Fehder and Hochberg (2014) show, the existence of an accelerator in a given region also has the indirect effect of increasing early-stage investments for non-accelerated participants. This KPI can be dissected into the number of early-stage investment deals and the amount invested in them.

Taxes paid Corresponds to the taxes paid by alumni startups in the locality of the accelerator. This KPI is relevant only for ecosystem accelerators, particularly those sponsored by governments. This measure can be estimated based on the sales and profits KPIs. As before, the only way to determine whether the return on investment of sponsor funding is positive is by comparing the *additional* taxes paid by the accelerator's alumni against a counterfactual group of non-participants. By focusing only on alumni taxes paid, accelerators sometimes make happy (but incorrect) calculations of the return on investment of sponsor funds.

Alumni demographic distribution Corresponds to the proportion of alumni who represent a given demographic category. For example, some ecosystem accelerators promote positive action toward female entrepreneurs. Thus, this KPI could compare the number of female alumni who continue to be as entrepreneurs some time after graduation from the program, against a valid counterfactual (e.g., by looking at the differential effect on a group of similar female entrepreneurs who did not participate in the program).

Community service   Corresponds to a measure of the activities ecosystem accelerator participants conduct to promote entrepreneurship or entrepreneurial thinking in the accelerator's locality. For example, one of the conditions for participation in Start-Up Chile is that entrepreneurs complete a series of community service tasks before graduation from the accelerator. Such tasks could include being a mentor to a domestic entrepreneur, giving a class at a local university, or giving a lecture to high school students. Thus, this KPI could be constructed as the number of given tasks and the number of people who benefited from each task.

Institutional change   Reflects the changes in the beliefs, behaviors, and regulations of the host locality. Unsurprisingly, cultures differ among societies. For example, Leatherbee and Eesley (2014) found Chilean entrepreneurs (from Santiago) had significantly different entrepreneurial behaviors than entrepreneurs from Silicon Valley. A key question that is particularly relevant for ecosystem accelerator sponsors is whether the accelerator prompts changes in the domestic institutions. Leatherbee and Eesley's (2014) findings suggest domestic entrepreneurs began behaving more like foreign entrepreneurs after the six-month interaction that was prompted by Start-Up Chile. Moreover, as soon as Start-Up Chile was created, the accelerator managers realized they needed to find a way to expedite the work-visa process. Otherwise, their foreign selected participants (roughly 75 percent of each cohort) would not be able to attend. Because the accelerator was government sponsored, the accelerator managers were able to find a way to drastically reduce the work-visa processing time, achieving a relevant change in the country's immigration norm.

HOW TO MEASURE ACCELERATOR KPIs

The typical way most of these KPIs are measured is by surveying accelerator participants and non-participants. Participants are more likely to provide high response rates during their tenure in the program. However, getting good response rates over time is not trivial. Response rates typically drop with alumni, and drop even further with non-participants. Therefore, the periodicity of surveys must be chosen with care. In general, the greater the frequency of surveys, the more annoyed the sampled population may get. The lower the level of perceived affiliation of the surveyed population, the higher this annoyance factor (i.e., participants will be more willing than non-participants to spend time on an accelerator survey). The same rings true for the length of the survey. The more KPIs an accelerator wants to keep track of, the longer the survey. Therefore, for better results, accelerator managers should think carefully about the most relevant KPIs they wish to keep track of and the survey frequency that maximizes the right combination of response rates and valuable data.

For many of the acceleration KPIs, an alternative (and less invasive) approach can be particularly useful. KPIs such as market traction, employees, fundraising, valuation, and survival can be captured from online sources. For instance, Gonzalez-Uribe and Leatherbee's (2018) study on the acceleration effects of ecosystem accelerators compares web-based metrics against survey-based metrics. Their results offer two key insights. First, their online metrics are significantly correlated with survey-based metrics, which implies the latter can be (at least partially) replaced by the former. This implication is important because online metrics can be captured with greater frequency without disturbing entrepreneurs. Second, as revealed in the authors' results, survey-based metrics can suffer from response bias (successful participants are more likely to respond). Moreover, socially desirable responding may also be at play. For example, non-participants may wish to over-represent their results as a way to signal to accelerator staff that they missed out by not accepting them into the program.

Other KPIs can also be captured without having to interact with entrepreneurs. For example, the data to build the vicarious founding or the venture investments KPIs aimed at testing spillover effects can typically be acquired from company registration government agencies.

ACCELERATOR SPILLOVERS AS A PUBLIC GOOD

The number of accelerators (whether investor-led, ecosystem, or match-maker) has grown considerably in the last decade. However, the programmatic design of accelerators is far from being consolidated. Accelerator managers are still working on figuring out the best model for their specific goals. For example, Start-Up Chile is currently undergoing a randomized control trial to test the performance-enhancing effects of specific programmatic interventions.

One question that emerges is how the programmatic changes that are being enacted will affect the spillover benefits for entrepreneurship ecosystems. While ecosystem accelerators will reshape their programmatic design to maximize the social benefits of accelerators, investor-led accelerators are starting to reshape their programmatic design to maximize the capture of individual benefits, potentially at the expense of spillovers. For example, investor-led accelerators currently do not encourage (and implicitly discourage) community service. However, they contribute to spillovers (perhaps unwittingly) by hosting demo-days. As Fehder and Hochberg (2014) argue, the periodic demo-days at which accelerators showcase their best startups among early-stage investors in the ecosystem (regardless of their formal affiliation with the accelerator) are an important contributor to the ecosystem. These demo-days seem to foster a unique cadence in the early-stage investment community, by which potential investors maintain active conversations about investment opportunities. Through these conversations, potential investors compare themselves socially (Festinger, 1954) and mimic investment behaviors.

The investor-led accelerator demo-day, as a programmatic activity that spills over to the entrepreneurship ecosystem, is currently under scrutiny. According to the manager of one investor-led accelerator, by helping start-ups grow and showcasing their potential to external investors (who are not affiliated with—and do not sponsor—the accelerator), the value created by the accelerator is being appropriated by third parties. Thus, these external investors are freeriding on the resources of accelerator sponsors. As a consequence, this accelerator was planning to discontinue its demo-day.

Whether other accelerators will mimic these programmatic changes conducted by a few accelerators is not evident. Nor is predicting whether these changes may cause further beneficial spillovers for entrepreneurship ecosystems trivial. However, it is important to realize that the existence of accelerators (as the organizational form they have today) adds value to the entrepreneurship ecosystem—and by extension to socioeconomic development. As individual forces find ways to capture the value created by accelerators, it behooves societies to keep an eye on the programmatic changes that may occur for the benefit of the individual, at the expense of the collective.

CONCLUSION

Business accelerator key performance indicators can be classified into three dimensions: recruitment, acceleration, and spillovers. Depending on the organizational goals of each accelerator, the different dimensions (and specific KPIs underlying them) will be more or less relevant. For KPIs to be meaningful, establishing a comparable baseline is important. This baseline can be a control group of comparable startups that do not receive acceleration services, similar startups within the same accelerator, other comparable accelerators, or measures of economic growth absent the accelerator. The key is to make sure the KPIs that are used are contrasted against a relevant backdrop. Otherwise, decision makers may fall into the trap of reaching inaccurate conclusions.

Choosing the right KPIs is key for organizational performance. On the one hand, the lack of meaningful KPIs can be detrimental because organizations need feedback about their actions in order to learn, adapt, and improve. On the other hand, having too many KPIs can also have a detrimental effect, because they increase operational costs (gathering and analyzing the KPIs) and cognitive load (confusing decision makers). Therefore, the optimal number of KPIs is most likely fewer than the number presented here.

Selecting meaningful KPIs from among multiple possibilities requires a deep understanding of the mission of the accelerator and the phenomenon underlying each KPI. On the one hand, if a given KPI does not help accelerators gauge progress toward their goals, managing that KPI is a waste of resources. On the other hand, a naïve belief in a given KPI (without understanding the underlying entrepreneurship phenomenon the KPI is reflecting) can lead an accelerator's decision-making down the wrong path. Therefore, when thinking about the select few KPIs an accelerator must work to include into its dashboard, carefully contemplating the organizational goals and the underlying phenomenon reflected by a given KPI is important.

The business accelerator is a key ingredient in healthy entrepreneurship ecosystems. A thoughtful analysis of KPIs will serve the purpose of improving the effectiveness of accelerator programs. A better understanding of the ways accelerators influence these ecosystems will help accelerator managers, their stakeholders, and entrepreneurs make better decisions, thus accelerating socioeconomic development.

NOTES

1. http://learn.onemonth.com/y-combinator-and-the-one-metric-that-matters (accessed May 2017).
2. http://startupchile.org/rva-points-theyre-not-a-bug-but-a-feature/ (accessed May 2017).
3. Recent studies focused on this question include Gonzalez-Uribe and Leatherbee (2017) and Hallen, Bingham, and Cohen (2016).
4. Unless acceptance into the accelerator is decided randomly, a comparison of average performance of participants against the average performance of non-participants is not helpful for causal inference, because the selection process may be screening innate high-performing applicants from low-performing ones.

REFERENCES

Clarysse B, Wright M, Van Hove J. 2015. *A Look Inside Accelerators: Building Businesses*, Nesta, London, February.

Cohen SG, Hochberg YV. 2014. Accelerating Startups: The Seed Accelerator Phenomenon. Working Paper. Available at SSRN: https://ssrn.com/abstract= 2418000 (accessed May 2017).

Fehder DC, Hochberg YV. 2014. Accelerators and the Regional Supply of Venture Capital Investment. Available at SSRN: https://ssrn.com/abstract=2518668 (accessed May 2017).

Festinger L. 1954. A Theory of Social Comparison Processes. *Human Relations* 7(2): 117–140.

Gonzalez-Uribe J, Leatherbee M. 2018. The Effects of Business Accelerators on Venture Performance: Evidence from Start-Up Chile. *The Review of Financial Studies* 31(4),: 1566–1603. hhx103, https://doi.org/10.1093/rfs/hhx103.

Hallen BL, Bingham CB, Cohen SLG. 2016. Do Accelerators Accelerate? A Study of Venture Accelerators as a Path to Success. Available at: https://ssrn.com/abs tract=2719810 (accessed May 2017).

Latham GP, Locke EA. 2006. Enhancing the Benefits and Overcoming the Pitfalls of Goal Setting. *Organization Dynamics* 35(4): 332–340.

Leatherbee M, Eesley CE. 2014. Boulevard of Broken Behaviors: Socio-Psychological Mechanisms of Entrepreneurship Policies. Available at: http:// ssrn.com/abstract=2488712 (accessed May 2017).

Leatherbee M, Frias R, Gonzalez M. 2016. *Diagnóstico y Recomendación del Método de Selección del Programa Capital Semilla*. Available at: http://epiclab.uc.cl/diag nostico-y-recomendacion-seleccion-capital-semilla/ (accessed May 2017).

Locke EA. 1996. Motivation through Conscious Goal Setting. *Applied and Preventative Psychology* 5: 117–124.

Locke EA, Shaw KN, Saari LM, Latham GP. 1981. Goal Setting and Task Performance: 1969–1980. *Psychological Bulletin* 90: 125–152.

Simon HA. 1991. Bounded Rationality and Organizational Learning. *Organization Science* 2(1): 125–134.

Wagner RA. 2016. Does Feedback To Business-Plans Impact New Ventures? Evidence from a Field Experiment. Working Paper. Available at SSRN: https:// ssrn.com/abstract=2766566 (accessed May 2017).

Yu S. 2016. How do Accelerators Impact the Performance of High-Technology Ventures? Working Paper. Available at: https://ssrn.com/abstract=2503510 (accessed May 2017).

7. Revolutionizing entrepreneurial ecosystems through US and European accelerator policy

Iris Vanaelst, Jonas Van Hove and Mike Wright

INTRODUCTION

European policies towards accelerators need to be seen as part of the attempts by the European Union (EU) to build and sustain global competitiveness by stimulating entrepreneurship, primarily science and technology based. These policies tie into a worldwide rise in interest by political leadership to address the building of science- and technology-based knowledge regions to enhance national economic competitiveness, particularly outside the USA (Mian, 2011). EU policies aimed at fostering the creation of technology (or knowledge) based firms are often perceived as a response to the US capacity to transform knowledge into new high-tech and high-growth firms. However, much of the US context that European policymakers have sought to emulate involves atypical high-tech clusters which seem to be absent from Europe (Mustar and Wright, 2010). Direct transfers of policy between the USA and Europe are therefore challenging because of the need to take into account the unique circumstances of high-tech clusters' history and surrounding communities.

Over the years, the EU has launched several new initiatives to foster entrepreneurship. The European Commission's initiatives promoting entrepreneurship are summarized in the Entrepreneurship Action Plan[1] adopted in January 2013. The aim is to reignite Europe's entrepreneurial spirit by (1) educating young people about entrepreneurship; (2) highlighting opportunities for women and other groups; (3) easing administrative requirements; and (4) making it easier to attract investors. The shift towards targeted policies to support high-growth entrepreneurship is identified as an important development in the public policy arena (Autio, 2007). Recent policies to reinforce accelerator activities tie into this trend as accelerator programs target and source these high-growth entrepreneurs. Many governments have adopted a focus on high-growth firms, having learned that only a small fraction of all new firms is responsible for creating the majority of new jobs (Bravo-Biosca and Westlake, 2009; Acs, Szerb and Autio, 2016b). As the output entrepreneurial ecosystems produce is high-growth new ventures (Acs et al., 2016b) and accelerators have become pivotal in the entrepreneurial ecosystem in which they are embedded, and are perceived as gateways for early-stage ventures, the development of an EU policy towards accelerators needs to be seen as part of its policy towards entrepreneurial ecosystems.

The EU encompasses a range of different institutional settings (informal and formal), cultures, norms and values, and attitudes toward entrepreneurship that affect the nature of entrepreneurial ecosystems (Autio, Kenney, Mustar, Siegel and Wright, 2014). Given that ecosystems comprise multiple participants bound by complex relations that often involve mutual interdependence, policy to stimulate and sustain entrepreneurial ecosystems needs to be aligned with the relevant context (Acs, Audretsch, Lehmann and Licht, 2016a). High-growth new ventures, as outputs of entrepreneurial ecosystems, are coproduced through a myriad of usually uncoordinated interactions between hierarchically independent yet interdependent stakeholders (Acs et al., 2016b). Therefore, policymakers need to engage the various stakeholders and co-opt them as active participants and contributors to policy intervention.

This chapter focuses on how EU policy currently engages with different stakeholders in order to support accelerator activity within the EU area. It should not be seen as an exhaustive overview of all the EU policies aimed at stimulating and supporting entrepreneurship in accelerators, but should rather be read as exemplary, highlighting the most relevant and recent EU initiatives aimed at fostering accelerator activity. The chapter commences with a brief overview of US policy towards accelerators.

GOVERNMENTAL SUPPORT FOR ACCELERATORS IN THE USA

Since accelerators originated in the USA, it is the first place to look for any kind of government policy aimed at accelerators. One distinctive funding program, aimed to fill geographic gaps in the accelerator and entrepreneurial ecosystem scene, is considered here as exemplary.

In 2014, the US Small Business Administration[2] (SBA) launched the first ever Growth Accelerator Fund Competition. The competition was designed to award select accelerator and incubator models[3] funding for their operating budgets worth a total of $2.5 million in cash prizes. Eight hundred and thirty-two entities submitted applications from every state (except Alaska, but including Washington DC and Puerto Rico). Accelerators and other entrepreneurial ecosystem models competed for awards of $50,000 each. One hundred finalists were whittled down by a panel of experts and 50 winners were selected. Of the 50 winners, 7 were in rural America and 9 were launching a new accelerator model. Twenty winners were active in general activities, 18 in science and technology, 5 in healthcare, 3 in manufacturing, 3 in education, 3 in agricultural, 3 in food and beverage, 2 in biotechnology, 2 in energy, 2 in tourism and 7 in other industries, with some accelerators having more than one focus. Those 50 winners are an ecosystem made up of about 1,500 geographically dispersed startups across a broad array of industries that employ close to 5,000 people and have collectively raised over $600 million.

Based on that success, SBA ran a second instalment of the competition in 2015[4] with $4 million in Congress-appropriated funds in support for accelerators in 39 states (plus Washington DC and Puerto Rico). The 80 accelerators selected as winners in the Growth Accelerator Fund received $50,000 each in cash from the SBA. The competition intentionally focused on increasing awareness and providing funding to "parts of the country where there are gaps in the entrepreneurial ecosystem". Additionally, in 2015, SBA's Office of Native American Affairs (ONAA) used this competition's framework to award an additional $400,000 to ecosystems primarily dedicated to Native American entrepreneurs and small businesses.

For its 2016 edition, more federal partners were included, such as the Office of Veterans Business Development, National Institutes of Health (NIH), National Science Foundation (NSF), Department of Education (DoED) and Department of Agriculture (USDA), to award additional prizes to accelerators that assist entrepreneurs with submitting proposals for the Small Business Innovation (SBIR) and Small Business Technology Transfer (STTR) programs. SBA's Office of Investment and Innovation (OII) is also partnering with the Inter-American Development Bank to provide prizes to US accelerators that assist the African descendant startup community in Latin America and the Caribbean. For its 2016 edition, special consideration was also given to any accelerator model that supports manufacturing and the White House Power Initiative, because they are considered critical to job growth and strengthening the nation's economy.[5] Sixty-eight winners[6] of SBA's third annual Growth Accelerator Fund Competition were awarded a total amount of $3.4 million in prizes to boost the economic impact of accelerators across 32 states and the District of Columbia.

To award the prizes, several panels composed of over 40 judges considered each applicant's stated mission, founding team members, and business goals, among other core components. The panel gave particular attention to, and the SBA encouraged, applicants that fill geographic gaps in the accelerator and entrepreneurial ecosystem scene. The most successful accelerators to date can be found on the coasts. Through this competition, SBA is looking to support the development of accelerators and startups in parts of the country where there are fewer conventional sources of access to capital, such as venture capital (VC) and other types of investors. This policy measure and its intended effect have recently been endorsed by scholars (Hochberg, 2016), showing that accelerators positively impact early-stage financing in the region (regardless of their direct effect on the limited number of companies that take part in these programs). In addition to accelerators that fill the gaps as indicated above, they also sought out accelerators that are run by and support women or other underrepresented groups to help increase Native American-owned, veteran-owned, women-owned and minority-owned small businesses.

THE EUROPEAN UNION'S POLICY TOWARDS ACCELERATORS

The evolution of accelerators in Europe is attracting policy support from the EU. For any Member State of the EU, European policy adds an additional layer of policy on top of national, regional or local policies (as extensively discussed in Chapter 8).

The Entrepreneurship 2020 Action Plan[7] is the European Commission's answer to challenges brought by the gravest economic crisis in the last 50 years. It is presented as a blueprint for action to unleash Europe's entrepreneurial potential, remove existing obstacles and revolutionize the culture of entrepreneurship in the EU. It aims to ease the creation of new businesses and to create a much more supportive environment for existing entrepreneurs to thrive and grow.

Startup Europe contributes to the Entrepreneurship 2020 Action Plan. The European Commission's Startup Europe[8] initiative was created to foster tech entrepreneurship by connecting tech entrepreneurs across Europe, providing networks, resources and information to help them start up their business and grow, creating new jobs and transforming the economy and society. Startup Europe's objectives are (1) to reinforce the links between people, business and associations who build and scale up the startup ecosystem (e.g. the Web Investors Forum, the Accelerator Assembly, the Crowdfunding Network); (2) to inspire entrepreneurs and provide role models (e.g. the Leaders Club and their Startup Manifesto, the Startup Europe Roadshow); (3) to celebrate new and innovative startups (with Tech All Stars and Europioneers), help them to expand

Table 7.1   European Union's funding of accelerator activity

Recipients	Examples of funded initiatives
Networking activities	ATALANTA project – European Accelerator Summit
	Accelerator Assembly
Programs	EU-XCEL – European Virtual Accelerator
	IoT Accelerator Startup Scaleup program
	Copernicus Accelerator Programme
Startups/SMEs	FIWARE – EuropeanPioneers
	SME Instrument

their business (e.g. Startup Europe Partnership), and give them access to funding under Horizon 2020.

In what follows, only those initiatives taken by the EU to strengthen entrepreneurial activity with a main focus on accelerator activities[9] are considered. Some of these initiatives were promulgated under the EU's Seventh Framework Programme (e.g. the ATALANTA project and the European Accelerator Summit, the FIWARE project and EuropeanPioneers) while others developed under the more recent Entrepreneurship 2020 Action Plan. The ways in which the EU interacts with accelerators can be interpreted as a confirmation of the recognition of the pivotal role of accelerators in entrepreneurial ecosystems. These interactions are threefold: (1) the EU supports the setup of accelerator networks to create momentum for accelerators to meet and exchange experiences, expertise and knowledge (e.g. Accelerator Assembly); (2) the EU supports and funds accelerator programs (e.g. EU-XCEL –European Virtual Accelerator, IoT Accelerator Programme, Copernicus Accelerator Programme); (3) accelerators serve as intermediaries between the EU and startups looking for funding (e.g. EuropeanPioneers) in addition to the small and medium-sized enterprise (SME) funding instruments of the EU (e.g. SME Instrument). Interesting examples of each of these initiatives will be discussed in more detail below.[10] Table 7.1 presents an overview of the examples of EU funded accelerator activities discussed.

Networking Activities

The ATALANTA project and the European Accelerator Summit

The ATALANTA project[11] supports groups of leading accelerators for delivering cross-border services to innovative SMEs and entrepreneurs and links these groups to knowledge creators and education organizations (e.g. mentors, trainers, service providers, and partners) on the one hand

and investors (e.g. VC organizations) and the business world (e.g. potential clients, partners, suppliers and venture capitalists) on the other. Via the ATALANTA project the European Accelerator Summit[12] is organized. In 2013, five accelerators (Beta-i, H-Farm, Sillicon Sentier, Tetuan Valley and Balkan Unlimited) from five different European countries came together to share best practices and exchange experiences in an industry that was just being born. At different stages of development, and operating in ecosystems with different challenges, these five accelerators were themselves able to accelerate through collaboration with each other. During the European Accelerator Summit 2016, leading accelerators from across Europe discussed and debated the current status and future of acceleration through collaborative workshops and interactive talks. The purpose of this one-day conference was to identify the major trends and challenges facing the accelerator sector as well as generate ideas and viable models to reinforce the future of accelerators.

Accelerator Assembly

As part of the Startup Europe initiative, the European Commission started a scheme[13] to support and promote web-friendly accelerators in Europe, with the aim of stimulating the growth of web startups and enabling them to become successful, sustainable businesses that will contribute to economic growth and to the creation of employment. This has been done because, despite the rapid growth of the digital economy in Europe, many tech entrepreneurs still lack access to adequate resources and support to launch their startup. Three of Europe's leading web-friendly support programs – Seedcamp, Startup Weekend and Bethnal Green Ventures – have formed a consortium with Seed-DB, the seed accelerator database, in response to this opportunity, with the aim of delivering an industry-led forum with maximum pan-European reach and impact. The key aims are (1) to increase awareness of the existing accelerator programs in Europe and their benefits among web entrepreneurs; (2) to attract other accelerators to support web businesses to grow the overall number of web-friendly accelerators in Europe; (3) to foster valuable linkages within the accelerator community in Europe; (4) to stimulate a policy dialogue to inform both policymakers and practitioners; (5) to improve the evidence base and provide insights and knowledge on accelerators and web startups in Europe; and (6) to increase understanding on how to participate in future EU policy to improve the environment for web entrepreneurship. The initiative is called the Accelerator Assembly[14] and brings the accelerator community together through the organization of events and workshops. Its activities include the creation of an online community to share learning and best practices, as well as to gather research evidence to improve the knowledge on accelerators and web startups in Europe. The Accelerator Assembly is delivered by WELCOME[15] and BISITE Accelerator, with the support of Nesta, How to Web, Techstars London, UPGlobal, Betahaus, Wayra UK, Basekit, Microsoft and dpixel.

Accelerator Programs

EU-XCEL – European Virtual Accelerator

The EU-XCEL – European Virtual Accelerator[16] is a network initiative of Startup Europe[17] which supports aspiring young tech entrepreneurs interested in co-founding new international information, communication and technology (ICT) startups through a new startup scrum training and mentored virtual accelerator initiative. This initiative seeks to identify and empower aspiring young tech entrepreneurs to become "incubator ready" with real products of promise in the areas of the Internet of Things (IoT), health informatics, big data, ICT4development, predictive analytics and E-/M- Commerce. The action plan consists of the following: (1) deliver a week-long intensive entrepreneurial training named "Start-up Scrum" across the six European countries of Ireland, Denmark, Germany, Greece, Poland and Spain; (2) provide online mentoring and technical support to EU-XCEL teams to develop their startup ideas through a European Virtual Accelerator; and (3) select the best startup scrum teams to compete in an EU-XCEL Ultimate Challenge Final where they will pitch to leading venture capitalists, angel investors and successful entrepreneurs.

The IoT Accelerator Startup Scaleup program

Startup Europe's IoT Accelerator Startup Scaleup[18] received funding from the EU's Horizon 2020 Research and Innovation Programme.[19] Startup Scaleup is a pan-European IoT Accelerator that provides a broad range and quality of services to ambitious entrepreneurs who want to launch and grow companies focused on IoT. The aim is to build a European ecosystem around four consolidated ecosystems in Spain (Cartagena), the Netherlands (Zoetermeer), Lithuania (Vilnius) and Ireland (Dublin) together with F6S[20] – a social network for startups in the EU that also comprises a data-driven tool for accelerators to let startups apply (first stage of selection process). These four ecosystems, which have a track record and complementary strengths, are supporting startups by enhancing the basic business skills of entrepreneurs as well as increasing technological advancement to accelerate the accepted startups. Startup Scaleup[21] is run by Universidad Politécnica de Cartagena, Crosspring Lab, Open Coffee Club Lithuania, the Ryan Academy, F6S and BluSpecs.[22]

Startup Scaleup is a six-month accelerator program, enabling accepted startups to receive support and mentorship from IoT people. Startup Scaleup is a no-strings attached program: no equity, no cost. Participants will get to work with other IoT startups, startup incubator hubs in Ireland, Spain, the Netherlands and Lithuania, and are supported by mentors working on design, prototyping, manufacturing, licensing and fundraising for their products. The journey begins with the IoT'ers week in all four hubs and consists of an intense schedule of activities, lectures and workshops that cover all the basics for scaling their business and expanding to international markets. Monthly events allow them to make sure they have reached key performance indicators (KPIs) and give them a chance to meet other teams developing their product (see Chapter 6 in this book by Leatherbee and Gonzalez-Uribe for further details on KPIs). The program ends at each hub with a local pitching event, and the best teams get to participate at one of the largest European IoT conferences – Connected Conference[23] in Paris.

For the first batch, ran in 2015, they received 179 applications; 49 teams were selected from 11 countries, raising €3,035,500. The selection process for the second batch ran from April to May in 2016 and received about 370 applications. The greatest number of applicants are in the prototype stage (143), some have customers (94), others have developed products (86), and very few (3) have a large-scale production. On average, the startups that have applied to this acceleration program are founded by between two and four people. From the applications received, the average revenue generated by most of those startups (85) so far amounts to €1,000, while about 40 have already raised between €1,000 and €50,000. In June 2016 the 84 accepted applicants started the program, with 20 in both Cartagena and Vilnius and 22 in both Dublin and Zoetermeer. The IoT verticals are in various sectors including home (18), health and medical (15), wearables (11), transportation (9), retail (5), agriculture (5), clean tech (4), logistics (1) and others (16).

The Copernicus Accelerator Programme
EU support is not limited to web-related accelerator programs to generate economic growth. The Copernicus Accelerator Programme[24] aims to speed up the user uptake of the EU's Earth observation program Copernicus as it fosters the development of commercial space applications and products. Tremendous amounts of data from space – especially the kind produced by Copernicus – present countless opportunities, and are becoming an increasingly common component of commercial products and applications in numerous sectors of the economy. Fascinated by the possibilities in intelligent data analysis, young startups and scientists in particular are developing a growing interest in Earth observation and the big data it

generates from space. The Accelerator Programme is an initiative funded by the Directorate-General for Internal Market, Industry, Entrepreneurship and SMEs (DG GROWTH) of the European Commission.[25]

In July 2016, individuals and teams from startups, SMEs, industrial companies, research institutes and universities were invited to apply online for the Copernicus Accelerator Programme while submitting their business ideas to the Copernicus Masters.[26] The 40 best entrants in the competition, which must be either citizens of one of the Copernicus participating countries (all the EU Member States, in addition to Norway and Iceland) or have established their company in the territory of one of the participating countries, were then selected for the program by an international panel of experts. Through the Copernicus Accelerator, participants receive tailored support from experienced mentors and work with them on advancing their innovations over a period of several months. They are able to determine the focus of this coaching, such as creating a business plan, acquiring their first customers and raising capital. Scheduled to last six to eight months, the Copernicus Accelerator kicked off with a boot camp[27] in Madrid in October 2016 bringing 40 pioneering entrepreneurs, 31 mentors and representatives of the European Commission and the European Space Agency together. In search of synergies, this event created momentum for mentees to meet their mentors and connect with industry leaders, renowned institutions and startups. This event forms part of the Satellite Masters conference and the Awards Ceremony of the Copernicus Masters competition.[28]

Accelerator Programs as Intermediaries for SME Funding

FIWARE and EuropeanPioneers
The European Commission[29] has some funding opportunities and has helped create networks within the European technology ecosystem to promote growth and share best practice. There was almost €850 million available for ecosystems builders as well as funding opportunities for startups and SMEs. Via its FIWARE Accelerator Programme,[30] worth €80 million (in 2014–2015), the European Commission launched a massive call for web entrepreneurs, SMEs and startups owning an innovation idea able to penetrate the market and be the basis of a sustainable business. The call targeted seed-type activities that generate actual take-up of innovative internet services and applications. As of September 2014, the 16 selected FIWARE accelerator projects[31] published open calls for the distribution of grants to SMEs and web entrepreneurs. The predefined industrial sectors for these accelerator projects were smart cities, ehealth, transport, energy and environment, agrifood, media and content, manufacturing and logistics, and social and learning.

The FIWARE Community is presented as an independent open community whose members are committed to materialize the FIWARE mission: to build an open sustainable ecosystem around public, royalty-free and implementation-driven software platform standards that will ease the development of new smart applications in multiple sectors. This community was not only formed by contributors to the technology – the FIWARE platform[32] – but also by those who contribute in building the FIWARE ecosystem and making it sustainable over time. As such, individuals and organizations committing relevant resources in FIWARE Lab[33] activities or activities of the FIWARE Accelerator, FIWARE Mundus[34] or FIWARE iHubs[35] programs are also considered as members of the FIWARE Community. "Think globally but act locally" is a distinguishing mark of the FIWARE ecosystem.

EuropeanPioneers[36] was one of the above mentioned 16 programs across Europe fostering innovative businesses on the basis of breakthrough FIWARE Future Internet technologies. EuropeanPioneers received funding[37] from the EU's Seventh Framework Programme for research, technological development and demonstration as part of the EU's Future Internet Public Private Partnership Programme (FI-PPP). EuropeanPioneers distributed funding provided by the EU. It was public money, so beneficiairies did not have to give away equity in their business in order to benefit. Total grants ranged from €50,000 to €250,000 per project (depending on the business model, current status and financial needs). Participants were supported in developing cutting-edge business skills via face-to-face workshops, online webinars, mentoring activities and a shared project management platform. Review workshops were conducted to discuss and analyze progress on both technical and financial levels. Selected teams were supported in building minimum viable products assessed through systematic user tests with a total of at least a thousand users across Europe.

EuropeanPioneers was the Berlin-based accelerator eight-month program that developed the participants' wide-ranging business skills through coaching and mentoring activities. Benefits also arose from the strong network of business experts and other startups involved in the FI-PPP. The accelerator was led by Berlin-based startup builder etventure in partnership with technology expert partner Fraunhofer IAIS (Germany), ThoughtBox (Ireland), Weblify (Poland) and F-Secure (Finland). This accelerator program aimed to boost the development of digital SMEs and web entrepreneurs in the media and content sector in Europe. Participants were connected with the platform and technologies of FIWARE – cutting-edge applications developed at the European level to enable fast and effective web developments. A co-working space was not provided. Participants became part of the team, but remotely, so had to be prepared to travel to Berlin several times. The infrastructure was provided to guarantee effective communication and exchange of best practices throughout the program. Participants who needed support were visited.

In the final round in 2015, EuropeanPioneers[38] funded 13 startups chosen out of 660 applications from a European-wide selection process. Each of the chosen teams received €175,000 in funding without giving up equity. Thirteen startups from the European tech hubs in Berlin, Barcelona, London, Copenhagen and Tel Aviv started the second round of this EU accelerator program in August 2015 in Berlin. During the "welcome days" the startups were introduced to lean startup and design thinking method-ologies. The "training weeks" were held in Tel Aviv, London and Berlin. The startups of this round were focused on the business areas of smart city, media and content, and social and learning.[39]

THE EUROPEAN UNION AND SME FUNDING

EU funding support for SMEs through accelerator programs sits alongside other direct funding for SMEs provided by the EU, like for instance via the SME Instrument.[40] At least 20 percent, nearly €9 billion, from Horizon 2020's "leadership in industrial technologies" and "societal change" funding pillars is expected to benefit SMEs directly in the form of grants, including the funding via the SME Instrument. SMEs from EU Member States or countries associated to Horizon 2020 can apply. With a budget of €77 billion over seven years, Horizon 2020 is the largest EU research and innovation program and envisages record funding for SMEs. The latest round brings the total number of companies funded by the SME instru-ment so far to 2,116, with more than €694.8 million in EU grants. Through the SME Instrument, the EU wants to finance the most innovative small companies with a high-growth potential to bring ideas from the lab to the market and help generate growth and jobs in Europe. The Instrument is worth around €3 billion over seven years and offers fast and simple grants for business innovation feasibility studies (Phase 1) and demonstration projects (Phase 2). Investment-mature concepts can, in addition, benefit from business development advice and other support services (Phase 3).

In July 2016 it was announced that the European Commission will invest €86 million, in 236 innovative SMEs from 31 countries. Out of the €86 million, €77.7 million will be given to 58 highly innovative SMEs from 16 countries under Phase 2 of the scheme – in which SMEs will further develop their submitted proposal in Phase 1 of the scheme through inno-vation activities. Each project, 48 in total, will receive between €0.5 and

€2.5 million (€5 million for health projects) to bring their product from pilot phase to the market. They can also ask for up to 12 days of free business coaching. Nine hundred and sixty-one proposals were received under Phase 2 by the cut-off date of 14 April 2016. UK companies have been particularly successful in this call, with 13 projects. They are closely followed by Spain (11) and Italy (9). Most of the projects funded will be in the area of ICT (9) and transport (9) followed by low-carbon energy systems (8). Since the launch of the program on 1 January 2014, 373 projects involving 464 SMEs have been selected for EU grants under Phase 2 of the SME Instrument, totaling more than €619.5 million.

Another 166 projects involving 178 SMEs from 28 countries have been selected in the latest round under Phase 1 of the SME Instrument. Each project will receive €50,000 to finance feasibility studies for new products that can disrupt the market. They can also request up to three days of free business coaching. The SMEs will receive €8.3 million in total for this cut-off. One thousand, nine hundred and seventy-five proposals were received under Phase 1 for the 3 May 2016 cut-off. Spain ranks first, with 32 projects selected for funding, followed by the UK (23) and Italy (22). Most projects will be funded in the area of ICT (30) followed by transport (22) and low-carbon energy systems (22). Since the launch of the program on 1 January 2014, 1,652 SMEs have been selected under Phase 1 of the SME Instrument and shared almost €75.3 million. The next cut-off is 7 September 2016 for Phase 1 and 13 October 2016 for Phase 2.

THE CLIMATE-KIC ACCELERATOR: A CASE STUDY[41]

The EU-funded Climate-KIC program is discussed in detail below as an illustrative case study. This program has been studied in depth through desktop research and semi-structured interviews with the program managers and participating startups.

Climate-KIC is one of five Knowledge and Innovation Communities (KICs) set up by the European Institute of Innovation and Technology (EIT),[42] an EU body assigned with creating sustainable European growth while dealing with climate change, one of the major global challenges of our time. This particular KIC is Europe's largest public–private innovation partnership that comprises support schemes for students, businesses and entrepreneurs. Through various mechanisms, the KIC focuses on proving the feasibility of concepts and transforming cleantech ideas into investable business cases.

When looking at its portfolio of support activities for entrepreneurs, it comprises four main elements: (1) business plan competitions such as the ClimateLaunchpad, which is Europe's largest cleantech business plan competition; (2) education-intensive workshops; (3) placement programs for professionals to work on innovative projects; and (4) the Climate-KIC (pre-) Accelerator, acknowledged as the number one cleantech accelerator worldwide.

The last is an intervention program operated as a pan-European stage-gate process linked with a grant funding mechanism that is open to academic researchers, students and external entrepreneurs. It is designed to fit the particular needs of research-driven ventures. Design highlights are, for instance:

- Stage-gate approach with open milestones in order to better suit the pace of each startup. Up to €95,000 "grant" funding is awarded over three stages: (1) Stage I for drafting the initial business model and market prioritization hypothesis (~ €20,000); (2) Stage II to verify assumptions and get customer feedback to validate the business model (~ €25,000); and (3) Stage III to gain market traction, that is, customer- and investor-wise (~ €50,000).
- Iterative market-driven approach with a process that systematically determines the specific barriers for success for a venture using market feedback.
- Co-location of the ventures in university-centered ecosystems with access to its advanced technical facilities and technology support vouchers.
- Pre-incubation support to help budding entrepreneurs develop climate innovative ideas combined with a sustainable business model. Each project will have an assigned coach with a fixed number of coaching hours, up to €5,000 of funding and additional project support. It provides an informal and flexible environment to assess the market potential of a business idea, develop a business model and find out whether entrepreneurship is a prospective future career for the participant.
- Tailored coaching by a core team, support from expert commercial advisors and an Entrepreneur-in-Residence (EIR) following the participants from day one. EIRs are selected based on their entrepreneurial track record and their expertise in the complex and heavily regulated cleantech industry.

Following its launch in 2010, it runs activities in multiple locations across Europe (France, Germany, the Netherlands, Nordics, the UK and Switzerland) and supports over 120 startups in Europe each year. Within the UK only, this unique program has so far supported 45 European cleantech startups to collectively raise €59 million in external investment, a median of €1.15m per startup (last updated figures end of 2015). For instance, one of the 45 startups, UK-based Aqdot, has developed an intelligent encapsulation platform technology and know-how which enables valuable active products to be protected, delivered and chemically programmed to release where and when required. Aqdot has now raised around €8.5 million in VC funding.[43]

To summarize, the Climate-KIC (pre-) Accelerator supports new ventures at key points of the commercialization journey using an ecosystem approach. This approach co-locates participants in university-centered ecosystems with a focus on the community aspect, and grants them access to advanced technical facilities and technology support vouchers. These are considered key elements in order to be able to deliver a responsive and connected support program. For instance, the technology support vouchers of up to €50,000 enables startups to leverage the ecosystem by accessing critical expertise and know-how.

To be eligible, a technological proof-of-concept is required that has climate impact and scalability. Three open calls are publicized each year and application is by submission of a four-page document including details of the market problem and opportunity, product or service, innovation, business model, climate impact, team, roles and commitment, development status and references. The application undergoes a multi-stage selection procedure comprising a desk assessment, a review by an expert panel and an interview with the accelerator management team. Of the startups entering through the 2015 calls, Climate-KIC received 62 applications of which 10 were selected onto the program.

Importantly, in order to secure the future support of early-stage ventures, accepted applicants are asked to sign an Investment Agreement that will come into effect once they enter Stage III. A fair equity percentage is requested in return for the grants and all other in-kind support.

This case study on the Climate-KIC program highlights the role of the EU in entrepreneurial ecosystems and how this role is evolving over time. Originally, and in line with EU policy, the Climate-KIC Accelerator program was primarily funded by the EU. This seems to be under evolution as current Climate-KIC programs are in active search for funding from private partners to reinforce, complement and eventually take over the funding role of the EU. A shift has been initiated from EU funding towards funding from private partners as the Climate-KIC program has long outgrown its infancy stage and has evolved into maturity, and is now dealing with the challenge of self-sustainability. As such, the role of the EU is evolving from safeguarding the setup of the initiative to, once proven viable, transferring it to the private sector to safeguard its longevity.

CONCLUSIONS

EU policy is often positioned as reactive and an attempt to emulate US policy. Looking at the examples of US and EU policy on accelerators, similarities and differences become apparent. Clearly, policies on both sides of the Atlantic are aimed at increasing entrepreneurial activity and economic growth, with both sides looking to increase awareness and provide funding where there are gaps in the entrepreneurial ecosystem.

The aim of the US policy to support accelerator activity is to fill geographical gaps in the accelerator and ecosystem scene, as in some parts of the country there are fewer conventional sources of access to capital, such as VC and other types of capital. So, location is a distinguishing factor. Additionally, in the US more policy attention seems to go to underserved groups, such as women, Native Americans and veterans.

The EU policy towards accelerators differs from the US policy as it responds to differing needs. The EU accelerator policy is not merely a reaction to US policy as it is part of a broader macro-economic plan – the European Commission's Entrepreneurship 2020 Action Plan – to answer to challenges brought by the gravest economic crisis in the last 50 years. EU funding of accelerator programs seems to be more focused on particular industry sectors, such as ICT, IoT and commercial space applications and products, as these are supposed to hold great potential for economic growth and to leverage Europe's economy out of its economic crisis. This objective can only be reached through policymakers taking a long-term budget view and providing finance for a number of years to support accelerators in creating flourishing entrepreneurial ecosystems.

NOTES

1. https://ec.europa.eu/growth/smes/promoting-entrepreneurship_en (last consulted on 4/8/2016).
2. https://www.sba.gov/offices/headquarters/ooi/resources/1428931 (last consulted on 1/6/2016).
3. For the purpose of this competition, Growth Accelerators include accelerators, incubators, co-working startup communities, shared tinker-spaces or other models to accomplish similar goals.
4. http://www.kauffman.org/blogs/policy-dialogue/2015/august/accelerators-across-us-get-4-million-from-sba (last consulted on 1/1/2016).

5. https://www.sba.gov/about-sba/sba-newsroom/press-releases-media-advisories/sba-lau nches-3rd-annual-growth-accelerator-fund-competition-award-395-million-small-busi ness (last consulted on 21/12/2016).
6. https://www.sba.gov/offices/headquarters/ooi/resources/1428931 (last consulted on 22/12/2016).
7. http://ec.europa.eu/growth/smes/promoting-entrepreneurship/action-plan/index_ en.htm(last consulted on 5/7/2016).
8. https://ec.europa.eu/digital-single-market/en/startup-europe (last consulted on 5/7/2016).
9. Taking a narrower delineation than in the exemplary case of the USA. For instance, the ACE Acceleration Programme (2013–2015) that delivered new value-added support to high-potential ICT startups and SMEs to accelerate their international growth by networking leading incubators, accelerators, clusters and living labs throughout Europe, who committed to pooling their knowledge and expertise in internationalization and opening up their existing facilities and support services to each other's local companies, was considered outside the scope of this chapter as accelerators were only one of many support systems involved. http://europeanace.eu (last consulted on 5/7/2016).
10. Programs under the European Institute of Innovation and Technology (EIT) are discussed in more detail in the Climate-KIC Accelerator case study further on in this chapter.
11. Community Research and Development Information Service Agreement number 611878 (2013–2016), http://cordis.europa.eu/project/rcn/189039_en.html (last consulted on 20/7/2016).
12. http://www.europeanacceleratorsummit.com/ (last consulted on 14/7/2016).
13. https://ec.europa.eu/digital-single-market/node/66623 (last consulted on 5/7/2016).
14. http://www.acceleratorassembly.eu/ (last consulted on 29/6/2016).
15. WELCOME is one of the connectors projects of Startup Europe. WELCOME is aimed at breaking down the barriers between five different major EU startup ecosystems (Berlin, Dublin, Milan, Madrid and Salamanca) by teaming up with local partners present in these ecosystems to identify and engage the most relevant players of the tech entrepreneurial world (e.g. investors, mentors, media, corporates, successful entrepreneurs) and connect them with prospective, emerging and successful tech startups. In addition, WELCOME also aims to bridge the divide between the tech entrepreneurial world and policymakers. In Berlin, the organizations that ensure this connection are The Factory, etventure and Betahaus. http://startupeuropeclub.eu/connectors/; http://startupeuropeclub.eu/berlin/ (last consulted on 18/7/2016).
16. http://euxcel.eu/ (last consulted on 18/7/2016).
17. EU-XCEL received funding from the EU's Horizon 2020 Research and Innovation Programme under Grant Agreement number 644801.
18. http://startup-scaleup.eu/ (last consulted on 6/7/2016).
19. Under Grant Agreement number 644023.
20. https://www.f6s.com/ (last consulted on 7/7/2016).
21. Scaleup is a connectors project of Startup Europe, next to DIGISTART, ePlus, TWIST and WELCOME. http://startupeuropeclub.eu/connectors/ (last consulted on 18/7/2016).
22. Consultancy firm – http://bluspecs.com/ (last consulted on 7/7/2016).
23. http://connectedconference.co/ (last consulted on 7/7/2016).
24. http://www.copernicus-masters.com/ (last consulted 7/7/2016).
25. The DG GROWTH is responsible for completing the Internal Market for goods and services; helping turn the EU into a smart, sustainable, and inclusive economy by implementing the industrial and sectorial policies of the Europe 2020 initiative. Next to actions towards SMEs, brought together in the Small Business Act, and towards IPR rights, it implements the EU's space policy via its two large-scale satellite programs Copernicus (for Earth observation) and Galileo (for global navigation), as well as research actions designed to spur technological innovation and economic growth.

http://ec.europa.eu/growth/about-us/, http://www.copernicus-masters.com/index.php? kat=copacc.html&anzeige=copacc-mentors.html (last consulted on 24/11/2016).

26. An international competition in the commercial use of Earth observation data. This competition is on the hunt for outstanding ideas, applications and business concepts that use such information in everyday life. Along with cash prizes, the winners will receive access to a leading international network, corresponding data, startups funding and other support. Over the past five years, the Copernicus Masters has already selected a total of 40 winners from among more than 700 cutting-edge business ideas from 60 different countries. www.copernicus-masters.com (last consulted 24/11/2016).

27. http://www.space-of-innovation.com/first-copernicus-accelerator-bootcamp/ (last consulted on 24/11/2016).

28. The team around Grega Milcinski from Slovenia's Sinergise Ltd, whose *Sentinel Hub* – a cloud-based web service for satellite data – won the 2016 Copernicus Masters competition. http://www.space-of-innovation.com/smart-data-access-pathbreaking-web-service-sentinel-hub-wins-2016-copernicus-masters-competition (last consulted on 24/11/2016).

29. https://ec.europa.eu/digital-single-market/en/capital (last consulted on 5/7/2016).

30. https://ec.europa.eu/digital-single-market/en/fiware-accelerator-programme (last consulted on 5/7/2016).

31. https://www.fiware.org/accelerators (last consulted on 5/7/2016).

32. The FIWARE platform provides a set of application programming interfaces that ease the development of smart applications in multiple vertical sectors. The specifications of these interfaces are public and royalty-free. An open source reference implementation of each of the FIWARE components is publicly available so that multiple FIWARE providers can emerge faster in the market with a low-cost proposition. https://www.fiware.org/accelerators (last consulted on 5/7/2016).

33. The FIWARE Lab is a non-commercial sandbox environment where innovation and experimentation based on FIWARE technologies take place. Entrepreneurs and individuals can test the technology as well as their applications on FIWARE Lab, exploiting open data published by cities and other organizations. FIWARE Lab is deployed over a geographically distributed network of federated nodes leveraging on a wide range of experimental infrastructures. https://www.fiware.org/accelerators (last consulted on 5/7/2016).

34. Although it was born in Europe, FIWARE has been designed with a global ambition, so that benefits can spread to other regions. The FIWARE Mundus program is designed to bring coverage to this effort engaging local ICT players and domain stakeholders, and eventually liaising with local governments in different parts of the world, including North America, Latin America, Africa and Asia. https://www.fiware.org/accelerators (last consulted on 5/7/2016).

35. The network of FIWARE iHubs will play a fundamental role in building the community of adopters as well as contributors at local level. The FIWARE iHubs program aims at supporting the creation and the operations of iHubs nodes worldwide. https://www.fiware.org/accelerators (last consulted on 5/7/2016).

36. http://www.europeanpioneers.eu/en/ (last consulted on 7/7/2016).

37. Under the Grant Agreement number 632871.

38. Press release 13 August 2015, http://www.etventure.de/wp-content/uploads/2015/08/20150813_EuropeanPioneers-Accelerator_Start-2nd-Batch.pdf (last consulted on 7/7/2016).

39. Although the EuropeanPioneers accelerator is no longer active, it appears to still support another new accelerator program based in London, named MarathonArtist Labs.

40. https://ec.europa.eu/easme/en/news/sme-instrument-european-commission-invest-86-million-236-innovative-businesses (last consulted on 8/7/2016).

41. http://www.climate-kic.org/national-centres/london-uk/ (last consulted 1/11/2016).

42. See explanation on EU programs at the beginning of the chapter.

43. Crunchbase and Climate-KIC London Salesforce database (last consulted 15/03/2016).

REFERENCES

Acs, Z.J., Audretsch, D.B., Lehmann, E.E. and Licht, G. (2016a). National systems of entrepreneurship, *Small Business Economics*, 16(4): 527–535.

Acs, Z.J., Szerb, L. and Autio, E. (2016b). Enhancing entrepreneurial ecosystems: A GEI approach to entrepreneurship policy. In: Acs, Z.J., Szerb, L. and Autio, E., *Global Entrepreneurship Index 2016*, Chapter 4 (63–72), The Global Entrepreneurship and Development Institute, Washington, DC, USA.

Autio, E. (2007). *Global Entrepreneurship Monitor: 2007 Global Report on High-Growth Entrepreneurship*. Global Entrepreneurship Research Association (GERA), London, UK.

Autio, E., Kenney, M., Mustar, P., Siegel, D. and Wright, M. (2014). Entrepreneurial innovation: The importance of context. *Research Policy*, 43(7): 1097–1108.

Bravo-Biosca, A. and Westlake, S. (2009). The vital six per cent: How high-growth innovative businesses generate prosperity and jobs. Nesta, London, UK.

Hochberg, Y.V. (2016). Accelerating entrepreneurs and ecosystems: The seed accelerator model. *Innovation Policy and the Economy*, 16(1): 25–51.

Mian, S.A. (2011). *Science and Technology Based Regional Entrepreneurship: Global Experience in Policy and Program Development*. Edward Elgar Publishing, Cheltenham, UK and Northampton, MA, USA.

Mustar, P. and Wright, M. (2010). Convergence or path dependency in policies to foster the creation of university spin-off firms? A comparison of France and the United Kingdom, *Journal of Technology Transfer*, 35: 42–65.

8. Use of the "ecosystem model" by accelerators at country and regional levels

Jonas Van Hove, Iris Vanaelst and Mike Wright

INTRODUCTION

It should come as no surprise that context is important when considering entrepreneurship (Autio, Kenney, Mustar, Siegel and Wright, 2014) as it tends to take place within a network of public and private partners that nurture and sustain entrepreneurs. Prior research provides evidence that entrepreneurial ecosystems are increasingly vital to the success of national entrepreneurship initiatives (Drexler et al., 2014) as they offer highly collaborative ways to solve challenges by bringing together within the ecosystem community the potential to build, solve, share and exchange goals. An ecosystem community consists of human, financial and professional resources that an entrepreneur requires, and an institutional environment in which government encourages and safeguards entrepreneurs (Isenberg, 2010). In other words, high-potential ventures are coproduced through a myriad of usually uncoordinated interactions between different stakeholders, all stimulating innovation by entrepreneurial firms. Examples of such stakeholders are initiatives such as startup support programs (e.g. incubators/accelerators) focused on helping early-stage ventures. These are of particular interest as they are considered to be strong instruments for promoting innovation and entrepreneurship (Aernoudt, 2004).

Young or new ventures increasingly choose to join business assistance programs as entrepreneurs are facing high levels of ambiguity during their search for solutions to problems that are still imperfectly defined. As these programs have become very heterogeneous (cf. Barbero, Casillas, Wright and Garcia, 2014), startups have a range of business assistance programs to choose from. However, as shown by their rapid growth in recent years, one kind of model seems to stand out as the preferred option for entrepreneurs to kick-start their ventures and decrease market/technology uncertainties:

the business accelerator. Such startup support programs are defined as a new generation of incubation models (Pauwels, Clarysse, Wright and Van Hove, 2015) that beyond the conventional incubator offering consisting of basic office space and financial support provide knowledge-intensive services essential for startups in their early growth phase dominated by an iterative search process.

Contemporary research revealed mostly beneficial effects of accelerator programs on participating startups and the overall ecosystem (e.g. Gonzalez-Uribe and Leatherbee, 2017; Spigel, 2015). These effects are related to accelerating mechanisms such as structured accountability, magnification of quality signals to potential investors, and access to networking and mentorship. The last mechanism – that is, mentoring by and networking with (former) entrepreneurs and investors, potential corporate clients that contribute their knowledge, time and connections to the startup – is key to the accelerator concept. As entrepreneurial ecosystems drive social and economic development by enabling access to markets, human capital and funding for startups, accelerators need to operate in an ecosystem in order to be effective over the course of new ventures' entrepreneurial trajectories. Furthermore, accelerators are crucial in building supportive commercial infrastructure, and there is growing interest from policy makers and corporates to utilize such programs as catalysts in entrepreneurial ecosystems (e.g. Sivonen, Borella, Thomas and Sharapov, 2015).

For entrepreneurship policies to nurture and facilitate entrepreneurial ecosystems effectively, policy makers must become more aware of how the different elements of these ecosystems interact (Acs, Szerb and Autio, 2016). Moreover, to do this successfully, the relative strengths and weaknesses of the multiple factors making up the entrepreneurial ecosystem need to be understood (cf. Acs, Audretsch, Lehmann and Licht, 2016). Considering the surge in business accelerators, we aim to understand the importance, activities and the benefits of such programs as part of an entrepreneurial ecosystem. The resulting insights can advise policy on business creation and entrepreneurial initiatives. This chapter revolves around the concept of a "connected ecosystem" and the blend of various startup support initiatives to advance our understanding of entrepreneurship and policy. It speaks primarily to new forms of incubation supporting new technology ventures.

The chapter unfolds as follows. First, we provide a brief background on entrepreneurial ecosystems. This is followed up with a discussion of the country- and regional-level policies using the case of United Kingdom (UK) to illustrate the most relevant policies stimulating the development of an entrepreneurial ecosystem. We identified these policy instruments by screening the web using a set of key words related to acceleration, policy and United Kingdom. In the last section, we outline policy implications and our recommendations.

LITERATURE REVIEW

Entrepreneurial ecosystems are typically viewed from a national and regional level as the idiosyncratic nature of regional economies and their entrepreneurial ecosystems makes a uniform approach irrelevant. Policies that have been successful in one European country cannot feasibly be adopted successfully in other European countries (Mustar and Wright, 2010; Audretsch and Peña-Legazkue, 2012; Acs and Szerb, 2007). National differences built upon different evolutionary trajectories or path dependencies may be deep-rooted and difficult to alter. Industrialized countries, like the UK, Germany, France and Italy, have large pools of developed manpower, higher incomes, developed basic infrastructure and large national markets, which provide them with enabling environments to establish science and technology oriented entrepreneurial regions. Mian (2011) shows an emerging history and considerable level of policy and program activity in these large developed nations. In all of these cases any renewed policy efforts were primarily triggered by national concerns about attaining and/or sustaining global competitive advantage through science and technology based high value added innovation and entrepreneurial activity. In the post-1980s scenario, most of the efforts have been directed towards more decentralized and grassroots-level science and technology research results transfer and diffusion programs. Another common element is the type of organizational mechanisms developed to address the perceived market or system failures, which predominantly included umbrella organizations, science and technology parks, incubators and firm clusters. The efforts to improve talent, technology, capital and entrepreneurial infrastructure issues clearly play a dominant role in the development of policies and their implementation programs (Mian, 2011).

Other industrialized nations, such as the Netherlands and Israel, maintain somewhat similar high levels of knowledge economy characteristics, but their smaller population size provides them with limited local market potential and hence they generally place more emphasis on the internationalization of their economies (Mian, 2011).

FINDINGS

Government policy at the national level – the United Kingdom

Since accelerator programs came ashore in the UK, resulting in the setup of the first accelerator programs in Europe and the strongest European accelerator ecosystem, a closer look will be taken at how the government in the UK supports accelerator programs, as an example of national government involvement.

We focused only on the most relevant instruments of national government policy towards accelerators and actors within the accelerator ecosystems such as government-backed accelerators, the visa policy for foreign startups, tax relief schemes and government-backed venture capital schemes.

Government-backed accelerators aim to stimulate local economic development or achieve social and/or environmental impact (Walters, Stacey, Haley and Roberts, 2014). One of the UK's most recent government-backed accelerator programs, HutZero,[1] was announced in June 2016 and is aimed at cybersecurity innovation. Since cybersecurity is of national importance, the national government's involvement is not counterintuitive. The idea is to reduce cyber threats in the country while also developing the UK's position in security innovation by encouraging entrepreneurs, students and others starting out in business to develop solutions to fight cybercrime. The initiative is funded by the Department for Culture, Media and Sport (DCMS) as part of the government's National Cyber Security Programme. HutZero is a free two-stage early-stage accelerator program that will help transform early-stage ideas into viable propositions and potential new businesses. Run by Cyber London and the Centre for Secure Information Technologies (CSIT), HutZero will support individuals, not teams, interested in starting their own cyber business, connecting them with a range of like-minded entrepreneurs and domain experts.

In general, when setting up a business[2] a particular set of rules must be complied with. At the same time, government-backed support and finance for business such as grants, loans, mentoring and consultancy is offered under particular conditions.[3] Since accelerators recruit startups internationally, an additional set of rules needs to be complied with and different support programs are offered. The Sirius Programme,[4] for instance, is the UK's support program for graduate entrepreneurs from around the world looking to start their venture in the UK. The Sirius Programme is run by a consortium of private companies and charities on a not for profit basis in partnership with the Department for International Trade. The program offers a full support package to enable promising entrepreneurs with new ideas that have real growth potential to maximize their chances of success. Successful applicants are admitted to the program for 12 months, and the package of support includes seed funding, a fixed sum for every venture accepted on the program; training, including full pre-acceleration and acceleration stages; mentoring, from experienced entrepreneurs and investors; office accommodation, at one of twelve locations across the UK relevant to the business selected; and visa support – applicants will be helped through the UK visa process (see below) and may apply for a visa from a dedicated annual allocation.

Additional support to recruit startup teams internationally comes from the Department for International Trade. This department guides entrepreneurs setting up in the UK[5] and promotes the UK by stressing that it has one of the lowest corporation tax rates in the G20, that a company can register within 48 hours, that the labor force is the second largest in Europe and that the government offers support to startups and entrepreneurs including access to mentoring programs and funding through working with the private sector. The Department for International Trade's Global Entrepreneur Programme (GEP)[6] supports overseas entrepreneurs and early-stage technology businesses or startups that want to relocate their business to the UK. The program has so far helped to relocate 340 businesses to the UK, create over 1,000 jobs in the UK economy and raise over £1 billion of private investment for companies. Support is free and includes help to develop business plans, assistance with relocating to the UK, providing introductions to investors, guidance on how to grow internationally, mentoring from experienced entrepreneurs, and continued help once located in the UK. In return for this support, overseas entrepreneurs are encouraged to set up their headquarters in the UK. In order to be able to do so and to potentially take part in UK-based accelerator programs, candidates need a visa.

An entrepreneur, from outside the European Economic Area and Switzerland, who wants to set up or run a business in the UK needs to apply for a Tier 1 (Entrepreneur) visa.[7] In addition, access is required to at least £50,000 of investment funds from one or more of the following: (1) a UK entrepreneurial seed-funding competition endorsed by UK Trade and Investment (UKTI); (2) a UK government department making funds available for the purpose of setting up or expanding a UK business; (3) a venture capital firm registered with the Financial Conduct Authority (FCA). Alternatively, an entrepreneur can apply if an investment of £50,000 was made in a UK business. The Department for International Trade has endorsed certain Seed Competitions. Some of them are accelerators, which support applications for a Tier 1 (Entrepreneur) visa for entry to the UK,[8] such as Techstars London, Oxygen Accelerator, Collider, Emerge Education Accelerator and StartPlanet NI, as well as Wayra and Entrepreneur First.

The UK government issued several investment schemes to stimulate investment in enterprises. Investment schemes reside under the non-ministerial department of HM Revenue & Customs (HMRC). As well as the Collective Investment Schemes Center[9] (CISC) – that deals with all operational issues on behalf of HMRC – several investment schemes exist, such as the Social Investment Tax Relief, for investments in social enterprises; the Venture Capital Trust[10] (VCT) Scheme, to encourage investment in small unquoted enterprises; the Enterprise Investment Scheme[11] (EIS), designed to help smaller higher-risk unquoted companies to raise finance by offering a range of tax reliefs to investors who purchase new shares in those companies; and the Seed Enterprise Investment Scheme[12] (SEIS), aimed at small, early-stage ventures looking to attract equity finance. Since SEIS targets a similar audience as accelerator programs, confirmed in our own field research, this investment scheme will be discussed in more detail. SEIS is designed to help small, early-stage ventures raise equity finance by offering tax reliefs to individual investors who purchase new shares in those ventures. It complements the existing EIS which offers tax reliefs to investors in higher-risk small companies. The rules mirror those of EIS as it is anticipated that companies will go on to use EIS after an initial investment under SEIS.

Income tax relief is available to individuals who subscribe for qualifying shares in a company which meets the SEIS requirements, and who have a UK tax liability against which to set the relief. Investors do not need to be UK residents. The shares must be held for a period of three years, from date of issue, for relief to be retained. Relief is available at 50 percent of the cost of the shares, on a maximum annual investment of £100,000. The relief is given by way of a reduction of tax liability, providing there is a sufficient tax liability against which to set it. A claim to relief can be made up to five years after the 31 January following the tax year in which the investment was made.

For its investors to be able to claim and keep the SEIS tax reliefs[13] relating to their shares, the enterprise which issues the shares has to meet a number of requirements. Some of these apply only at the time the relevant shares are issued. Others must be met continuously, either for the whole of the period from date of issue of the shares or, in some cases, from date of issue of the shares to the third anniversary of their issue. If the enterprise ceases to meet one or more of these conditions, investors may have their tax relief withdrawn. Finally, there are requirements[14] as to how the enterprise must use the funding it has raised via the issue of relevant shares, and the enterprise needs to run a qualifying trade which is conducted on a commercial basis with a view to the realization of profit.

The Small Companies Enterprise Centre[15] (SCEC) decides if an enterprise and a share issue qualify, and is responsible for monitoring enterprises to ensure that they continue to meet the requirements of the scheme for the duration of the qualifying period for any share issue. HMRC operate an advance assurance facility for SEIS, as it does for the existing EIS. This facility allows enterprises to submit details of their plans to raise money, their structure and their activities in advance of an issue of shares, so that the SCEC can advise on whether or not the proposed share issue is likely to qualify for relief. If the SCEC accepts that the enterprise, its activities and the shares all meet the requirements of the scheme, it will issue the enterprise with a certificate to that effect, and will supply claim forms for the enterprise to send to the investors so they can claim tax relief. Research (Cowling, Bates, Jagger and Murray, 2008) on the impact of VCT and EIS found evidence of an increased rate of accumulation of fixed assets, an increased rate of job creation and increased sales turnover. Enterprises had lower profit margins and survival rates when compared to matched enterprises. Lower profit margins are to be expected for schemes investing in young, growth-oriented, and often pre-profit firms. Lower survival rates included both voluntary exits and the acquisition of attractive enterprises by larger firms, and should, therefore, not necessarily be interpreted negatively (Nightingale et al., 2009).

Research (Nightingale et al., 2009) demonstrates that there is a role for government-backed "hybrid" venture capital schemes to reach those young businesses that have difficulty accessing funds from purely private investors. These "hybrid" venture capital funds refer to arrangements where the state invests in a venture capital fund managed by a commercial venture capital fund. Government intervention to address any market failure or underinvestment would be warranted. This is particularly the case if funding problems constrain the growth of the very small number of high-growth enterprises that hold the potential of creating jobs and to be drivers of economic growth. By the mid-1990s, a portfolio of policy instruments was introduced, like, for instance, the above mentioned VCT and EIS schemes (Nightingale et al., 2009). In addition, the 1998 Competitiveness White Paper focused on supporting venture capital provision throughout the UK. It announced the formation of a £270 million Enterprise Fund working in partnership with the private sector to address market weaknesses through, for instance, Regional Enterprise Funds, a UK High Tech Fund of Funds and an Early Growth Fund (Nightingale et al., 2009). Later hybrid funds include the Enterprise Capital Funds (ECFs) developed following a 2003 consultation that pointed out that while funding had improved, a small and significant number of enterprises still faced funding difficulties (Nightingale et al., 2009). One of the organizational innovations with the ECF has been the semi-privatization of its operation. This was done through Capital for Enterprise Ltd, an enterprise originally fully owned by the Department for Business, Innovation and Skills[16] (Nightingale et al., 2009). The enterprise acted as a consultancy and asset management business for the government and managed the loan guarantee schemes as well as hybrid venture capital programs. The enterprise was a substantial investor in UK venture capital funds, and its close connections to the government, together with its independence, enabled it to stay away from some of the conflicts of interest that plague public-sector-run funds while still being responsive to government policy (Nightingale et al., 2009).

Policies at the Regional Level

The idiosyncratic nature of regional economies and their entrepreneurial ecosystems makes a uniform approach irrelevant. Systems of entrepreneurship are geographically bounded – London, Paris and Berlin serve as examples of thriving entrepreneurial ecosystems with prominent accelerator activity. Those cities are internationally acknowledged as local ecosystems that provide the best support for both startups and scale-ups. The European Digital City Index and the Regional Entrepreneurship and Development Index (REDI), both complex indicators of regional entrepreneurship that capture individual-level actions as well as contextual influences such as the financial possibilities of business, consistently rank the entrepreneurial performance of London, Paris and Berlin among the top in the European Union (Szerb, Acs and Autio, 2013).

The strength of each of the capitals' position as one the of the strongest and vibrant startup ecosystems in Europe is being underscored by the very existence of an amalgam of acceleration models conceptualized as Ecosystem Builders, Welfare Stimulators and Deal-flow Makers (Pauwels et al., 2015; see also Chapter 1). This is not surprising as the region created the conditions for accelerators to take off as they have a sufficiently dense population of entrepreneurial ventures to be attractive for accelerators and have developed a seed-stage funding supply resulting in improved circumstances for startups and startup programs to make an impact (Salido, Sabás and Freixas, 2013).

The three different types of incubation models identified by Pauwels et al. (2015) demonstrate how accelerator programs adopt different ways of structuring and running their programs depending on the objectives of their key stakeholders. For instance, the Ecosystem Builder tends to be backed or sponsored by large corporates and has a strong focus on (cor-

Table 8.1   Examples of incubation models in London, Paris or Berlin

Incubation models	Examples of acceleration programs
Ecosystem Builders	Fintech Innovation Lab
	Starburst Accelerator
	Grants4Apps Accelerator
Welfare Stimulators	MassChallenge
	NUMA Paris
	Eyefocus Accelerator
Deal-flow Makers	Deep Science Ventures
	TheFamily
	Axel Springer Plug & Play Accelerator

porate) customers by helping new ventures through the complex corporate decision-making structures. Deal-flow Makers are perceived as high-risk investment funds getting early-stage ventures ready for their follow-up investments. Finally, the Welfare Stimulators are tools typically supported by public institutions with the aim to foster their (entrepreneurial) ecosystems. Based on our research, Table 8.1 categorizes well-known accelerators representing each of these models, based in London, Paris or Berlin.

All three regions are considered to be well-developed ecosystems, each housing numerous accelerator programs which are active on different levels (local/regional/national/international). However, empirical data shows that the three startup ecosystem evolution paths (London, Paris and Berlin) exhibit distinct phases, each characterized by distinct challenges and arenas of activity. For instance, London underwent profound changes in the entrepreneurial finance landscape following the launch of the first accelerator in 2008. The focus was no longer only on venture capitalists and business angels. Traditional funds started to experiment early on by adopting similar accelerator activities as in the USA. Afterwards, policy makers and other ecosystem stakeholders followed the accelerator hype. When compared to Berlin and Paris, our fieldwork showed that each region had a different ecosystem stakeholder initiating the launch of the accelerator scene in order to spur ecosystem emergence. Early programs in London were launched primarily by venture capitalists experimenting with new forms of finance and seeking to develop deal flow. Furthermore, the arenas of activity differ mostly in terms of specialization. For instance, Fintech is a particularly popular sector among London-based accelerators (Bone, Allen and Haley, 2017).

As policy makers should take an ecosystem perspective when considering new actions for further ecosystem development, we reveal in the next subsection current regional policies and how accelerator activity is linked to other initiatives. We illustrate this with the case of London, as it has the highest degree of accelerator activity within a vibrant entrepreneurial ecosystem. Using information-rich cases such as London and a multi-source data collection approach strengthened the accuracy of our findings.

London's accelerator ecosystem
London's clear advantage over the rest of the country (and even the continent) can be explained by the intrinsic relation of London to key financial and advisory institutions. Furthermore, the metropolis is and has been the world center of financial technology for decades due to the presence of the woolly mammoths of finance located in the City and tech hubs nestling in their close proximity, such as Shoreditch. Although in the past few years government has been striving for a national equilibrium (e.g. the national network of Entrepreneurial Spark accelerator centers and the Sirius Program), the difference in startup support is still prevailing. While its centricity approach has left the rest of the UK mostly underserved, there is a trend towards new programs being launched in other cities such as Birmingham, Bristol, Cambridge and Manchester (Bone et al., 2017). Various policy measures implemented in the City of London have been vital in boosting the London startup ecosystem.

Up until the end of 2016, the region housed at least 57 accelerators, with 2016 being the most active year since the launch of the first privately funded accelerator Springboard (launched in 2009 and merged with Techstars in 2013) and the first university-based accelerator InnovationRCA in 2008. Moreover, our fieldwork indicates that more than half of the UK's total number of accelerators are based in London. The surge in new programs is partially due to the paradigm shift inside large corporates towards open innovation as they recognize the limits of "closed" internal R&D (West, Salter, Vanhaverbeke and Chesbrough, 2014). For instance, according to Bone et al. (2017), accelerators are now most commonly funded by corporates, including corporate venture capital units.

Complementary to the national-level pro-business environment created through talent recruitment practices, generous tax breaks for seed investors, reduced corporation tax and a regulatory framework that stimulates legal efficiency, the City of London is known for its "pay-it-forward" ethos and offers an additional set of coordinating initiatives which interconnects the different ecosystem stakeholders and facilitates co-opetition among them. These initiatives – backed by the Mayor of London and the UK government – also act as an institutional intermediary between policy makers and practitioners in order to preserve alignment of interests of the ecosystem stakeholders. By institutional intermediaries, we mean actors that link two or more parties to bring about activities that could not readily happen otherwise (see also Dutt et al., 2015; Armanios, Eesley, Li and Eisenhardt, 2017). Of interest here are institutional intermediaries that coordinate and/or influence ecosystem stakeholders by shaping the ecosystem, stimulating multi-party collaboration and adding value through their own capacities, such as to help entrepreneurs obtain public funding.

To illustrate such an institutional intermediary, Capital Enterprise[17] is a leading membership body for London-based universities, accelerators and incubators that support entrepreneurs. Capital Enterprise represents the interests and the views of its members to influential public sector bodies such as the Mayor of London, the former Department for Business, Innovation and Skills, and so on. It is funded through members' subscriptions, third-party sponsorship and income received from public/private sector partners to develop, pilot and manage innovative programs that support enterprises and entrepreneurs in London. Overall, it provides a support service and platform that identifies and then selects some of the best innovative and scalable startups in London to showcase and connect them to London's leading investors, advisers and accelerator programs. Furthermore, from 2015 onward it complemented its coordination role with the management of an early-stage investment fund, named the London Co-Investment Fund.[18] By developing and running a pipeline of investment-ready tech businesses to be referred to its selected co-investment partners, this £25 million fund aimed to co-invest 150 seed investments of £250,000–£1 million in the best tech startups by the end of 2015. Established accelerators, such as Techstars, Collider and Startupbootcamp, have been able to use this co-funding to massively expand their activities. Furthermore, investment brokerage services, such as Capital List, crowdfunding platform CrowdCube and the London Business Angel Network have been supported by the program. For instance, initiatives like Angels in MedCity and trade missions to Singapore, China and the USA have been co-funded. By the end of 2015 it had supported over 700 businesses and created over 400 new jobs in London. Capital Enterprise is in contact with other regions in the UK and Europe about how they could replicate the program's success in combining public and private money to stimulate the evolution and growth of a startup ecosystem.[19]

It is clear that London differs from other entrepreneurial ecosystems due to the outstanding quality and abundance of its startup support services. Nonetheless, critics are voicing concerns that an overall systemic policy approach to support startups is still lacking. For instance, the funding gap of between £250,000 and £500,000 (which is usually the amount of funding needed by early-stage ventures as they graduate from accelerators) still persists. Microsoft Accelerator, for instance, extends its support by offering a connected ecosystem, called Microsoft Accelerator Alumni Program (also known as the Microsoft Reactors' project), so startups can continue to leverage access to resources, networks and potential customers. Others aim to help bridge this gap between seed funding and the so-called Series A crunch, by designing an accelerator program specifically for scale-ups. For instance, the international accelerator and seed investment fund 500Startups launched Distro Dojo in London, a three-month program for "post-seed" startups. Only recently has this funding gap been addressed by policy makers. Coordinated by Capital Enterprise and funded with a grant from the European Regional Development Fund, the Capital Accelerate & Scale Tech Superstars program has been launched to support scale-ups in their growth ambition prior to applying for next round funding.[20]

Furthermore, within any given entrepreneurial ecosystem, substantial variation in startup quality remains. As more people become interested, an increasing number of people with diverse backgrounds and needs are seeking information and entrepreneurial education. For instance, university students, early-stage researchers and recent graduates from the STEM-fields[21] have recently been recognized as sources of new ventures. To this end, many universities are now adapting to facilitate this research-led commercialization by building pre-accelerators and active entrepreneurial communities. Leading universities such as Imperial College London and City University of London have started to tackle the lack of entrepreneurial guidance and now run pre-accelerator programs, respectively Imperial Create Lab and Fast Forward. Pre-accelerators offer a lot of freedom and space for creativity in order to explore viable market applications and fine-tune the opportunity identified by the entrepreneur. Besides the offerings of leading universities in London (to fast-track academic entrepreneurs), structured pre-acceleration programs are also created as standalone entities or as part of established accelerator programs. Examples are Startup Next (powered by Google for Entrepreneurs and Techstars), Climate-KIC Greenhouse and Incubus London. The last two pre-accelerators are backed by public institutions such as the European Commission, Tech City UK and Digital Business Academy. These initiatives seek to empower aspiring entrepreneurs to become "accelerator ready" in order to build up a thriving startup ecosystem.

ACCELERATOR CASE STUDIES

Presented below are examples of accelerator models illustrating respectively the financing challenge accelerators encounter and an overlooked element in the accelerator scene. They differ in their program design as well as objectives. The program has been studied in depth through desktop research and semi-structured interviews with the program managers and participating startups.

A Case Study on Financing Challenges: NUMA[22]

NUMA Paris is the by-product of Le Camping, one of the first French startup accelerators. The initial concept of an accelerator program in Paris was developed at La Cantine in 2010, the first co-working space. It was recognized that early-stage ventures search for more than office space, for example hands-on (mentor) support to process information from the environment and give it meaning. Inspired by the Anglo-Saxon models, more specifically Startupbootcamp, and backed by a range of public entities, one of the first French startup accelerators was launched.

The accelerator program was established originally as a non-profit entity sponsored by Silicon Sentier[23] and strategic partners such as Orange, BNP Paribas and Google, before changing into an equity-engagement model and finally moving to an organization offering a range of services such as startup acceleration, corporate innovation consultancy, event management and co-working space. The first change was linked to a misalignment between the strategic objectives of the sponsors (both public and private) and that of the startups within the program. Although governance of accelerators can afford the flexibility necessary to pursue goals beyond those of the main stakeholders, Le Camping's performance was not tied to its portfolio companies. After internal struggles, this resulted in a new investment scheme taking equity of as little as 3 percent to ensure full commitment by the accelerator management's team for the support of their ventures. The second change goes along with a transformation into a for-profit entity (taking 5 percent instead of 3 percent equity), named NUMA, implementing an international strategy on top of its regional activities. After a successful crowdfunding campaign[24] and seed-funding round collecting over €4 million, they aim to open 15 programs worldwide and accelerate 700 startups. International programs in Bangalore, Moscow and Casablanca are jointly set up with local partners such as local business angel networks and governmental entities. The ambition is that by creating such an international network, each program can feed off one another.

The focus of the accelerator remains fixed on young and scalable digital startups, and it selects on average 12 startups per cohort for an intensive four-month program followed up by two months of post-program support. In regard to financial support, the accelerator initially offered a financial grant of €4,500 ("pizza money"); however, this contribution changed into a €25,000 convertible loan after it transformed into a for-profit entity. Such a scheme was preferred over a conventional capital increase as such an increase entails complex and costly steps under French company law.

By implementing a matchmaking model, the accelerator stimulates peer-to-peer networking between the startups, mentors, volunteers, and industry and governmental partners. For instance, there is a direct collaboration with another Paris-based accelerator, TheFamily, that entails anything from sharing good practices with the stakeholders of the French entrepreneurial ecosystem to sharing startups. Within the program, each startup is connected with one "lead mentor" and a "brother", chosen after a matchmaking event (speed dating). These two guide the participating startups in their search processes for their optimal product–market fits. Typically, these two mentors are a business mentor with specific industry expertise and a product mentor with prior entrepreneurial experience. The other role of the mentors is to flag to the core team of the accelerator the startups that are not performing well.

In addition, the program hosts events such as "Adopt a CTO", which is a specific networking opportunity to connect technically-skilled individuals with aspiring entrepreneurs, and training sessions open for external partners to stimulate innovative activities. In this way, NUMA Paris is pursuing its mission to put in place tangible schemes and pooled resources for the benefit of innovation, while favoring the development of a network dedicated to different players in the digital sector.

From 2015 onward, they have worked with 30+ large corporates to carry out their digital metamorphosis, which has generated more than €2.5 million in annual turnover and accelerated 76 startups, who have raised over €30 million.

Case Study on Accelerating Impactful High-Technology Ventures (London): Deep Science Ventures[25]

Deep Science Ventures is a fully funded, full-time program launched in the summer of 2016 which works with scientists to make the transition from technical expert to founder of a high-tech startup. It aims to build a community of interdisciplinary scientists, industry experts and high-tech focused investors to build the next generation of high-growth science-based ventures. It is based on the success stories of Imperial Create Lab, a pioneering pre-accelerator program at Imperial College London, and Entrepreneur First, a technology accelerator and training school for entrepreneurs. Both programs acknowledged the potential of the UK's talented scientific staff to tackle real-world challenges and have the clear objective to "skill-up" (academic) entrepreneurs and start building companies from scratch by alleviating most of the risks.

As they focus on aspiring entrepreneurs with specific technical expertise, their approach is different compared to the more typical web-tech or digital-focused accelerators. The concept behind Deep Science Ventures is supporting individuals rather than fully formed teams, and the program is designed in two stages:

1. A three-month educational program providing individuals with intensive learning and supplemented with an equity-free cash infusion (i.e. "monthly stipend"). As individuals tend to possess (only) technical capabilities, they are likely to have inadequate skills to create a technology-based venture, that is, business capabilities. The aim of this stage is to develop an idea while receiving entrepreneurship know-how input, meet like-minded people and form a company based on a technology application or solution solving a "grand challenge". Educational workshops cover topics such as customer development, financial modeling, design thinking, patent strategies and transferrable skills.

2. A second three-month phase into which early-stage ventures enter (if selected), where the accelerator invests £70,000 for an equity stake (which is negotiable). Participants need to have a validated idea of the commercial side and a prototype in order to make the transition into stage 2.

This unique accelerator reduces risks by providing substantive benefits in the form of weekly mentoring, unique high-tech prototyping facilities (e.g. by partnering up with SynbiCITE[26]), such as wet-lab facilities, and sector experts. Participants can apply and choose between two tracks:

- The industrial brief model, which is co-created by the program team, the venture partners and sponsoring corporates such as Jaguar Land Rover and Arup. These briefs are developed to tackle "grand challenges" which can be described as highly significant yet potentially solvable, such as antibiotic resistance, intelligent and personalized healthcare and global famine. They affect vast numbers of individuals in often profound ways. As they may require working across disciplinary boundaries to solve technical problems, Deep Science Ventures implements a structured approach to gather talented individuals to ideate and validate potential concepts with end users and field experts.
- The cohort thought leadership model, whereby participants with specific technical expertise conduct workshops laying out the current

developments of cutting-edge technology and stimulating schooled peers within the program to creatively think about certain opportunities or viable market applications. Examples are next generation computing infrastructure, space technologies and cellular agriculture. This model is based on the so-called cohort-peer effect, whereby founding teams learn indirectly from the experience of others (see Hallen, Bingham and Cohen, 2014). It is an approach that has been designed to stimulate the formation of multi-disciplinary founding teams which tend to identify a larger number and more varied market opportunities.

Furthermore, the program team supports participants in obtaining public resources such as grants. They also impose regular meetings with founding teams, that is, structured accountability (Gonzalez-Uribe and Leatherbee, 2017), which serves as a way to commit participants to the achievement of business milestones. Although it looks promising, Deep Science Ventures is only currently running their first program and could be perceived as an accelerator experiment focused on high-technology ventures. A sneak peek at the cohort tells us that participants are working on technological matters from advanced materials based on algae biofuel waste to low-cost transistors for DNA sequencing.

DISCUSSION AND POLICY IMPLICATIONS

In this chapter, we have reviewed the evolution of the landscape of policy support for accelerators across national and regional/local levels.

The diversity of accelerator archetypes has implications for policy makers in evaluating the role of accelerators and how to support them. Rather than evaluating the effectiveness of all accelerators using the same criteria, there is a need to develop measures that take into account the different objectives of different types of incubation models.

While accelerators may help solve some of the challenges relating to previous generations of incubators, they are not without shortcomings from a policy perspective. Policy makers focusing on regional development and employment objectives need to recognize that the accelerators they finance cannot be profitable in the short or even medium term. The ventures they invest in, the programs they have to develop in order to be successful in their objectives and their strategic focus on the local environment do not allow this. The systematic research evidence is sparse, but only investor-led accelerators in very dense ecosystems such as Silicon Valley appear to have a proven, sustainable business model. Unfortunately, we often see that policy makers expect ecosystem accelerators to have similar outputs as investor-led ones. If, as seems likely, accelerators designed to help create entrepreneurial ecosystems will only be sustainable with continued financial support for a number of years, there is a need for policy makers to take a longer-term budget view of this form of support. Absent of this support, many accelerator initiatives are bound to disappear as soon as public finance is withdrawn. Otherwise, such accelerators are challenged to reconsider their incubation model in order to ensure longer-term sustainability. For instance, the very first accelerator founded in Paris spent considerable time searching for an optimal model. It was established originally in 2011 as Le Camping, a publicly backed entity, with a focus on employment creation and providing little financial support and not taking an equity stake in the ventures in the program. Subsequently it changed into a private accelerator fund, renamed NUMA, replicating its model internationally through joint ventures with local partners such as in Casablanca, Bangalore and Moscow (for more information, see the case study section above).

Although accelerators can be an effective way to shorten the startup journey, many potentially successful ventures may still not be investor-ready or commercially viable by the end of the accelerator program. Amid an abundance of startup support programs, the existence of a void has been acknowledged in terms of the lack of early-stage funding for entrepreneurs in their so-called scale-up phase. As a compensatory mechanism, we are seeing an evolution whereby some accelerators are allowing alumni to remain at the premises after the program has ended. On the one hand, this may be indicative of a creep towards the problem confronted by traditional incubators of ventures failing to leave. On the other hand, it suggests that there may need to be policy development that provides explicitly for continued active support within the accelerator and/or provides a connected ecosystem in which there are mechanisms for picking up still early stage ventures as they come off the end of the accelerator conveyor belt. In general, this focuses attention on the question of what are the funding and support gap(s) that accelerators are best placed to fill. Some accelerators, as we have seen, are now developing their support for scale-ups beyond the program, and some accelerators specializing in scale-ups are also emerging. This being the case, accelerators represent developments that serve to broaden the funding and support landscape rather than simply being a new step in the traditional linear funding and support escalator. As such, to the extent that competition from the evolving forms of accelerators provokes responses from more traditional equity providers to growing ventures, there may be systemic benefits for entrepreneurs.

The accelerator landscape is continuously evolving, the most recent trend being a rise in corporate programs exhibiting a variety of forms and approaches. These programs are an important open innovation tool for corporates to search for emerging technologies and talent. Another remarkable trend is the increased interest in building impactful high-technology ventures based on experiential and fundamental scientific research. By providing substantive benefits, these interventional programs try to enable scientists to turn their inventions into ventures with new products at the forefront of innovation, such as personalized cancer treatments and algae-based biofuel. One such initiative, the London-based Deep Science Ventures, aims to support entrepreneurial activities taking place at technology frontiers through an experimental accelerator program to "skill-up" academic entrepreneurs (see the case study in section above). However, the longer timelines and essentially higher capital requirements involved in these types of startups contradict the traditional characteristics of an accelerator – initially created to support fast-moving digital start-ups. With policies that promote technology transfer to support spin-offs, regulation should consider how to create an entrepreneurial ecosystem that can fuel a boom in "deep science" startups similar to the one observed in software and app spaces over the last decade.

Finally, in line with creating a connected ecosystem, institutional inter-mediaries have been proven to be useful to policy makers with the goal to create a resource munificent environment for entrepreneurial activity. Those intermediaries can help build supportive commercial infrastructures by interconnecting and facilitating cooperative and competitive challenges among ecosystem actors such as accelerators, incubators, crowdfunding platforms and early-stage investors. Besides coordination, such intermediaries tend to be well positioned to shape the ecosystem through the preservation of the aligned interests between policy makers and practitioners.

Overall, we can conclude that government policy is not just reacting to entrepreneurial ecosystem trends but the government is an active key stakeholder that through its accelerator policy, on different levels, revolutionizes entrepreneurial ecosystems to safeguard sustainable economic growth. But accelerators alone will not ensure the successful growth of an ecosystem. It takes a more systematic approach for startups to thrive.

NOTES

1. http://www.hutzero.co.uk/ (last consulted on 09/09/2016).
2. https://www.gov.uk/set-up-business (last consulted on 21/09/2016).
3. https://www.gov.uk/business-finance-support-finderr (last consulted on 21/09/2016).
4. https://www.gov.uk/government/collections/sirius-programme-for-graduate-entrepreneurs (last consulted on 21/09/2016).

5. https://www.gov.uk/government/publications/entrepreneurs-setting-up-in-the-uk/entre preneurs-setting-up-in-the-uk (last consulted on 08/09/2016).
6. https://www.gov.uk/government/publications/dealmakers-for-the-global-entrepreneur-programme (last consulted on 28/09/2016).
7. https://www.gov.uk/tier-1-entrepreneur (last consulted on 28/09/2016).
8. https://www.gov.uk/government/publications/entrepreneurs-setting-up-in-the-uk/entre preneurs-setting-up-in-the-uk (last consulted on 28/09/2016).
9. https://www.gov.uk/guidance/collective-investment-schemes-centre-contacts (last consulted on 16/09/2016).
10. https://www.gov.uk/hmrc-internal-manuals/venture-capital-schemes-manual/vcm50010 (last consulted on 04/10/2016). Similar to an investment trust, a VCT is an HMRC-approved company which subscribes for shares in, or lends money to, small unquoted companies. Under the VCT scheme, VCTs and their investors enjoy certain tax reliefs.
11. https://www.gov.uk/government/publications/the-enterprise-investment-scheme-introd uction/enterprise-investment-scheme (last consulted on 16/09/2016).
12. https://www.gov.uk/topic/business-tax/investment-schemes; https://www.gov.uk/guidan ce/seed-enterprise-investment-scheme-background (last consulted on 16/09/2016).
13. https://www.gov.uk/guidance/seed-enterprise-investment-scheme-how-companies-quali fy (last consulted on 19/09/2016).
14. https://www.gov.uk/guidance/seed-enterprise-investment-scheme-investment-and-inves tor-requirements (last consulted on 19/09/2016).
15. https://www.gov.uk/guidance/seed-enterprise-investment-scheme-procedures (last consulted on 19/09/2016).
16. On 1 October 2013, Capital for Enterprise Ltd transferred its operations and staff to the British Business Bank Programme. Source: https://www.gov.uk/government/organisa tions/capital-for-enterprise-ltd; http://british-business-bank.co.uk/ (last consulted on 07/10/2016). The Department for Business, Innovation and Skills (BIS) and the Department of Energy and Climate Change (DECC) merged to form the Department for Business, Energy and Industrial Strategy (BEIS) in July 2016. Source: https://www. gov.uk/government/organisations/department-for-business-innovation-skills; https:// www.gov.uk/government/organisations/department-for-business-energy-and-industrial -strategy (last consulted on 19/09/2016).
17. http://capitalenterprise.org (last consulted on 01/11/2016).
18. http://lcif.co (last consulted on 01/11/2016).
19. Source: https://journolink.com/release/the_london_tech_scenes_best_kept_secret_594 (last consulted on 01/11/2016).
20. Source: https://www.linkedin.com/pulse/launch-londons-74m-programme-support-sca le-up-london-tech-spindler (last consulted 01/11/2016).
21. STEM refers to Science, Technology, Engineering and Mathematics.
22. https://paris.numa.co/en/ (last consulted on 24/11/2016).
23. Silicon Sentier is a non-profit association founded by entrepreneurs in 2000 as an entity that stimulates networking between enterprises and embodies the digital identity in Ile de France. It is sponsored by strategic partners such as R&D Orange, Ile de France, Mayor of Paris and Cap Digital.
24. https://yeswecrowd.co (last consulted 29/11/2016).
25. http://deepscienceventures.com (last consulted 01/11/2016).
26. http://www.synbicite.com (last consulted 24/11/2016).

REFERENCES

Acs, Z.J., Audretsch, D.B., Lehmann, E.E. and Licht, G. (2016). National systems of entrepreneurship, *Small Business Economics*, 16(4): 527–535.

Acs, Z.J. and Szerb, L. (2007). Entrepreneurship, economic growth and public policy, *Small Business Economics*, 28(2): 109–122.

Acs, Z.J., Szerb, L. and Autio, E. (2016). Enhancing entrepreneurial ecosystems: A GEI approach to entrepreneurship policy. In: Acs, Z.J., Szerb, L. and Autio, E. (eds), *Global Entrepreneurship Index 2016*, Chapter 4 (pp.63–72), The Global Entrepreneurship and Development Institute, Washington, DC, USA.

Aernoudt, R. (2004). Incubators: Tool for entrepreneurship?, *Small Business Economics*, 23(2): 127–135.

Armanios, D.E., Eesley, C.E., Li, J. and Eisenhardt, K.M. (2017). How entrepreneurs leverage institutional intermediaries in emerging economies to acquire public resources, *Strategic Management Journal*, 38(7): 1373–1390.

Audretsch, D.B. and Peña-Legazkue, I. (2012). Entrepreneurial activity and regional competitiveness: An introduction to the special issue, *Small Business Economics*, 39: 531–537.

Autio, E., Kenney, M., Mustar, P., Siegel, D. and Wright, M. (2014). Entrepreneurial innovation: The importance of context, *Research Policy*, 43(7): 1097–1108.

Barbero, J.L., Casillas, J.C., Wright, M. and Garcia A.C. (2014). Do different types of incubators produce different types of innovations?, *Journal of Technology Transfer*, 39(2): 151–168.

Bone, J., Allen, O. and Haley, C. (2017). Business incubators and accelerators: The national picture. BEIS research paper 7. London, UK.

Cowling, M., Bates, P., Jagger, N. and Murray, G. (2008). Study of the impact of the Enterprise Investment Scheme (EIS) and Venture Capital Trusts (VCTs) on company performance, HMRC Research Report 44. London, UK.

Drexler, M., Eltogby, M., Foster, G., Shimizu, C., Ciesinsik, S., Davila, A., Hassan, S.Z., Jia, N., Lee, D., Plunkett, S., Pinelli, M., Cunningham, J., Hiscock-Croft, R., McLenithan, M., Rottenberg, L. and Morris, R. (2014). *Entrepreneurial Ecosystems around the Globe and Early-Stage Company Growth Dynamics*, World Economic Forum, Geneva, Switzerland.

Dutt, N., Hawn, O., Vidal, E., Chatterji, A.K., McGahan, A.M. and Mitchell, W. (2015). How open system intermediaries address institutional failures: The case of business incubators in emerging market economies, *Academy of Management Journal*, 59(3): 818–840.

Gonzalez-Uribe, J. and Leatherbee, M. (2017). The effects of business accelerators on venture performance: Evidence from Start-Up Chile, *Review of Financial Studies*, hhx103, https://doi.org/10.1093/rfs/hhx103.

Hallen, B.L., Bingham, C.B. and Cohen, S.L. (2014). Do accelerators accelerate? A study of venture accelerators as a path to success?, *Academy of Management Proceedings*, 2014(1), 12955.

Isenberg, D.J. (2010). How to start an entrepreneurial revolution, *Harvard Business Review*, 88(6): 40–50.

Mian, S.A. (2011). *Science and Technology Based Regional Entrepreneurship: Global Experience in Policy and Program Development*, Edward Elgar Publishing, Cheltenham, UK and Northampton, MA, USA.

Mustar, P. and Wright, M. (2010). Convergence or path dependency in policies to foster the creation of university spin-off firms? A comparison of France and the United Kingdom, *Journal of Technology Transfer*, 35: 42–65.

Nightingale, P., Murray, G., Cowling, M., Baden-Fuller, C., Mason, C., Siepel, J., Hopkins, M. and Dannreuther, C. (2009). From funding gaps to thin markets: UK Government support for early-stage venture capital. Nesta, London, UK.

Pauwels, C., Clarysse, B., Wright, M. and Van Hove, J. (2015). Understanding a new generation incubation model: The accelerator, *Technovation*, 50–51: 13–24.

Salido, E., Sabás, M. and Freixas, P. (2013). The accelerator and incubator ecosystem in Europe. Telefónica Europe.

Sivonen, P., Borella, P., Thomas L.D.W. and Sharapov D. (2015). How an accelerator can catalyse your ecosystem, *European Business Review*, September 17.

Spigel, B. (2015). The relational organization of entrepreneurial ecosystems, *Entrepreneurship, Theory and Practice*, 41(1): 49–72.

Szerb, L.A., Acs, Z. and Autio, E. (2013). Entrepreneurship and policy: The national system of entrepreneurship in the European Union and its member countries, *Entrepreneurship Research Journal*, 3(1): 9–34.

Walters, K., Stacey, J., Haley, C. and Roberts, I. (2014). *Startup Accelerator Programmes: A Practice Guide*. Nesta, London, UK.

West, J., Salter, A., Vanhaverbeke, W. and Chesbrough, H. (2014). Open innovation: The next decade, *Research Policy*, 43(5): 805–811.

9. Emergence of accelerators and accelerator policy: the case of Australia

Martin Bliemel, Saskia de Klerk, Ricardo Flores and Morgan P. Miles

INTRODUCTION

This study describes the process by which accelerators and accelerator policy co-emerged in Australia. To illustrate the process, case studies are presented, with emphasis on accelerators headquartered in Sydney. Australia seems to be a particularly interesting context to explore the evolution of accelerators because it has historically had an underdeveloped venture capital (VC) industry (when compared to that of the US) and multiple "boomerang entrepreneurs" (Dana, 1996)—entrepreneurs who migrate overseas and return—who continuously try to improve Australia's entrepreneurial output. Scholars have highlighted that these incubators, accelerators, venture capitalists and policies and their relationships interdependently evolve over time in ways that are unique to each country (Geels, 2004). For instance, the emergence of venture capitalists in the US was a key contributor to their national innovation system (Kenney, 2011; Samila and Sorenson, 2010). This is supported by Kortum and Lerner (2000, p. 675), who found that a reinterpretation of the US Employee Retirement Income Security Act in 1979 "freed pensions to invest in venture capital," and from 1983 to 1992 resulted in "about 8% of U.S. industrial innovations of the decade." Similarly, the emergence of incubators significantly contributed to the development of Taiwan's innovation system (Tsai et al., 2009).

The Australian story, however, involves several false starts with VC and incubators. More recently, a diverse range of start-up support organizations have emerged, including accelerators, pre-accelerators, incubators and germinators (as defined in Bliemel et al., 2016). Only after the early emergence of these organizations did the federal government review their business models and develop policy in hopes of guiding the industry towards full-service support (i.e., acceleration).

BACKGROUND LITERATURE

Prior to reviewing and discussing the development of policy and organizations related to incubators and accelerators, some conceptual clarity is required in relation to organizational labels and their meaning. This is particularly the case as some organizations deliberately avoided using the most appropriate label to disassociate themselves from prior failures of that type of business, while others unintentionally used inconsistent labels without consideration of their actual definition.

Business Incubation

Broadly defined, business incubators (BIs) are facilities that shelter vulnerable new firms until they can survive in the environment. Hackett and Dilts (2004) define BIs as "a shared office space facility that seeks to provide its incubatees [. . .] with a strategic, value-adding intervention system of monitoring and business assistance" (p. 57). However, incubators have changed significantly over time (Grimaldi and Grandi, 2005), spanning three "generations" (Bruneel et al., 2012). The first generation of incubators focused on regional development, venture survival and employment, creating economies of scale which could be passed on to start-ups along with government subsidized rent, much like modern co-working spaces. Second generation BIs moved to a value-added model by directly providing coaching and professional services. By the third generation, discounted space was incidental in comparison to the intangible resources available via the incubator operators (Grimaldi and Grandi, 2005; Bruneel et al., 2012), at times including ad hoc investments into incubatees (von Zedtwitz, 2003; Carayannis and von Zedtwitz, 2005). Interestingly, a for-profit investment model through taking equity is sometimes seen as being in conflict with charging incubatees fees for rent and professional services. Despite this evolution, at their core, BIs are largely organizations that support businesses through subsidized rents, management assistance, technology assistance and in some cases funding.

Accelerators

Accelerators are a recent breed of organization resembling incubators. The term accelerator emerged in the academic literature with Price's early definition:

> A *Business Accelerator* is an organisation that provides relatively short-term support to companies that have already been formed and which have a

well-defined business purpose. Services may include anything that assists the business to optimise its growth, either through strengthening its infrastructure, redefining is products and services to answer the needs of its target market, or preparing it for exits and mergers. (2004, p. 466, emphasis in original)

Because of the newness of the phenomenon and literature, "there is little formal academic literature on the subject and no universally accepted definition of what an accelerator is" (Barrehag et al., 2012). Earlier references relate accelerators to incubators (von Zedtwitz, 2003; Carayannis and von Zedtwitz, 2005; Grimaldi and Grandi, 2005), despite there being "no evidence in the literature that accelerators examined incubators for guidance" (Hoffman and Radojevich-Kelley 2012, p. 57). Since 2011, an increasing number of articles have been adopting Miller and Bound's (2011) definition that "the accelerator programme model comprises five main features", consisting of: (1) "An application process that is open to all, yet highly competitive"; (2) "Provision of pre-seed investment, usually in exchange for equity"; (3) "A focus on small teams not individual founders"; (4) "Time-limited support comprising programmed events and intensive mentoring"; and (5) "Cohorts or 'classes' of start-ups rather than individual companies" (e.g., Barrehag et al., 2012; Los Kamp, 2013; Fehder and Hochberg, 2014; Pauwels et al., 2016). In order to disentangle the interdependencies of these factors, Bliemel et al. (2016) identify accelerators as a combination of "(i) Seed funding, (ii) cohort-based entry and exit, (iii) co-location, (iv) a structured programme, and (v) mentoring." Altogether, accelerators are structured as "primarily a funding mechanism [and] two critical factors differentiate them from other business development programs: (1) their focus on the development of scalable high-growth, high-value start-ups, and (2) the ability of graduates to access the program directors' vast social networks" (Porat, 2014, p. 2).

Pre-accelerators

A variant of an accelerator is the pre-accelerator, which does not require participants to be founders or to issue equity. Pre-accelerators focus more on entrepreneurial competency development than on business development and are popular with universities (Voisey, Jones and Thomas, 2013), particularly when supporting student-based ventures and the "entrepreneurial university" (Wright, Siegel and Mustar, 2017). As a result, most pre-accelerators often resemble coursework programs, and only temporarily need access to facilities, not full-time co-location or full-time commitment of the founders to their ventures.

Germinators

A hybrid form of accelerator is the "germinator," which (like incubators) provide space and do not operate on a cohort model. Like accelerators, germinators take equity and have a structured program through which to accelerate the start-up. The key feature of germinators is that they actively participate in the co-founding of the start-up (Hannon, 2004; Bliemel et al., 2016). Germinators are sometimes also referred to as labs or start-up factories, like IdeaLab, founded in 1996 "to test many ideas at once and turn the best of them into companies, while also attracting the human and financial capital necessary to bring them to market."[1]

RESEARCH DESIGN

This study is part of a larger project seeking to understand the evolution and performance of different start-up support organizations within Australia. The Australian context is interesting for several reasons. First, Australia shares many cultural aspects with the US, the global leader in VC and high-technology start-ups. Second, many Australians have easily assimilated into the Silicon Valley high-technology community, while some of these have returned to Australia as "boomerang" entrepreneurs. Third, Australia seems to lack international leadership in several high-technology sectors, but seems to have some relatively competitive sectors, particularly the information and communications technology (ICT) sector. Lastly, the VC, angel capital and accelerator organizations have only recently become more established. The last point makes it easier to find recent historical records and give researchers the opportunity to talk with key participants.

As a first step in this exploration, we have collected data on the emergence of accelerators in Australia, drawing on several secondary data sources including public media, industry and government reports, some academic theses, and other available sources. This data search is complemented by the first-hand experience of the authors with accelerators and pre-accelerators in Australia, Canada and New Zealand, as well as extensive contact with the technology entrepreneurship community in Sydney since July 2009.

This archival research is augmented with a mixed methods design (Creswell and Clark, 2011) conducted over a four-year period using a series of semi-structured and structured interviews with accelerators (of all types). Over this period, 82 organizations were identified in Australia as relating to acceleration and invited to participate in the interviews. The total sample as at the end of 2016 consisted of 36 organizations. These included 5 start-up support organizations (3 co-working spaces, 1 angel organization and 1 mentoring organisation) as reference points and 31 accelerators. As sub-classified by Bliemel et al. (2016), the accelerators included 16 archetypical accelerators, 6 university-based accelerators, 6 pre-accelerators, 2 incubators and 1 germinator. Notably, most of these organizations were start-ups themselves and changed business models, as revealed in greater detail below.

EVOLUTION OF THE AUSTRALIAN ENTREPRENEURIAL ECOSYSTEM

This section reviews the historic context (and co-evolutionary processes) in which accelerators emerged in Australia. Through archival research pivotal actors within the Australian innovation system were identified: 1) the commonwealth government (and associated agencies); 2) the private providers of capital (venture capitalists, angels, etc.), 3) some key start-ups and entrepreneurs (whose success and relevance reverberated over time within the ecosystem) and 4) the start-up supporters (incubators, accelerators, etc.). Four eras in this "history" of the evolution of the Australian innovation system are evident: 1) the dark ages (1983–1995); 2) the dawn of VC (1995–2003); 3) the emergence of accelerators (2004–2016) and 4) the "IdeasBoom" period (2016–current). It is important to note that these eras have no precise date at which they end and the next one begins because some events and organizations that define each era overlap. For each of these eras, we review key actors and events.

Figure 9.1 depicts the first three eras as a visual time line and indicates significant interrelations between start-ups and support organizations. Noteworthy, is that this is limited to only two interrelations. In other words, the early start-up success stories were not a product of the incubators and accelerators. And, only very recently did some of these role model start-ups start to support the incubators and accelerators. Likewise, while the VC industry has had some success with its investments, it has historically operated with limited connection to the ICT start-up scene and independently of incubators and accelerators.

Figure 9.2 reflects the early emergence of incubators in Australia up until 2001, after which point annual data was not available. The lack of data and the current absence of such high numbers of incubators indicates that the incubation industry crashed around the dot-com crash, likely as collateral damage to the bad reputation start-ups gained globally.

Figure 9.3 reflects the low rate of start-up creation leading up to the dawn of the Internet. In the last decade, following inspirations from

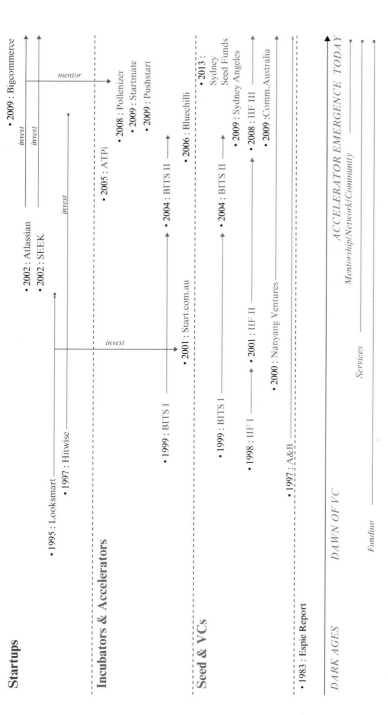

Figure 9.1   Evolution of the Australian innovation system

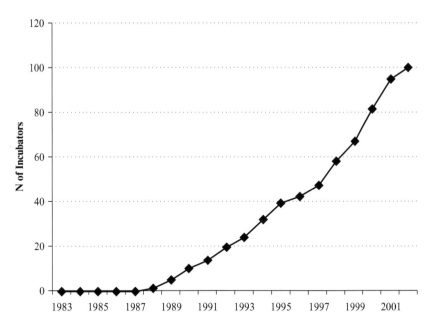

Figure 9.2   Total incubators over time

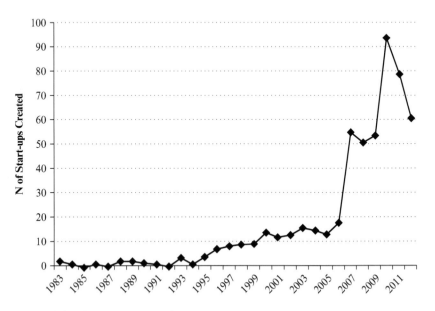

Figure 9.3   Start-ups created per year

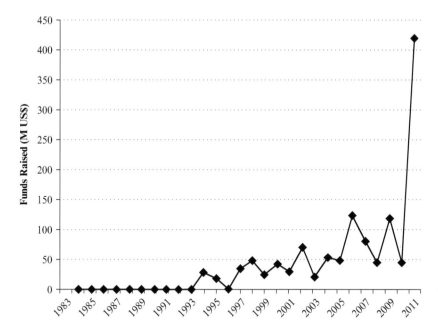

Source: Data from Suchard and Humphery-Jenner (2011).

Figure 9.4   VC funds raised per year

overseas, the rates have climbed dramatically, but remain low overall. The most recent estimates from an annual Australian start-up survey indicate that there are approximately 1,500 active start-ups (Startup Muster, 2016).

As with the emergence of a start-up sector, the VC industry has seen a marked increase in liquidity in recent years (Figure 9.4). For the first time ever, pension funds have voluntarily allocated a small portion of their capital to VC pools. Altogether there was an estimated A\$2 billion in VC in 2016 (Baldassarre, 2016).[2]

The Dark Ages (1983–1995)

This era is defined by a significant lack of local private VC. Two key events define this era:

1. An influential government report (the Espie Report) that laid out how the Australian government might help create an active VC industry; and

2. The formation of the Australian Private Equity and Venture Capital Association Limited (AVCAL).

Espie Report (1983)

In 1983, the High Technology Financing Committee of the Australian Academy of Technological Sciences (AATS) led by Sir Frank Espie provided a report to the Minister for Science and Technology. In particular, the report (AATS, 1983) recommended that the Australian government needed to facilitate the flow of risk capital by creating investment companies in the form of "Growth Business Investment and Management Companies (GBIMC's)". GBIMC's would play the role of start-up supporters analogously to the role played later by incubators and other private organizations, as visualized in Figure 9.5. In essence, a licensing board was expected to issue GBIMC's licenses, which in turn provide funds and management capabilities to promising new start-ups in exchange for equity. This report is commonly identified as the genesis of the current VC industry (AusIndustry, 2012).

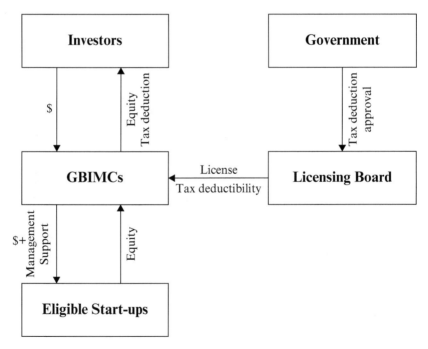

Figure 9.5   Espie model

Australian Private Equity and Venture Capital Association Limited (1992–1994)

In 1992, nearly a decade later, the Australian Private Equity and Venture Capital Association Limited (AVCAL) was eventually established. AVCAL's members comprised most of the active private equity and VC firms in Australia, ranging from firms who provided early stage capital for start-ups through to capital for management buyouts of established companies. Along with the creation of this organization, the first formal VC fund was created in 1994: Nanyang Ventures Pty Ltd. This fund was co-founded by Chris Golis, an individual who is considered "an elder statesman of the Australian venture capital community" (Riordan, 1996). Nanyang Ventures has been a key VC player throughout the early evolution of the Australian innovation system and had invested in 40+ new ventures by 2003.

The Dawn of VC (1995–2003)

While the response was not immediate, the Australian National Innovation System did eventually react to the Espie Report. We review these changes in the following sections.

Venture Capitalists and Innovation Investment Funds (1998 and 2001)

In 1998, 15 years after the Espie Report, the Australian government created the Innovation Investment Fund (IIF) program to encourage VC investments and commercialization of Australia's research. In the IIF model (summarized in Figure 9.6), the government matched funds raised by venture capitalists at a ratio of 1:1 or more, and passed the majority of the disbursements from an exit to the venture capitalists. The IIF programs were designed to be invested within the first five years, and were expected to generate returns over the next five years. In the first round of IIF, five funds were supported with a total funding of A$197.4 million, with the government providing $130 million and the private sector A$67.4 million (DIISR, 2011). A second round was launched in 2001, releasing a total of A$156.6 million in VC (A$90.7 million from government funds matched by A$65.9 million from the private sector). The second round of funds was hit by two external shocks: first by the dot-com bubble, which reduced the rate and scope of investments, then second by the Global Finance Crisis (GFC), which restricted the capacity of IIF fund managers to raise new capital and reduced exit possibilities for existing investments.

Trying to respond to the IIF funds, VC organizations were quickly created by notable individuals. Allen & Buckeridge (formed 1997) and Macquarie Bank (formed 1998) created two of the most influential funds.

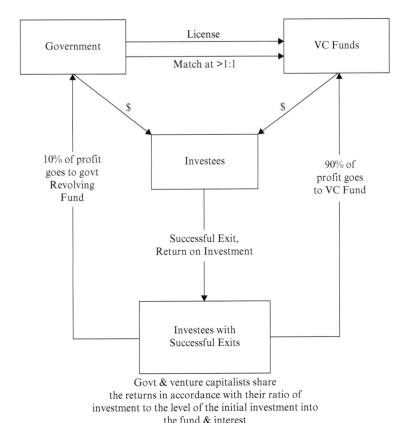

Figure 9.6   IIF model

Collectively, these venture capitalists represented a new set of organizations that were able to channel over A$300 million into over 70 new ventures (Lowe, 2001a, 2001b).

Start-ups
In the late 1990s and early 2000s, a handful of Australian companies started to stand out as success stories within the ICT and VC industry, including *Looksmart* (founded 1995), *Hitwise* and *Seek* (both founded in 1997). Each of these firms received a mix of VC from Australia and the US, with most later-stage funding coming from the US. Only one of these ventures received IIF funding: *Looksmart*. Throughout the process of developing their businesses, the entrepreneurs generally relocated to the US and remained there for several years. Some of these entrepreneurs

wanted to help other "mates" to follow in their footsteps. For instance, three months after their initial public offering (IPO) in 1999, Looksmart bought a controlling share of start.com.au, a small Australian free email service provider. Another (later) success story was *Atlassian*, which was launched in 2002. Atlassian did not receive angel or venture capital through any organized program. It was initially funded using only a credit card and some revenues from contract programming. While relatively unremarkable at the time, Atlassian's founders would later become Australia's youngest ever recipients of the Ernst & Young Entrepreneurs of the Year award. In 2010, they raised US$60 million from the US and eventually had an IPO in 2015 at a market capitalization of US$4.37 billion.

Incubators
While the "Dawn of VC" era is dominated by the emergence of venture capitalists and the IIF program, it also includes the genesis of the first generation of technology BIs. By 1997, business incubation was relatively established in Australia (Schaper and Lewer, 2009), and a BI association (then "ANZABI") had published best practices (Dowling and ANZABI, 1997). At the time, the bulk of the incubators were entirely focused on supporting small businesses and on their own survival by "aim[ing] to operate at greater than 90% occupancy" (ibid., p. 1–15). A high-growth mind-set was absent, as evidenced by only one mention of *equity* as a single aside in the section about incubator financial plans. Technology start-ups were only one of many tenants, and were not yet an exclusive focus of any incubators. A lack of specialized focus on technology start-ups could likely be because the popularization of the Internet and related start-ups (e.g., the dot-com era) had not yet occurred.

BITS I and BITS II (1999 and 2004)
In 1999 the Australian government launched the *Building on Information Technology Strengths* (BITS) program as a continued commitment to develop the IT sector in Australia. The BITS program consisted in the establishment of 11 incubators across Australia to help entrepreneurs turn their ideas into globally competitive businesses. The program was backed by A$158 million over five years (ending in June 2004) to establish BIs in conjunction with seed stage funding. Each incubator facility was managed by a consortium of investors (including KPMG, the Commonwealth Scientific and Industrial Research Organisation (CSIRO) and universities) and provided tenants with professional services (mentoring, consulting, capital-raising advice, business model development). Table 9.1 summarizes which BITS incubators were set up in which states, and who operated them, including some recipients of the IIF funds. To a certain extent, the

Table 9.1   BITS program and incubators

Incubator name	Location	Consortium
Allen & Buckeridge Seed Stage Ventures Pty Ltd	NSW/VIC	Allen & Buckeridge Pty Ltd
Australian Distributed Incubator (ADI) Pty Ltd	VIC	EMERGE CMC Ltd; Ernst & Young; Babcock & Brown (via its subsidiary AIDC Ltd); Greyhair.com Pty Ltd
BlueFire Group Incubator Pty Ltd/ Divergent Capital	NSW	BlueFire Group Pty Ltd BlueFire Innovation Pty Ltd
Entrepreneurs in Residence (EiR) Pty Ltd	WA	Imago Multimedia Centre Ltd; Zernike (Australia) Pty Ltd; Software Engineering Australia (WA) Ltd
Epicorp Ltd	ACT	Anutech Pty Ltd; CSIRO; University of Canberra Australian National University
Information City Victoria (ICV) Pty Ltd	VIC	Joint Technology Partners; Melbourne IT; Photonics RedCentre (a spin off from Australian Photonics); University of Ballarat—Greenhill Enterprise Centre; Ericsson Australia Pty Ltd
inQbator	QLD	Timsco Pty Ltd is the owner and operator of inQbator.
ITem3 Pty Ltd	NSW	Iplus Development Pty Ltd; Lateral Concepts International Pty Ltd Software Engineering Australia (NSW) Ltd
Original IT Investments Pty Ltd	NT	Nexus Energy Limited (formerly eNTITy1 Limited); Darwin International Textile Pty Ltd; Northern Territory University
Playford Capital Pty Ltd	SA	The Playford Centre; Ngapartji Pty Ltd
Intellinc Pty Ltd	TAS	ITem3 Pty Ltd; KPMG (Tasmania); University of Tasmania

Note: States: Australian Capital Territory (ACT), New South Wales (NSW), Northern Territory (NT), Queensland (QLD), South Australia (SA), Tasmania (TAS), Victoria (VIC) and Western Australia (WA).

Source: Allen Consulting Group (2003).

business models of these BITS BIs were closer to accelerators than many of the other BIs that later emerged. By November 2003, the performance of the BITS I encouraged the government to extend the program for a second round (BITS II). The second round was funded by A$36 million and the program was renamed the ICT Incubators Program (ICTIP). In June 2008, the eight remaining incubators and the program were restructured, and most of these BIs are no longer active.

ATPi, Mark I

Conceptualized in 1991 and officially opened in 1996 (Farrelly, 1996), Australian Technology Park (ATP) in Sydney would become a key organization within the Australian National Innovation System. In 2000, ATP Innovations (ATPi) was formed as a formal incubator subsidiary of ATP. ATPi was given a 99-year lease, rumored to be for an extremely low symbolic amount. It was formed by a consortium of four research-intensive universities with the goal to focus on incubating new early stage ventures. In its early days, ATPi resembled a pure first generation incubator, with a strong emphasis on providing space to early stage ventures at favorable rates and with minimal emphasis on access to professional services or capital. As is common for incubators following a landlord–tenant business model, ATPi's initial operations revolved around renting out as much space as possible: "In the early days, if you had a heartbeat and more than a dollar in the bank account, you were welcomed in with loving arms" (interview data). However, that operating model was deemed as unsustainable after a few years of operation. In the following five years, ATPi transitioned to an operating model emphasizing the creation of value for the ventures they attracted. This transition implied churning the "space fillers [and] zombie companies" (ibid.) and "replacing them with high quality, high-growth businesses, refining our value proposition to our portfolio companies and really focusing on the value that we can create as an incubator for our incubatees" (ibid.). This value proposition included providing in-house professional advice and mentoring, and introductions to external investors. Due to the transition to a value-added model, they managed to accumulate modest profits and were "doing a really good job at running a sustainable high growth business ourselves, as well as having a portfolio of companies that were doing the same thing" (ibid.).

Other government programs

In addition to the IIF and BITS programs, the Australian government launched a few additional programs related to start-ups and technology commercialization. Commercialising Emerging Technologies (COMET) was a merit-based grant program tailored to early-growth-stage companies, spin-off companies and individuals. COMET commenced in 1999 and closed to new applications on 1 January 2010. The Australian Technology Showcase (ATS) commenced in the lead-up to the 2000 Olympics, with a focus on identifying innovative, market ready Australian technologies with global market potential. Part of the ATS program was an overseas road show to meet with potential industrial clients. In 2001 the Pre-Seed Fund (PSF) program was designed to encourage private sector involvement in the commercialization of publicly funded early stage research. The establishment of the PSF program was predicated on the view that research institutions, including universities, Cooperative Research Centres (CRCs) and publicly funded research agencies lacked appropriate commercialization expertise, and that more funding would be necessary to make a given technology "investment-ready."

The Emergence of Accelerators (2004–2015)

This era is driven mainly by entrepreneurs, some of whom became angel investors or otherwise got involved in accelerating or germinating more new ventures. Meanwhile, venture capitalists moved upstream to keep their older investments alive given the difficulties of raising large sums of funds due to the GFC (Business Review Australia, 2011). The government continued its involvement by providing additional institutional changes and fresh funds. Key issues within this era are discussed below.

Extended government intervention: VCLP, ESVCLP and IIF Round 3
The Early Stage Venture Capital Limited Partnerships (ESVCLP) and Venture Capital Limited Partnerships (VCLP) provide tax benefits to private investors. They remove the necessity for the government to provide up-front capital. The VCLP program was introduced in 2002 to provide a world-class investment vehicle to encourage new foreign and domestic investment into the Australian VC industry. The program provides flow through back-end tax benefits (i.e., benefits are only accessed when investments are sold, not when they are made) to foreign and domestic investors, as well as fund managers. The VCLP program is continuously open for new applications. As of June 2011, the program has committed A\$4.98 billion—approximately 20 percent is foreign sourced. It has A\$2.1 billion invested in 578 eligible deals, of which 63 percent of the deals are pre-seed, seed, start-up and early expansion. The ESVCLP program was introduced in 2007, and is continuously open for new applications. As of June 2011, a total of A\$120 million has been raised through the ESVCLP program, with 67 percent being from the IIF program. Unlike the previous two rounds of IIF, Round 3 used a staged approach for licensing with a target of up to ten

new funds to be licensed over a five-year period—nominally two per year. This approach provides a more consistent flow of VC over time (i.e., new investment will be supported for a period of nine years rather than just five years, which would have been the case if all the funds were licensed simultaneously) and avoids momentary flooding of the market.

Grassroots organization of the start-up sector

Commencing around 2009, the start-up sector started becoming more self-organized, leading to active lobbying for policy change and engagement with policy makers. A catalyst for this self-organization was the formation of Fishburners.org, a large co-working space centrally located in the city. While the space focuses on housing tech start-ups, it is also home to a new lobbyist organization, StartupAus.org, and home to StartupMuster.com, who run an annual survey about the start-up ecosystem. StartupAus's main output is an annual report, the Crossroads Report, which provides an increasingly detailed account of the state of the start-up sector as well as funding levels, along with several well-researched policy recommendations (e.g., changes to Employee Stock Option Plans, visa programs, tax incentives for investors, R&D tax concessions, support for incubators, accelerators and industry organizations, and more). In parallel to StartupAus (supported by Google Australia, who developed Google Maps and Google Wave), other industry associations, societies and lobbyist groups have emerged, which have common interests. These include TheStartSociety.com and TechSydney.com.au.

The impact of this self-organization of the start-up sector, including incubators and accelerators, is evidenced by their frequent commentary in documents such as Tech Startups Action Plan by the City of Sydney (Recke and Bliemel, 2018) and by the level of interaction between government and the sector at events like PolicyHack.com.au.

Angel capital

A 2006 review of angel investing in Australia identified 12 angel organizations (Vitale, Everingham and Butler, 2006). In the same year, Innovation Bay was formed, which runs angel/investor dinners four times per year across three cities, each with four to five presenting start-ups. In 2007, the Australian Association of Angel Investors (AAAI) was founded with the aim of driving the growth, success and sustainability of angel investing as a professional practice in Australia. In 2008, Sydney Angels, a Sydney-based risk capital organization, was co-founded by members of the angel investing community, including the then CEO of ATPi.

ATPi, Mark II

As ATPi transitioned from a first generation to a third generation incubator, providing seed capital and mentoring was never the *primary* focus of their business model. Nonetheless, it remains a key differentiating factor in comparison to other incubators and accelerators. With regards to mentoring, ATPi seems to be

> slightly different to [. . .] an accelerator or other incubators, where [. . .] the majority of those are set up where there is a group of mentors who sit *around* the accelerator or incubator that provide a lot of value. We, through our scale, have chosen to take a different approach by bringing that talent in-house. So the vast majority of the value that's delivered to our portfolio of companies is from people who are on the payroll of ATPi. (Interview data, emphasis in original)

In terms of seed capital, ATPi provides small amounts, typically between 1 and 5 percent. The rationale for the seed investment is to share in the upside of the venture's success and capture some of the value that is being delivered.

Providing seed capital is also important as a mechanism

> to introduce some mutual obligation to our clients. [. . .] We know that if we have a small piece of equity in the business, we are on [a] level playing field with the founders. We're aligned with them. They'll listen to us because they don't see us as a landlord sitting in the room, we're a shareholder. (Interview data)

The share of equity taken is also deliberately small:

> The problem is that if you're taking 20–30% you're going to find a lot of unhappy people that don't think they've got the value. That's the trap when you are taking significant equity stakes. You become a co-founder. And we have 55 companies in our portfolio. We can't be co-founders to 55 people. It's not possible. I have a team of 5 executives and we struggle with a portfolio of 55 companies. So if you're over-promising and under-delivering, you'll have very unhappy customers. We under-promise and way over-deliver because we're aligned with the founders. (Ibid.)

ATPi also hosts the operations of two accelerators, or as they call them, "programs" (Startmate and IgnitionLabs). For both "programs," they contribute some of the seed capital, space and mentorship, and provide a full-time staff member to help with operations. The rationale for ATPi to host the accelerators includes the ability for ATPi to learn how to run a more structured cohort-based program, while opening their doors to a sector of ventures they typically had not focused on. The rationale for the accelerator to be located at ATPi (instead of in any other popular co-working space) includes being physically co-located with other ventures in ATPi and benefiting from the value-added services already delivered "on demand" by ATPi.

In terms of labeling, ATPi currently uses the label "incubator" liberally. However, this was not always the case due to perceptions of the meaning of the label:

> There was *a lot* of baggage with the word "incubator". So, for a long time, we didn't call ourselves an incubator because it was very negative. We called our-selves a commercialization hub. We called ourselves an accelerator (before any of the current accelerators started using that label), a precinct, an ecosystem . . . lots of words [. . .] but *not* the I-word. (Interview data, emphasis in original)

Since 2006, ATPi has worked with more than 80 businesses, helping them raise over A$121 million in private investment and secure more than A$28 million of competitive government grants, leading to seven exits via acquisition and one initial public offering (IPO). Notably, ATPi won the Randall M. Whaley Incubator of the Year Award, granted by the National Business Incubator Association. In 2016, ATPi was rebranded to Cicada Innovations to make more symbolic reference to its focus on emerging and "deep" technology.

Overall, ATPi's story reflects the extent to which many incubators and accelerators are new ventures themselves, and how they evolve in pursuit of their own survival and growth. It also highlights a potential source for confusion since some of these organizations using the incubator label can include features associated with accelerators without cohort-based seed investment being their primary focus or even ultimate aim. In this respect, the physical space of incubators provides benefits as well as drawbacks. While physical space is an asset to incubators, and gives them the option to host not only entrepreneurs and their incipient ventures but also other potentially reinforcing organizations such as accelerators, the operating costs of maintain the building and lease (if applicable) can also become a liability.

Startmate accelerator

During this era, multiple seed accelerators emerged, often derivatives of the Y Combinator or Techstars model in the US, but without formal con-nections to these US accelerators. The most prominent one was Startmate, which laid the groundwork for others to follow (e.g., using the same lawyers to figure out the corporate structure). Startmate was founded in 2010 by a returning Australian entrepreneur and two of his old friends, who happened to be the co-founders of Atlassian. The decision to start the accelerator was a by-product of one of the founders returning to Australia with the intention to launch another venture of his own, and to invest in a small number of others on the side. When reconnecting with local entrepreneurs he knew from his university days, the decision to collaborate on an accelerator became a natural extension of those initial intentions and was driven more by impulse than analysis. In their words,

> The idea was to move back to Australia and start another company, another software business [. . .] So that was the plan. And invest in one or two companies per year and try to help the startups. I came back. And I was catching up with [the other founder] and we said "F**k it!" Let's just invest in five companies. (Interview data)

The other founder argued that since

> Y-Combinator had just done a few of their batches. It was an interesting mechanism, particularly to learn how to be a good investor: invest a small amount of money in a large amount of companies and try to be helpful to them. It gives you a lot of data points as to who's a good team, who's a bad team. It felt right in terms of where Australia was [. . .] So, the idea was not written down in any form, it was really just a coffee. And it was just like "OK, let's get this and network with people and get them to invest a small amount of money each [. . .] but even if they don't, you and I, let's just invest in 5 companies and see how it goes." That was the extent of the planning. (Interview data)

Startmate quickly gained momentum with the entrepreneurial community and grew to approximately 40 investors who all agreed to mentor all of the portfolio companies. As reflected in the above quotation, the accelerator model devised for Startmate was primarily focused on investment and advice, and did not involve renting out physical space to start-ups. It could therefore be started without first becoming a landlord or office manager and worrying about maximizing occupancy or deal flow at the expense of deal quality. As of 2013, Startmate has graduated 21 ventures over multiple cohorts, many of which have gone on to raise significant follow-on capital.

Germinators

While most accelerators take in existing ventures with advanced prototypes in exchange for a small percentage of equity, another type of "accelerator" has emerged that takes on a more active managerial role by co-founding the venture prior to a functional prototype in exchange for a much larger stake in the incipient venture. Because this type of organization co-creates the venture while it is still in the idea stage, it has been labeled "germinator" (Hannon, 2004). Two organizations in our sample, Pollenizer and BlueChilli, initially fitted with this germinator type before morphing into even more hybridized organizations.

Pollenizer and BlueChilli both originated from the founders' prior experiences as entrepreneurs and their interest in supporting other entrepreneurs at a larger scale. Early on, both businesses relied heavily on service revenues as digital agencies, and eventually raised modest and then significant funds. These funds enabled them to launch more start-ups of their own, for which they would recruit co-founders who were rewarded with equity (5 to 15 percent) and a modest salary. The funds also allowed them to invest in entrepreneurs who approached them with little more than an idea, for which the germinator would help develop the underlying technology.

While the core aspects of these organizations represent a distinct form of technical co-founding organization, their similarities and hybridization with other organizational forms can make them difficult to classify. The founders of these organizations initially resisted being labeled an accelerator or incubator while acknowledging similarities to both models, with one of the founders describing his organization as a "combination of an incubator, accelerator, digital agency and venture capital all rolled into one." Both of these organizations also hybridized into providing acceleration as a service to corporate and other organizations, including the nation's largest research institute, CSIRO. While the fate or success for BlueChilli remains to be seen, Pollenizer ultimately announced it would "shut down after conceding that it had failed to find a sustainable business model for its operations."[3] The high overhead costs to facilitate a cohort-based program were also noted by Singapore's premier accelerator when it abandoned the program components in mid-2016,[4] with 500 Startups following suit in late 2016.[5] Taken together, this continuous morphing of business models[6] questions whether the survival of start-up support programs is entirely dependent on either early "home runs" or government support.

IdeasBoom (2016–Current)

In late 2015, the new Australian Prime Minister was voted in through a leadership spill, only nine months before a federal election. In an attempt to gain popular support, the new Prime Minister's election campaign proposed a National Innovation and Science Agenda (NISA), affectionately called IdeasBoom. As part of this campaign for a transition to an innovation-based economy, a promise was made to develop an Incubator Support Programme, commencing in 2016. In preparation for this program, a report was commissioned by the authors to clarify the state of the industry, aims, business models and performance metrics of different support organizations, along with policy implications (Bliemel et al., 2016). Despite the incubator label in the title, the resulting policy strongly favored accelerators, or other organizations with strong mentoring, community engagement and capability development components. The initial program was announced at A$8 million, but soon increased to a total of A$23 million, with preference for supporting sectors and regions for which there were not already accelerators. Funding was intended to support the cost of operations, and was not available for co-investment like the IIF or ESVCLP programs. Consistent with an end-user empathic approach to developing policy (Mintrom and Luetjens, 2016), several public consultation sessions were held across the country. While the intentions and design of the policy have been well received by the community, several noted that the level of funding was insufficient to even cover the bond required for a commercial lease.

Complementary to the Incubator Support Programme, changes were made to the employee stock option plans and investment taxation, with many other policy changes remaining under review. Noting that Australia is far from the rest of the world, several international Landing Pads were set up under the NISA scheme, where entrepreneurs could temporarily reside, conduct business and foster connections to other clusters, including Berlin, San Francisco, Shanghai, Singapore and Tel Aviv.

Somewhat simultaneously, state governments are launching similar incubator and accelerator support programs, such as the A$12 million Boosting Business Innovation program in New South Wales (NSW), which "aims to accelerate innovation in New South Wales (NSW) by supporting greater collaboration between research organisations and their business communities."[7] In late 2016 and early 2017, competing bids were announced to create the country's largest "hub" or "precinct" where multiple accelerators, incubators and co-working spaces could be co-located; one supported by the private sector,[8] and the other by the state government.[9]

DISCUSSION

The evolution of the Australian innovation system has been at the core of many public and policy discussions. In particular, the lack of funds and management/business skills has been singled out as one of the key drawbacks of this system for a long time. However, in the last few years, the amount of funds available and the number of new start-ups launched have grown explosively. Along the way, accelerators have emerged as a new phenomenon within the Australian Ecosystem, as have germinators. While policy has lagged the emergence of the phenomenon internationally, new policies were developed during the early evolution of the accelerator industry in Australia and remain in a state of flux as complementary policies are reviewed at the federal level and new policies are introduced at the state level.

The literature on accelerators reveals that current conceptualizations of accelerators as new organizations tend to link them with incubators. However, the founders, mentors and members of the Australian seed accelerators depict a different picture. If one considers that angel investors are "wealthy individuals who acts as an informal venture capitalist, placing his or her own money directly into early stage new ventures" (Wiltbank et al., 2009, p. 116), then accelerators are in essence more like angel investors than incubators. The link between accelerators and angels is reinforced by the motivations to invest. For instance, angels tend to be former entrepreneurs motivated by helping out the next generation of entrepreneurs, investing a relatively small part of their individual wealth (Wiltbank et al., 2009; Wong, Bhatia and Freeman, 2009).

Meanwhile, accelerators also have a strong mentoring and competency development aspect that is more aligned with higher education and vocational training. This makes accelerators difficult to associate with any one form of support. The policy implications reflect this complexity. While new policies support accelerators and their respective portfolios of activities (e.g., co-working space, seed capital, mentoring, training), their development in Australia has also triggered reconsideration of complementary policies regarding R&D concessions, immigration, bankruptcy protection and investment capital.

CONCLUSION

This study has explored the emergence of accelerators and related policy in the context of the Australian innovation system. Accelerators first appeared in 2010 with little formal coordination between them, followed by the development of accelerator policy in 2015 and its implementation in 2016. In comparison, the VC industry and VC policy in Australia started off with a neglected government report (i.e., the 1983 Espie Report), followed by the emergence of AVCAL in 1992 and the first formal VC fund in 1994, culminating in the introduction of VC policy 15 years after the report (1998). The evolution of the VC industry also suffered setbacks due to unfortunate timing with the burst of the dot-com bubble and GFC. Meanwhile, accelerators appeared in Australia largely independent of policy efforts, with only a few being capitalized via early stage VC policy programs. The federal and state governments were comparatively quick to learn about accelerators and design policy for accelerators while also reconsidering changes to complementary policies. Simultaneously, the total number of accelerators has been growing rapidly and accelerator business models are evolving at an incredible pace and hybridizing with incubation, co-working, VC, mentoring, higher education, professional services and other organizational types.

NOTES

1. http://www.idealab.com/about_idealab/timeline.html (last accessed Feb 2016).
2. 1 Australian dollar (A$1) has typically been the equivalent to 0.8 US dollars (US$0.8), with levels as low as US$0.5 in 2001 and as high as US$1.1 in 2011.
3. http://www.afr.com/technology/end-of-an-era-as-aussie-startup-pioneers-pollenizer-call-it-a-day-20170228-gun90e (last accessed Feb 2017).
4. https://www.techinasia.com/jfdi-accelerator-no-more (last accessed Feb 2017).
5. https://techcrunch.com/2016/11/18/500-startups-ditches-the-accelerator-brand-as-it-looks-to-differentiate/ (last accessed Feb 2017).
6. See the authors' summary of the six evolutions of their business model: https://www.bluechilli.com/blog/six-evolutions-learning-from-failure/ (last accessed Mar 2018).
7. http://www.industry.nsw.gov.au/business-and-industry-in-nsw/innovation-and-research/boosting-business-innovation-program (last accessed Feb 2017).8
8. https://www.lighthouse.sydney/ (last accessed Feb 2017).
9. https://www.jobsfornsw.com.au/how-we-help/the-sydney-startup-hub (last accessed Feb 2017).

REFERENCES

AATS (1983). *Developing High Technology Enterprises for Australia (Espie Report)*. Canberra.

Allen Consulting Group (2003). *Evaluation of the BITS Incubator Program and the Intelligent Island Incubator: Final Report to the Department of Communications, Information Technology and the Arts.*

AusIndustry (2012). *Investment, Innovation and Venture Capital.* Commonwealth of Australia. https://www.business.gov.au/~/media/Business/VC/Investment-Innovation-Venture-Capital-PDF.ashx?la=en (last accessed Feb 2017).

Baldassarre, G. (2016, 21 Dec). Australian startups to see further corporate involvement and growing international investment in 2017. *Startup Daily.* http://www.startupdaily.net/2016/12/australian-startups-see-corporate-involvement-growing-international-investment-2017/ (last accessed Feb 2017).

Barrehag, L., Fornell, A., Larsson, G., Mardstrom, V., Westergard, W. and Wrackefeldt, S. (2012). Accelerating success: A study of seed accelerators and their defining characteristics. Bachelor Thesis TEKX04-12-10, Chalmers University, Sweden.

Bliemel, M.J., Flores, R., De Klerk, S., Miles, M.P., Costas, B. and Monteiro, P. (2016). *The Role and Performance of Accelerators in the Australian Startup Ecosystem (Funder Ref. No. ACCEL01).* Commissioned report for the Department of Industry, Innovation & Science. Canberra, ACT.

Bruneel, J., Ratinho, T., Clarysse, B. and Groen, A. (2012). The evolution of business incubators: Comparing demand and supply of business incubation services across different incubator generations. *Technovation*, 32(2), 110–121.

Business Review Australia (2011, 8 Mar). An overview of Australia's venture capital industry. *Business Review Australia*. http://www.businessreviewaustralia.com/finance/522/An-Overview-of-Australias-Venture-Capital-Industry (last accessed Feb 2017).

Carayannis, E.G. and von Zedtwitz, M. (2005). Architecting gloCal (global–local), real-virtual incubator networks (G-RVINs) as catalysts and accelerators of entrepreneurship in transitioning and developing economies: Lessons learned and best practices from current development and business incubation practices. *Technovation*, 25(2), 95–110.

Creswell, J.W. and Clark, V.L.P. (2011). *Designing and Conducting Mixed Methods Research*. Los Angeles, CA: SAGE Publications.

Dana, L. (1996). Boomerang entrepreneurs: Hong Kong to Canada and back. *Journal of Small Business Management*, 34(2), 79–83.

DIISR (2011). *Innovation Investment Fund Program Progress Report*. Canberra, ACT: Department of Innovation, Industry, Science and Research. https://industry.gov.au/industry/IndustrySectors/VentureCapital/Documents/InnovationInvestmentFundProgramProgressReport.pdf (last accessed Feb 2017).

Dowling, P. and ANZABI (1997). *Establishing and Operating Incubators in Australia: A Guide*. Wollongong, NSW: Australia and New Zealand Association of Business Incubators Inc.

Farrelly, E. (1996, 6 Aug). Home for technology confounds pessimists. *Sydney Morning Herald*. http://search.proquest.com/docview/363351966 (last accessed Feb 2017).

Fehder, D.C. and Hochberg, Y.V. (2014). Accelerators and the regional supply of venture capital investment. http://ssrn.com/abstract=2518668 (last accessed Feb 2017).

Geels, F.W. (2004). From sectoral systems of innovation to socio-technical systems: Insights about dynamics and change from sociology and institutional theory. *Research Policy*, 33(6), 897–920.

Grimaldi, R. and Grandi, A. (2005). Business incubators and new venture creation: An assessment of incubating models. *Technovation*, 25(2), 111–121.

Hackett, S.M. and Dilts, D.M. (2004). A systematic review of business incubation research. *Journal of Technology Transfer*, 29(1), 55–82.

Hannon, P.D. (2004). A qualitative sense-making classification of business incubation environments. *Qualitative Market Research: An International Journal*, 7(4), 274–283.

Hoffman, D.L. and Radojevich-Kelley, N. (2012). Analysis of accelerator companies: An exploratory case study of their programs, processes, and early results. *Small Business Institute® Journal*, 8(2), 54–70.

Kenney, M. (2011). How venture capital became a component of the US National System of Innovation. *Industrial and Corporate Change*, 20(6), 1677–1723.

Kortum, S. and Lerner, J. (2000). Assessing the contribution of venture capital to innovation. *RAND Journal of Economics*, 31(4), 674–692.

Los Kamp, M. (2013). Betaspring: Entrepreneurship in startup accelerators. Senior Capstone Project, Bryant University, Smithfield, Rhode Island, USA.

Lowe, S. (2001a, 23 Apr). Venture capital retains its magic. *Sydney Morning Herald*. http://search.proquest.com/docview/363680179 (last accessed Feb 2017).

Lowe, S. (2001b, 29 Sep). Allen & Buckeridge delivers the goods, plus a bit extra.

Sydney Morning Herald. http://search.proquest.com/docview/363815456 (last accessed Feb 2017).

Miller, P. and Bound, K. (2011). The Startup Factories: The rise of accelerator programmes to support new technology ventures. Discussion paper: June 2016, NESTA, London.

Mintrom, M. and Luetjens, J. (2016). Design thinking in policymaking processes: Opportunities and challenges. *Australian Journal of Public Administration*, 75(3), 391–402.

Pauwels, C., Clarysse, B., Wright, M. and Van Hove, J. (2016). Understanding a new generation incubation model: The accelerator. *Technovation*, 50–51, 13–24.

Porat, J. (2014). Exploring the policy relevance of startup accelerators. Office of Advocacy, Issue Brief, Number 4, Washington, DC: US Small Business Administration.

Price, R. (2004). The role of service providers in establishing networked regional business accelerators in Utah. *International Journal of Technology Management*, 27(5), 465–474.

Recke, M. and Bliemel, M. (2018). Policy making versus policy research: The case of the City of Sydney's Tech Startups Action Plan. In Miles, M., Battisti, M., Lau, A. and Terziovski, M. (eds), *Economic Gardening: Entrepreneurship, Innovation and Small Business Ecosystems in Regional, Rural and International Development*. SEAANZ Annual Research Book Series (pp. 58–79). Prahran, VIC: Tilde University Press,

Riordan, D. (1996, 17 Nov). Answer to business quiz. *Sunday Star – Times*, Wellington, NZ. http://search.proquest.com/docview/313887392 (last accessed Feb 2017).

Samila, S. and Sorenson, O. (2010). Venture capital as a catalyst to commercialization. *Research Policy*, 39(10), 1348–1360.

Schaper, M.T. and Lewer, J. (2009). Business incubation in Australia: Policies, practices and outcomes. *Asia Pacific Journal of Innovation and Entrepreneurship*, Special Topic: National Innovation System and Business Incubation Policy: Best Practices and Challenges (II), 3 (3), 37–46.

Startup Muster (2016). *Startup Muster 2016 Annual Report*. https://www.startup muster.com/ (last accessed Feb 2017).

Suchard, J.-A. and Humphery-Jenner, M. (2011). *An Overview and Trends in the Venture Capital and Private Equity Sector in Australia: 1984–2011*. Report prepared for the Industry and Innovation Division, Department of Industry, Innovation, Climate Change, Science, Research and Tertiary Education.

Tsai, F.S., Hsieh, L.H., Fang, S.C. and Lin, J.L. (2009). The co-evolution of business incubation and national innovation systems in Taiwan. *Technological Forecasting and Social Change*, 76(5), 629–643.

Vitale, M., Everingham, B. and Butler, R. (2006), *Study of Business Angel Market in Australia*. Study commissioned by the Department of Industry, Tourism and Resources, November.

Voisey, P., Jones, P. and Thomas, B. (2013). The pre-incubator: A longitudinal study of 10 years of university pre-incubation in Wales. *Industry and Higher Education*, 27(5), 349–363.

von Zedtwitz, M. (2003). Classification and management of incubators: Aligning strategic objectives and competitive scope for new business facilitation. *International Journal of Entrepreneurship and Innovation Management*, 3(1), 176–196.

Wiltbank, R., Read, S., Dew, N. and Sarasvathy, S.D. (2009). Prediction and control under uncertainty: Outcomes in angel investing. *Journal of Business Venturing*, 24(2), 116–133.

Wong, A., Bhatia, M. and Freeman, Z. (2009). Angel finance: The other venture capital. *Strategic Change*, 18(7–8), 221–230.

Wright, M., Siegel, D.S. and Mustar, P. (2017). An emerging ecosystem for student start-ups. *Journal of Technology Transfer*, 42(4), 902–922.

10. Accelerators: insights for a research agenda

Massimo G. Colombo, Cristina Rossi-Lamastra and Mike Wright

INTRODUCTION

In this chapter, we take stock of the nascent literature on accelerators and set out an agenda for further research on the topic. The chapter documents that, given the embryonic stage of the phenomenon and of the related scholarly debate (e.g., Hochberg, 2016; Kanbach and Stubner, 2016; Pauwels, Clarysse, Wright, and Van Hove, 2016), ample room exists for both theory development and application of multiple empirical research methods (von Krogh, Rossi-Lamastra, and Haefliger, 2012). Moreover, our research agenda takes fully into account the nature of the phenomenon and revolves around three main pillars. First, an accelerator involves and links many actors/elements at different levels of analysis – the accelerator *as a whole*, the accelerator program (with its mentors and trainees), the startups and entrepreneurs participating in the program, and so on (Miller and Bound, 2011). Accordingly, we invite researchers to approach the accelerator phenomenon at different levels of analysis and propose a *multiple-level* research agenda. Second, the phenomenon of accelerators is evolving rapidly. We can trace its birth back to the foundation of Y Combinator in 2005 in Cambridge, Massachusetts, by a successful entrepreneur, Paul Graham[1] (see again Miller and Bound, 2011). Since its inception, Y Combinator has supported over 1,000 startups, including Dropbox and Airbnb. More generally, Seed-DB[2] reports 187 accelerators active worldwide, which have supported approximately 6,495 startups. Such a lively dynamic makes it mandatory to consider the time dimension and thus to adopt a life-cycle approach.

Third, nowadays accelerators operate in many diverse geographical contexts. The phenomenon originated in the Silicon Valley in the United States (Wei, 2017), but it quickly spread to many countries and regions. In particular, since the creation of the first European competitor of

Y Combinator, Seedcamp,[3] an accelerator founded in 2007 by Saul Klein and Reshma Sohoni in London, accelerators have diffused rapidly across Europe (see Clarysse, Wright, and Van Hove, 2016 for an assessment of the phenomenon in London, Berlin, and Paris). Consequently, we advise scholars working on the topic to acknowledge the prominent role of local contexts.

Moving from these premises, in the next section we outline directions for future research on accelerators at diverse levels of analysis, namely, the accelerators *as a whole*, the accelerator programs, the startups, and the associated entrepreneurs. In the third section we discuss the importance of adopting a life-cycle perspective and the research questions it raises. The fourth section focuses on the prominence of the geographical context in the studies of accelerators. Finally, the fifth section concludes the chapter.

A RESEARCH AGENDA ON ACCELERATORS: A MULTILEVEL APPROACH

Directions for Future Research at the Accelerator Level

To date, studies that have focused on the level of the accelerator *as a whole* have mainly explored their impact on accelerated startups. The overarching research question is: does such a novel form of support for startups accrue benefits? Hallen, Bingham, and Cohen (2016) find evidence that many accelerators do indeed aid and accelerate startups' development and that their effects are neither due purely to selection nor credentialing. The authors also show that participation in accelerators complements rather than substitutes for other forms of prior founders' experience. The work of Hallen et al. (2016) is also highly interestingly from a methodological perspective. The authors use both quantitative and qualitative data, focusing on privately backed accelerators based in North America and Europe, with these accelerators operating almost exclusively in high-technology industries. Interestingly, one of their samples includes proprietary data on 262 ventures that made it to the final selection rounds in four cohorts at top accelerator programs, of which 45 were accepted onto the program and 217 were not, enabling identification of the causal impact of accelerators on venture performance and survival. To examine in detail how founders' human capital and other contingencies shape the effects of accelerator participation, the authors also compile a sample of 328 ventures from public data sources that include a greater number of accelerator participants. Finally, they also gather qualitative evidence from site visits and 75 semi-structured interviews with accelerator directors, venture founders, and mentors associated with nine US accelerators and four international accelerators. We believe that such a mixed method approach is highly appropriate for studying new phenomena.

Other works contrast accelerators and other forms of support for startups, including incubators or angel investors. For instance, Smith, Harrigan, and Gasiorowski (2015) compare the effects on startups of participating in accelerators and of receiving angel investing. The authors use data for the universe of startups that participated in the Y Combinator and Techstars[4] accelerators and a complementary sample of startups backed by angel investors covering the period 2005–2011. They find that accelerator-backed startups receive the first round of follow-up financing significantly sooner; are more likely to be acquired or to fail; are founded by entrepreneurs from a relatively elite set of universities; and exhibit substantially greater founder mobility among other accelerator-backed startups.

Despite these interesting early studies, many research directions are still underexplored; we sketch some of them in the following. First, accelerators are new entrants into the (crowded) space of actors providing support for startups (Hochberg and Fehder, 2015, p.1202). These actors include traditional incubators, venture capitalists, business angels, crowdfunding platforms, and so on. Current studies that have compared accelerators and angel investors or business incubators (e.g., Stagars, 2015) have left largely unanswered the question of accelerators' *additionality*. In line with the debate on the impact of measures to stimulate entrepreneurship (e.g., Clarysse, Mustar, and Wright, 2009), we invite scholars to investigate what is the incremental benefit of accelerators. Do they really support startups or are they just the latest fad in the support landscape? Do accelerators really fill a gap in the provision of entrepreneurial support or do they crowd-out existing support forms?

Second, and partially in line with the former point, an interesting area of inquiry deals with how accelerators position themselves within entrepreneurial ecosystems and relate with the other support providers. In particular, being newcomers, accelerators must distinguish themselves from other actors and establish their legitimacy. To this end, organizations usually resort to narratives (Garud, Gehman, and Giuliani, 2014). Hence, to distinguish themselves from existing support providers, like for instance incubators, accelerators may need either to replace existing competing narratives about what incubators do or to accommodate elements of such narratives (Holstein, Starkey, and Wright, 2016).

Third, several definitions of accelerator exist (Cohen, 2013; Cohen and Hochberg, 2014; Hochberg and Fehder 2015; Lewis, Harper-Anderson, and Molnar, 2011). However, no definition is recognized as definitive, given also the heterogeneity of accelerators. In such a situation, a comprehensive taxonomy, which makes sense of accelerators' variety along various dimensions (e.g., ownership, goals, scope), would be a crucial milestone for knowledge advancement. In particular, we think that ownership, that is, the nature of the organization running the accelerator, should be a focal element of this taxonomy. As we have seen in Chapter 1, currently diverse organizations own and operate accelerators, including large corporations (Kohler, 2016), financial institutions, or public sector organizations (like, for instance, universities: York, Metcalf, and Katona, 2016). These differences in accelerators' ownership likely result in heterogeneity in their goals. Usually, large corporations set up accelerators as they view startups as sources of novel ideas and organization models which can rejuvenate the corporate knowledge base and organizational design (Bauer, Obwegeser, and Avdagic, 2016). Conversely, we expect that financial investors are much more attentive to financial returns, while public sector organizations mainly care about employment creation or development of entrepreneurial ecosystems. Accordingly, we need further research on whether and how diverse types of accelerators achieve their diverse goals. In turn, such goal heterogeneity calls for the development of diverse key performance indicators (KPIs) for assessing accelerators' outcomes. In this regard, a general caveat is that, given the early stage of startups typically passing through and graduating from accelerators, the financial performance of accelerated startups has limited applicability as a KPI. More specifically, scholars should recognize that one size does not fit all in this realm and we envisage KPIs development as a fourth promising research avenue which can pave the way to further studies on accelerators' performance and sustainability. Suitable KPIs can alert accelerators on whether and how they should adjust their programs and internal organization.

Finally, we think that there is much more to study on corporate accelerators (Kohler, 2016) than just their goals. Starting from the early 2010s, major corporations – such as Microsoft, Citrix, or Telefonica – were the first to launch programs to accelerate startups. Currently, the Corporate Accelerator Database[5] reports 72 active corporate programs (out of the 80 launched since 2010) all around the world. Such a booming tendency poses numerous research questions. Given the profit-oriented nature of large corporations, to what extent are corporate accelerators beneficial for the startups that they accelerate? Does the presence of large corporations behind accelerators scare-off startups and make corporate accelerators less attractive than accelerators run by other organizations? Conversely, is the presence of a powerful incumbent an element of attraction? How should corporate headquarters design the relations with their accelerators to maximize startups' attraction and unleash their innovation potentials?

Does granting the accelerator as much autonomy as possible serve this purpose? To what extent should headquarters involve corporate managers in accelerator programs? What are the effects of such involvement?

In the realm of corporate accelerators, another interesting research area deals with the relations between corporate accelerators and corporate venture capital programs (Dushnitsky and Lenox, 2005, 2006; Sykes, 1990). Some large corporations, which have well-established corporate venture capital programs, are now launching accelerators. Google is a case in point. In October 2009, it launched its corporate venture capital program (Dushnitsky, 2012); then, in 2015, it launched the Google Launchpad Accelerator,[6] its corporate accelerator. Thus, what are the advantages and disadvantages of one form of startup support over another? What factors drive the choice of one form over another? Does it depend on industries, with corporate venture capital being the preferred form in the company's main industry and accelerators being the way of exploring new industries or strengthening the competitive position in peripheral markets?

In term of methods and research design, answering research questions which focus on the accelerator level would require making a census of accelerators currently active worldwide. Apart from Seed-DB and the Corporate Accelerator Database, mentioned above, there are other databases (e.g., the Database of Accelerators and Corporate Innovation[7] by Kauffman Fellow or the OpenAxel Initiative[8] founded by the European Community under the 7th Framework Programme). Some of these databases, like Seed-DB, have gained prominence among researchers and practitioners. However, to date, none have emerged as the definitive data source. Therefore, an idea would be to build a comprehensive database by integrating and triangulating information from different sources, thus resorting to a methodology similar to the one that Dushnitsky, Guerini, Piva, and Rossi-Lamastra (2016) applied for making a census of crowdfunding platforms in Europe. We conceive this database as the starting point for understanding how diverse accelerators position themselves in their entrepreneurial ecosystems, building a taxonomy of accelerators, comparing and contrasting the diverse types of accelerators, understanding which KPIs are appropriate for them, and so on.

Directions for Future Research at the Accelerator Program Level

We envisage ample room for further inquiry focusing on the level of the accelerator program. Currently, knowledge is accumulating on the main phases of an accelerator program (Pauwels et al., 2016). Some insights also exist on how these phases vary across diverse types of accelerators (see, for instance, Chapter 1). Nevertheless, we still have more to learn on how an accelerator program works.

Overall, we can define an accelerator program as "a fixed-term, cohort-based program, including mentorship and educational components, that culminates in a public pitch event or demo-day" (i.e., the so-called gradu-ation, Cohen and Hochberg, 2014). Moving from this definition, we sketch here future research directions for three main phases in accelerator programs: selection, acceleration, and exit.

Selection. Nascent literature and anecdotal evidence suggest that accel-erators typically apply well-defined selection criteria for admitting startups. These criteria are based on the main principles of *openness* and *competi-tion* (Miller and Bound, 2011). The selection process aims to attract many applicants and then provides for a strong selection. Usually, startups apply by filling a simple online form with information about their entrepre-neurial team and their business idea. After a first screening, accelerator managers undertake face-to-face interviews with a subset of applicants and admit the most promising startups in the program. Accelerators also need a strong selection process because they usually support only a few startups per batch or cohort.[9] However, apart from these few facts, we still know little on the selection phase, while extensive research exists on how venture capitalists and business angels select startups (e.g., Muzyka, Birley, and Leleux, 1996; Van Osnabrugge and Robinson, 2000; Zacharakis and Meyer, 1998). Accordingly, we welcome research which explores differ-ences and similarities between the criteria adopted by traditional support providers and those adopted by accelerators. Along this line of reason-ing, an interesting issue concerns whether and how accelerator managers can leverage the experience they have accumulated with other forms of startup support to improve accelerators' selection processes. Specifically, we expect that accelerator managers who have been venture capitalists and business angels enjoy advantages in selecting startups. However, given the differences among these support forms, is there any risk of inappropriate generalization? Furthermore, how do accelerator managers learn from the experience they gained in selecting prior cohorts of startups? Based on this experience, do they adapt their selection criteria over time?

Accelerating. Once admitted to an accelerator program, startups usually receive training, mentorship, access to offices and conference rooms, and, in some cases, financial capital. We advise scholars to examine the ante-cedents and consequences of the provision of these diverse support forms by putting also in this case accelerators' heterogeneity at the core of the analysis. In particular, mentors play an important role in the offering of accelerators (Memon, 2014), but we know little about them. This opens interesting research issues. How do accelerators select their mentors? What is their expertise and what value do they add? What are their goals in being mentors? Given the heterogeneity of accelerators, we expect differential ability to identify and attract mentors, as well as differences in the capabilities of the mentors who are attracted. Anecdotal evidence reports that sometimes mentors also invest in ventures, and we need more work to gain insights into this aspect. To what extent do mentors invest in the startups they mentor and how does the investment process work?

Exit. We view the phase after the end of the accelerator program as critical and as raising numerous research issues. How can accelerators maintain links with their graduated startups? Providing an answer to this question is crucial as it relates to a fundamental point: how the owner appropriates value out of the accelerator. As mentioned above, different types of accelerators have different goals. In the case of corporate accelerators, for instance, large corporations view accelerated startups as a source of novel ideas. How can they leverage this innovation potential after the graduation? Do they allow graduated startups to continue to use the accelerator spaces for continuing (informal) knowledge transfer through face-to-face interactions? To what extent does this undermine the graduation principle? What reflections does this trigger on the appropriate length of the accelerator programs? Indeed, a key characteristic of such programs is that they have a limited time span, but a short duration may undermine the creation of stable linkages with startups. Do accelerators create alumni associations with periodical networking events for keeping these linkages alive after graduation? Do they adopt more structured and long-term approaches by engaging in corporate venture capital or acquiring the most promising startups?

As to research design, studies having the accelerator program as the level of analysis should benefit from qualitative research and longitudinal studies. The former would allow rich evidence to be gained on how accelerator programs work, which can inform further quantitative inquiry. Through a longitudinal approach, scholars can get insights on the processes which unfold within an accelerator program, from selection to exit, and can single out those that are the main critical junctures in these processes.

Quantitative research also has much value in the study of accelerator programs. By collecting samples of selected and non-selected startups in diverse types of accelerators and in diverse industries, one can compare their characteristics in terms of entrepreneurial teams, business ideas, organization, and so on. One can study the matching among the characteristics of mentors and that of the acceleration program or the effectiveness of the diverse post-graduating strategies on the maintenance of the linkage between startups and the organization running the acceleration program.

Directions for Future Research at the Startup Level

Having the accelerated startups as the level of analysis is one of the most promising research avenues in the field of accelerators. Indeed, accelerators exist to have an impact on startups and add value to them. Grounding on the aforementioned paper by Hallen et al. (2016), we welcome further contributions that study survivorship, financial and innovation performance, access to further finance, and sale or stock market flotation of accelerated startups. Provided scholars gauge the peculiarities of accelerators, they can borrow ideas and methods from the ample research strands assessing the effects of venture capital financing (Bertoni, Colombo, and Grilli, 2011), angel investing (Kerr, Lerner, and Schoar, 2014), incubators (Colombo and Delmastro, 2002), or of other forms of startup support. In order to provide robust insights into the real contribution of accelerators, a suitable research design consists in comparing accelerated startups to a well-constructed control group of non-accelerated startups and to carefully control for endogeneity to assess rigorously the treatment effect. Along this line of reasoning, one can develop and test hypotheses on the differential effects of the diverse forms of support. In their study, Hallen et al. (2016) do include controls for different accelerators, but there is room for digging deeper on this aspect. Do the diverse types of accelerators have different impacts on startups depending on their diverse goals? For instance, do corporate accelerators have stronger effects on startups' innovation performance compared with accelerators run by other organizations? More specifically, does startups' innovation performance correlate positively with that of the parent company? Similarly, are the financial performances of accelerated startups higher when an investment fund runs the accelerator program? Furthermore, a key decision when setting up an accelerator deals with the choice between a *generalist* program and a *specialist* one which focuses on a given technology or industry. The assessment of differences in terms of effectiveness and value-added to the startups between generalist and specialist accelerators can improve our understanding of the possible benefits of these two forms.

Finally, we contend that startups' characteristics do matter in this realm, as some startups are likely better able than others to obtain the most from accelerators. Investigating such an issue also has interesting practical implications in that it allows for the identification of best practices for implementing customized acceleration strategies to propel diverse types of startups. Thus, we invite scholars to study the startup-level factors that boost accelerators' impact. Does this effect depend on the fit between startups and the organization running the program? In our view, such an issue is highly interesting in the case of corporate accelerators. For instance, do we observe better performance in the case of startups operating in the same industry/technology domain as the corporation running the accelerator or in the case of startups funded by former employees?

Directions for Future Research at the Entrepreneur and Entrepreneurial Team Level

The vast literature on entrepreneurial teams recognizes the challenges of building teams with the requisite variety of expertise as well as adapting that composition as the startup evolves (Gruber, MacMillan and Thompson, 2012, 2013; Ucbasaran, Lockett, Wright, and Westhead, 2003; Vanaelst, Clarysse, Wright, Lockett, Moray, and S'Jegers, 2006).

This may be especially an issue for technology-based startups emerging from academia and education programs (Rasmussen, Mosey, and Wright, 2011). Usually, technicians founded these startups and struggle to add commercial competences to their teams due to their limited social networks (Colombo and Piva, 2012).

At present, we know little about whether and how accelerators favor or hamper the process of entrepreneurial team formation and thus the evolution for startups admitted into their programs. Do accelerators make it easier for entrepreneurs to add competences to their teams by allowing them to access novel social networks? We expect that corporate accelerators are particularly beneficial to this end as large corporations are the core of a large network of partners, suppliers, customers, and communities of practices. Likewise, one may wonder whether the allegedly positive effect of accelerators on entrepreneurial teams' formation is stronger for generalist accelerators, where entrepreneurs can come across startups and mentors from diverse industries. We also expect that accelerators, which enable the addition of new competences to entrepreneurial teams, also enhance the cognitive variety of the accelerated startups. Accordingly, it would be of interest to investigate how this variety affects startups' evolutionary path, including the evolution of their business models.

A second promising research stream focuses on *individual entrepreneurs* of startups involved in accelerator programs. Such a stream can add novel nuances to the study of the differences between accelerated and non-accelerated startups. Are entrepreneurs of accelerated startups different in terms of human, social, and cognitive capital in comparison with entrepreneurs who apply but fail to get selected by accelerators or who never apply? This investigation is a first step in answering a more general question: who applies for accelerator programs?

A third, and partially related, research area concerns the differences and similarities between entrepreneurs of accelerated startups and entrepreneurs supported by venture capitalists and business angels. For instance, given the frequent focus of accelerators on early stage startups operating in high-technology industries, we may expect that entrepreneurs in accelerators are younger, less experienced, and more likely to be in or to have just come out of education.

Fourth, it is interesting to study why and how entrepreneurs approach accelerators. This research question is the mirror image of the one on why and how accelerators select startups and sheds further light on the matching process between accelerators and startups. For instance, do entrepreneurs approach accelerators after a rejection by other support providers or are accelerators their first choice? Evidence exists that often entrepreneurs are turned down by venture capitalists and business angels (Cosh, Cumming, and Hughes, 2009), especially in the early stage of their ventures. We need further evidence on whether entrepreneurs in accelerators have approached traditional financiers or other support providers (e.g., university incubators, business plan competitions), which turned down them.

Finally, one may want to investigate whether and how entrepreneurs prepare pitches and business plans which can meet the accelerators' selection criteria. This issue becomes particularly intriguing when considering different types of accelerators. Does a heterogeneity in business plans exist which mirrors the heterogeneity in accelerators' goals? One can imagine that a business plan is more likely to meet the selection criteria of a corporate accelerator if it stresses the innovation potential of the startup and its linkages with the technologies of the corporation running the accelerator.

Given the nascent nature of this research area, we argue that studies at the entrepreneurial team/entrepreneur level can benefit from the application of multiple methods. For instance, the comparison between individual characteristics of accelerated and non-accelerated entrepreneurs can leverage both quantitative and qualitative approaches. While the former allows for generalizability through the collection of large and representative samples and endogeneity controls, the latter are particularly useful for gauging why entrepreneurs apply to accelerator programs. Finally, a narrative approach that explores the ways in which entrepreneurs convey what their venture is about (Martens, Jennings, and Jennings, 2007) may hold particular potential for understanding how entrepreneurs construct their business plans to enter accelerators.

ACKNOWLEDGING THE TIME DIMENSION: STUDYING ACCELERATORS THROUGH A LIFE-CYCLE APPROACH

We advise scholars to adopt a life-cycle approach when studying accelerators as we think that such an approach brings several advantages. First, it allows for inquiry about the time horizon and survival of accelerators. Are accelerators permanent or transient organizations? Furthermore, in the case of accelerators with a finite time horizon, do the owners plan their duration or does this duration depend on accelerators' results?

Second, we need more research on how accelerators evolve. Do selection criteria, mentorship approaches, management of the post-graduation phase vary as accelerators achieve legitimacy within their entrepreneurial ecosystems? Does legitimacy result in the attraction of better startups so that we observe an increase in the quality of accelerated startups over time? Do specialist accelerators evolve into generalist ones as time passes and accelerator managers accumulate new knowledge and expertise? In addition, we expect that accelerators encounter several challenges over time and variously respond and adapt to them. Likely, these challenges vary across accelerator types and this again speaks in favor of the importance of developing a taxonomy of accelerators. Do accelerators change their goals in consequence of these challenges and depending on trends in their KPIs? These are just a sample of the questions that researchers studying the evolution of accelerators should answer.

Third, we know little about the long-term sustainability of accelerators in general and of different types of accelerators in particular. We expect that the diverse goals, programs, and funding regimes of accelerators affect their sustainability. For example, public sector funded accelerators may be susceptible to policy decisions and budgeting. Do these accelerators die when the initial funding runs out or do they adapt their models and if so how? Does the creation of corporate accelerators depend, among other things, on top executives' attitudes towards entrepreneurship to the extent that change in senior management leads to the discontinuation of previously approved initiatives? More generally, we conjecture that the sustainability of corporate accelerators depends on the strategies of the corporations running them, as it happens for traditional corporate venturing programs (Phan, Wright, Ucbasaran, and Tan, 2009). The higher the integration and fit between the accelerator and the company's strategy, the higher the probability of the accelerator's survival.

Finally, we should explore accelerators' diffusion, focusing also on similarities and differences with the diffusion of traditional incubators and of other forms of entrepreneurial support. Specifically, in recent years, as observed in Chapter 1, accelerators' diffusion has been rapid and massive. Will the accelerators boom continue in the following years? Conversely, will there be a shakeout in the coming years as some accelerators fail or cannot secure funding or revenue streams to remain active? Will this shakeout involve the diverse types of accelerators differently?

Despite its potential, the adoption of a life-cycle approach poses the challenges of collecting data over time. As the phenomenon is still nascent, qualitative studies which closely monitor the evolution of one or few accelerators, seem a good methodological approach for beginning to answer the aforementioned research questions. The study of accelerators' diffusion and shakeout would benefit from the creation of the census of worldwide accelerators that we mentioned above. Such a census can report, for every year, the number of created and closed accelerators, thus grasping the dynamics of the phenomenon.

ACCELERATORS IN GEOGRAPHICAL CONTEXTS

Scholars concur that geography strongly influences entrepreneurial ecosystems (Autio, Kenney, Mustar, Siegel, and Wright, 2014). We argue that, as part of such ecosystems, accelerators are not an exception. Therefore, an overarching research issue is: do the answers to the research questions which we have put forth in this chapter, vary depending on countries and regions? Overall, we envisage here two important and highly related research streams. The first one deals with the *impact of local contexts on accelerators*, while the second one deals with the *impact of accelerators on local contexts*.

Examples of questions in the first stream are as follows. How does the local context influence the creation, functioning, evolution and sustainability of accelerators by forging favorable (or unfavorable) socio-economic conditions? Are some regions more germane to the creation and sustainability of accelerators? Are these favorable conditions contingent on accelerator types? Do accelerators attract mainly local startups or does their attraction manifest at long distance? In this regard, one may expect that corporate accelerators run by large multinationals have a "wide ray of attraction" independently of their location as they can leverage the international network and reputation of their parent organizations for attracting distant startups. Furthermore, it is also important to recognize that both developed and developing regions are heterogeneous in terms of socio-economic conditions (Hoskisson, Wright, Filatotchev, and Peng, 2013). Researchers therefore should focus on how accelerators can be successful in regions with less favorable socio-economic conditions in both developed and emerging economies. A key question relates to the attraction of mentors in such circumstances. From a regional perspective, how can accelerator managers persuade mentors to cross borders from more developed areas to less developed ones? To what extent can they persuade returnee entrepreneurs to play mentoring roles in emerging economies? In less developed regions, new forms of microfinance, such as crowdfunding, may also be important in absence of traditional forms of entrepreneurial finance (Bruton, Khavul, Siegel, and Wright, 2015). Integrating accelerators with these microfinance providers may be crucial for unleashing the potential of accelerators.

The second research stream should study how accelerators shape the local contexts in which they operate. Does the presence of a high-performing accelerator in a peripheral area attract into the area high-quality startups and mentors, thus contributing to local development? Does such a presence raise the awareness of residents towards entrepreneurship to the extent that we observe high rates of startup creation in the area over time? Finally, a further challenge for the regional impact of accelerators concerns potential mismatches between regional entrepreneurial ecosystems and regional administrative boundaries. What challenges does this pose especially for publicly funded accelerators?

Assessing the importance of the geographical context in research on accelerators requires accessing data from spatially dispersed sources, a task which is far from simple. The study of whether accelerators boost differently the performance of accelerated startups in different countries due to diverse socio-economic conditions is a case in point. Indeed, given their early stage, startups in accelerator programs are often privately held. These firms are subject to formal financial reporting only in some countries and thus this lack of financial data may render cross-country comparison impossible. Challenges in data accessibility may call for the introduction of novel methodologies, such as experiments or web scraping procedures that may take advantage of accelerator program websites and the websites of the ventures concerned.

CONCLUSIONS

In this chapter, we have proposed a structured agenda for further research on accelerators at various levels of analysis. Our agenda also acknowledges the moderating role of the time dimension and of the geographical context. Research on the topic will likely develop further over time beyond the ways we have envisioned here, but we hope that we have elaborated a basis on which scholars can build their future work on such a fascinating and multifaceted phenomenon.

NOTES

1. http://www.ycombinator.com (accessed January 14, 2018).
2. http://www.seed-db.com (accessed December 28, 2016).
3. http://seedcamp.com/ (accessed January 1, 2017).
4. http://www.techstars.com/ (accessed January 14, 2018).
5. https://www.corporate-accelerators.net (accessed December 28, 2016).
6. https://developers.google.com/startups/accelerator (accessed January 14, 2018).
7. http://startupaccelerator.vc/accelerator-corporate-innovation-sig (accessed January 14, 2018)/.
8. http://openaxel.com/ (accessed January 14, 2018).
9. For instance, whereas Y Combinator accepts up to 60 startups per cycle, Techstars opts for 10 startups per batch. Evidence exists that just one out of ten startups succeeds in entering the program.

REFERENCES

Autio E., Kenney M., Mustar P., Siegel D., Wright M. (2014). Entrepreneurial innovation ecosystems and context. *Research Policy*, 43(7), 1097–1108.

Bauer S., Obwegeser N., Avdagic Z. (2016). Corporate accelerators: Transferring technology innovation to incumbent companies. *MCIS 2016 Proceedings*. 57. http://aisel.aisnet.org/mcis2016/57 (accessed January 14, 2018).

Bertoni F., Colombo M.G., Grilli L. (2011). Venture capital financing and the growth of high-tech start-ups: Disentangling treatment from selection effects. *Research Policy*, 40(7), 1028–1043.

Bruton G., Khavul S., Siegel D., Wright M. (2015). New financial alternatives in seeding entrepreneurship: Microfinance, crowdfunding, and peer-to-peer innovations. *Entrepreneurship Theory and Practice*, 39(1), 9–26.

Clarysse, B., Mustar P., Wright M. (2009). Behavioural additionality of R&D subsidies: A learning perspective. *Research Policy*, 38(10), 1517–1533.

Clarysse B., Wright M., Van Hove J. (2016). A look inside accelerators in the United Kingdom: Building businesses. In Phan P., Mian S., Lamine, W., (eds), *Technology Entrepreneurship and Business Incubation: Theory, Practice, Lessons Learned*. Imperial College Press, London, UK.

Cohen S. (2013). What do accelerators do? Insights from incubators and angels. *Innovations*, 8(3–4), 19–25.

Cohen S., Hochberg Y.V. (2014). Accelerating startups: The seed accelerator phenomenon. SSRN Working Paper. Available at SSRN: https://ssrn.com/abstract=2418000 (accessed March 30, 2014). https://dx.doi.org/10.2139/ssrn.2418000

Colombo M.G., Delmastro M. (2002). How effective are technology incubators? Evidence from Italy. *Research Policy*, 31(7), 1103–1122.

Colombo M.G., Piva E. (2012). Firms' genetic characteristics and competence-enlarging strategies: A comparison between academic and non-academic high-tech start-ups. *Research Policy*, 41(1), 79–92.

Cosh A., Cumming D., Hughes A. (2009). Outside entrepreneurial capital. *Economic Journal*, 119(540), 1494–1533.

Dushnitsky G. (2012). Corporate venture capital in the 21st century: An integral part of firm's innovation toolkit. In Cumming D. (ed.) *The Oxford Handbook of Venture Capital*, Oxford University Press, Oxford, UK.

Dushnitsky G., Lenox M.J. (2005). When do firms undertake R&D by investing in new ventures? *Strategic Management Journal*, 26(10), 947–965.

Dushnitsky G., Lenox M.J. (2006). When does corporate venture capital investment create firm value? *Journal of Business Venturing*, 21(6), 753–772.

Dushnitsky G., Guerini M., Piva E., Rossi-Lamastra C. (2016). Crowdfunding in Europe: Determinants of platform creation across countries. *California Management Review*, 58(2), 44–71.

Garud, R., Gehman, J., Giuliani, A. (2014). Contextualizing entrepreneurial innovation: A narrative perspective. *Research Policy*, 43, 1177–1188.

Gruber M., MacMillan I.C., Thompson J.D. (2012). From minds to markets: How human capital endowments shape market opportunity identification of technology start-ups. *Journal of Management*, 38(5), 1421–1449.

Gruber M., MacMillan I.C., Thompson J.D. (2013). Escaping the prior knowledge corridor: What shapes the number and variety of market opportunities identified before market entry of technology start-ups? *Organization Science*, 24(1), 280–300.

Hallen, B., Bingham, C.B., Cohen, S.L. (2016). Do accelerators accelerate? If so, how? The impact of intensive learning from others on new venture development (July 8). Available at SSRN: https://ssrn.com/abstract=2719810 (accessed January 14, 2018).

Hochberg Y.V. (2016). Accelerating entrepreneurs and ecosystems: The seed accelerator model. *Innovation Policy and the Economy*, 16(1), 25–51.

Hochberg Y.V., Fehder D. (2015). Accelerators and ecosystems. *Science*, 348, 1202–1203.

Holstein J.C.A., Starkey K., Wright M. (2016). Strategy and narrative in higher education. *Strategic Organization*, https://doi.org/10.1177/1476127016674877 (accessed January 14, 2018).

Hoskisson R., Wright M., Filatotchev I., Peng M. (2013). Emerging multinationals from mid-range economies: The influence of institutions and factor markets. *Journal of Management Studies*, 50(7), 1295–1321.

Kanbach D.K., Stubner S. (2016). Corporate accelerators as recent form of startup engagement: The what, the why, and the how. *Journal of Applied Business Research*, 32(6), 1761–1776.

Kerr W.R., Lerner J., Schoar A. (2014). The consequences of entrepreneurial finance: Evidence from angel financings. *Review of Financial Studies*, 27(1), 20–55.

Kohler T. (2016). Corporate accelerators: Building bridges between corporations and startups. *Business Horizons*, 59(3), 347–357.

Lewis D.A., Harper-Anderson E., Molnar L.A. (2011). *Incubating Success. Incubation Best Practices that Lead to Successful New Ventures*. Report of the U.S. Department of Commerce Economic Development Administration.

Martens M.L., Jennings J.E., Jennings, P.D. (2007). Do the stories they tell get them the money they need? The role of entrepreneurial narratives in resource acquisition. *Academy of Management Journal*, 50(5), 1107–1132.

Memon J. (2014). A theoretical framework for mentor–protégé matchmaking: The role of mentoring in entrepreneurship. *International Journal of Green Economics*, 8(3/4), 252–272.

Miller P., Bound K., (2011). The startup factories: The rise of accelerator programs to support new technology ventures. NESTA Discussion Paper: June 2011.

Muzyka D., Birley S., Leleux, B. (1996). Trade-offs in the investment decisions of European venture capitalists. *Journal of Business Venturing*, 11(4), 273–287.

Pauwels C., Clarysse B., Wright M., Van Hove J. (2016). Understanding a new generation incubation model: The accelerator. *Technovation*, 50–51, 13–24.

Phan P., Wright M., Ucbasaran D., Tan W. (2009). Corporate entrepreneurship: Current research and future direction. *Journal of Business Venturing*, 24(3), 197–205.

Rasmussen E., Mosey S., Wright M. (2011). The evolution of entrepreneurial competencies: A longitudinal study of university spin-off venture emergence. *Journal of Management Studies*, 48(6), 1314–1345.

Smith S.W., Harrigan T.J., Gasiorowski L. (2015). Peering inside: How do peer effects impact entrepreneurial outcomes in accelerators? *Academy of Management Proceedings*, http://proceedings.aom.org/content/2015/1/17072.short (accessed on January 1, 2017).

Stagars M. (2015). *University Startups and Spin-offs: Guide for Entrepreneurs in Academia*. Apress, New York, USA.

Sykes H. (1990). Corporate venture capital: Strategies for success. *Journal of Business Venturing*, 5(1), 37–47.

Ucbasaran D., Lockett A., Wright M., Westhead P. (2003). Entrepreneurial founder teams: Factors associated with member entry and exit. *Entrepreneurship Theory and Practice*, 28(2), 107–127.

Van Osnabrugge M., Robinson, R.J. (2000). *Angel Investing: Matching Start-Up Funds with Start-Up Companies: The Guide for Entrepreneurs, Individual Investors, and Venture Capitalists*. Jossey-Bass, San Francisco, USA.

Vanaelst I., Clarysse B., Wright M., Lockett A., Moray N., S'Jegers R. (2006). Entrepreneurial team development in academic spinouts: An examination of team heterogeneity. *Entrepreneurship Theory and Practice*, 30(2), 249–271.

von Krogh, G., Rossi-Lamastra, C., Haefliger S. (2012). Phenomenon-based research in management and organisation science: When is it rigorous and does it matter? *Long Range Planning*, 45(4), 277–298.

Wei J. (2017). State of hardware incubators and accelerators in the United States. *IEEE Consumer Electronics Magazine*, January 2017, 22–23.

York J., Metcalf L., Katona T. (2016) University accelerators: Entrepreneurial launchpads or unsustainable fads? *Proceedings of the United States Association for Small Business and Entrepreneurship Conference*, DG1–DG8, Boca Raton, USA.

Zacharakis A.L., Meyer G.D. (1998). A lack of insight: Do venture capitalists really understand their own decision process? *Journal of Business Venturing*, 13(1), 57–76.

Index